Persuasive Legal Writing

A Storytelling Approach

EDITORIAL ADVISORS

ASPEN COURSEBOOK SERIES

Persuasive Legal Writing

A Storytelling Approach

SECOND EDITION

Camille Lamar Campbell
Professor of Law
Nova Southeastern University
Shepard Broad College of Law

Olympia R. Duhart
Professor of Law
Associate Dean for Faculty Development
Nova Southeastern University
Shepard Broad College of Law

ASPEN PUBLISHING

Cover image credit: iStock.com/Yevgeniya Kolnobritskaya

To contact Customer Service, e-mail customer.service@aspenpublishing.com, call 1-800-950-5259, or mail correspondence to:

Aspen Publishing
Attn: Order Department
1 Wall Street
Burlington, MA 01803

Printed in the United States of America.

1 2 3 4 5 6 7 8 9 0

ISBN 978-1-5438-2521-3

Library of Congress Cataloging-in-Publication Data

Library of Congress Cataloging-in-Publication Data application is in process.

About Aspen Publishing

Aspen Publishing is a leading provider of educational content and digital learning solutions to law schools in the U.S. and around the world. Aspen provides best-in-class solutions for legal education through authoritative textbooks, written by renowned authors, and breakthrough products such as Connected eBooks, Connected Quizzing, and PracticePerfect.

The Aspen Casebook Series (famously known among law faculty and students as the "red and black" casebooks) encompasses hundreds of highly regarded textbooks in more than eighty disciplines, from large enrollment courses, such as Torts and Contracts to emerging electives such as Sustainability and the Law of Policing. Study aids such as the *Examples & Explanations* and the *Emanuel Law Outlines* series, both highly popular collections, help law students master complex subject matter.

Major products, programs, and initiatives include:

- **Connected eBooks** are enhanced digital textbooks and study aids that come with a suite of online content and learning tools designed to maximize student success. Designed in collaboration with hundreds of faculty and students, the Connected eBook is a significant leap forward in the legal education learning tools available to students.
- **Connected Quizzing** is an easy-to-use formative assessment tool that tests law students' understanding and provides timely feedback to improve learning outcomes. Delivered through CasebookConnect.com, the learning platform already used by students to access their Aspen casebooks, Connected Quizzing is simple to implement and integrates seamlessly with law school course curricula.
- **PracticePerfect** is a visually engaging, interactive study aid to explain commonly encountered legal doctrines through easy-to-understand animated videos, illustrative examples, and numerous practice questions. Developed by a team of experts, PracticePerfect is the ideal study companion for today's law students.
- The **Aspen Learning Library** enables law schools to provide their students with access to the most popular study aids on the market across all of their courses. Available through an annual subscription, the online library consists of study aids in e-book, audio, and video formats with full text search, note-taking, and highlighting capabilities.
- Aspen's **Digital Bookshelf** is an institutional-level online education bookshelf, consolidating everything students and professors need to ensure success. This program ensures that every student has access to affordable course materials from day one.
- **Leading Edge** is a community centered on thinking differently about legal education and putting those thoughts into actionable strategies. At the core of the program is the Leading Edge Conference, an annual gathering of legal education thought leaders looking to pool ideas and identify promising directions of exploration.

Summary of Contents

Contents

Acknowledgments

General Acknowledgments

The authors express their gratitude to all those who provided support, read, offered comments, or assisted in the editing, proofreading, and design of this text. Special thanks to students Alberto Leal, Lizza Maldonado, and Kristin Vara for their invaluable input and hard work.

Personal Acknowledgments

Camille Lamar Campbell

I'm grateful to God for the way that He holds my life in His hands.

I'm also grateful to my parents, Aaron and Hattie Lamar, who showed me that good teachers are storytellers who engage, motivate, and inspire students to become their best selves; to my husband, Dwight, who guided me through those dark nights of the soul when I questioned if the work was worth the sacrifice; to Judge Karon Bowdre, who inspired my love for legal writing, and to Judge Charles Coody, who taught me discipline, focus, and the elegance of brevity.

And last, but certainly not least, to the "Lovely Ones," my students who allow me to show them the beauty and majesty of the law—the clients and their stories.

Olympia R. Duhart

Christian Duhart, Lexy Semino, and Blake Frame deserve recognition for the important time they invested in this project. I also thank my dedicated co-author Camille Lamar Campbell. Thanks to Jessica Barmack, Suzanne Rapcavage, and the team at Aspen Publishing for their guidance. And to Chris Duhart, Cai Duhart, Linda Ross, and Carlyn Ross for their encouragement. Finally, I am so lucky to have the support of my colleagues at Nova Southeastern University Shepard Broad College of Law. I appreciate all the teachers and students who continue to inspire me.

How to Use This Book

Writing is not a spectator sport.

To master the art of writing, we must all roll up our sleeves, dig in, and prepare to do some heavy lifting. Legal writers have the additional burden of keeping a constant eye toward weaving compelling narratives. The goal is ambitious: to create an engaging, truthful, persuasive, and thematically cohesive narrative. To that end, this book is not intended for the casual reader. It is in-depth, detailed, and carefully designed to offer specific, relevant, and practical advice for the novice legal writer.

It is also different. This book endorses a three-stage framework for integrating storytelling into any type of persuasive writing. Chapter 1 introduces these three stages—processing, packaging, and revising—and makes the substantive argument for why legal storytelling is the most effective backdrop for efficient advocacy.

But before you jump into our world, we want to give you a quick primer on how to best use this book. This section unpacks the "toolbox" we have assembled for you in this text. More importantly, it gives you instructions on how to use these tools.

Stories help people understand new or abstract concepts. Our book is informed by the strength of storytelling in many ways. The book's organization is designed to make the material accessible and highlight the intuitive nature of legal storytelling. Your instructor may elect to modify some coverage, emphasize other parts, or skip a few sections entirely. Like in real law practice, make sure you take your cues from the supervisor. This text gives you enough resources to engage with the legal storytelling process in a meaningful way. Use this book as a constant guide in class and an important resource throughout your early career.

Our sincere hope is that you will highlight, underline, mark up, and tab the book. By the end of the course or assignment, it should reflect the wear and tear of constant readings and annotations. You are not reading a magazine; rather, you are reading a legal writing textbook. That distinction alone should merit more engagement and attention.

At various places throughout the book appear what we call Cognitive Corners, which direct you on some important self-reflection throughout the writing process. These questions do not test your knowledge of the material in the book; instead, they encourage you to carefully reflect on the material and make important connections, a method of metacognition. Metacognition is often described as "thinking about thinking."[1] The Cognitive Corner features will help you think explicitly about the knowledge construction process, as well as boost your ability to take your own "meta-cognitive pulse."[2]

Why build these features into a book about legal writing? Lawyers are lifelong learners. The best lawyers are expert learners who reflect on how they best learn. These Cognitive Corners encourage you to jump-start your journey to self-evaluation. Take the extra time to think about your answers to these questions. Writing can be exhausting and stressful. In recognition of those challenges, we deliberately build in small breaks for you to reflect. A little break and reflection along the way is important to keep up your momentum.

Throughout the text, you will also see testimonials from students, practicing lawyers, and judges that reinforce the saliency of the particular skill discussed in a chapter. You are perfecting your writing skills to one day use them in practice. It is valuable to hear from your future colleagues and judges who use these skills every day. In recognition that both women and men work as lawyers and judges, we have alternated the use of pronouns for generic references throughout the book; odd-numbered chapters will use masculine pronouns and even-numbered chapters will use feminine pronouns to promote gender balance.

In addition, this book leverages familiar literary and pop culture references—everything from *Catcher in the Rye* to *Star Wars*—to make storytelling techniques accessible to you. After all, this is nothing new. According to cognitive theorists, using nonlegal examples to teach legal skills improves the velocity of learning by allowing learners to build on existing knowledge—as opposed to "starting from scratch" each time a new challenge is presented.

Even though this book on persuasive legal storytelling focuses primarily on the trial briefs most attorneys use in practice, we have made a serious effort to be comprehensive in our coverage. We address the gamut of persuasive writing documents, such as motion briefs, appellate briefs, oral argument outlines, and even cover letters. We also give you some Bonus Materials on soft skills related to writing, such as time management, editing, revising, and formatting and writing professional e-mails. These inclusions reflect our commitment to create a full toolbox for the whole legal writer. We also want to be a resource to readers who will soon transition from law students to legal interns. The Bonus Materials should help you when you take that leap.

Furthermore, you will no doubt note the graphics, images, and visual aids featured throughout the text. Yes, we know that these are not the typical additions to a law school textbook. But we also know that visual aids are essential to learning. Visual aids help people learn better because of the way images interact with the brain.[3]

These additions evince our commitment to a "show, don't tell" approach. We include the visuals and other features to keep you engaged and informed. The book's

---

[1] Anthony Niedwiecki, *Teaching for Lifelong Learning: Improving the Metacognitive Skills of Law Students through More Effective Formative Assessment Techniques*, 40 Cap. U. L. Rev. 149 (2012).

[2] *See* Michael Hunter Schwartz et al., Teaching Law by Design (2009).

[3] Hillary Burgess, *Deepening the Discourse Using the Legal Mind's Eye: Lessons from Neuroscience and Psychology that Optimize Law School Learning*, 29 Quinnipiac L. Rev. 1, 38 (2011) ("Because of the way synaptic networks connect information nodes, however, once a person remembers the visual, she has access to any node that is connected to the visual by an existing pathway.").

multiple tools, charts, and checklists will appeal to people of different learning styles. Review the charts and build your own. Of course, there is more than one way to do things, and we want you to take ownership of the writing process.

And as every teacher has learned, a picture is worth a thousand words. For example, we could talk to you all day about the love and attention a mother shows her baby through simple gestures. We could describe her as "attentive" and "caring" and "affectionate." Or we could share this single picture.

Finally, no book can work if you don't take full advantage of the resources available. By working through the book as an active participant—rather than a passive spectator—you will be able to master the storytelling approach to persuasive writing. Your active engagement with the material is the best way to use this book.

Part I

Processing the Story: The Nuts and Bolts of Legal Storytelling

Chapter 1

Introduction to Legal Storytelling

"[E]very lawsuit is a story. I don't care if it's about a dry contract interpretation; you've got two people who want to accomplish something and they're coming together. That's a story. And you've got to tell a good story."—John Roberts, Chief Justice of the United States Supreme Court

"This case is about cotton. B.B. King once called cotton a force of nature—[T]here's a poetry to it, he wrote, hoeing and growing cotton. Here, the poetry of the hoeing and growing has given way to a nasty little feud over the selling."[1] —The Honorable Kevin C. Newsom, Eleventh Circuit Court of Appeals

Everything about the law begins with a story. And, as Justice Roberts observes, successful advocates transform the client's legal dilemma into a story that grabs the judge's attention. The second quote is from a case about the interpretation of a liquidated damages clause—one of those dry contract cases that Justice Roberts references. It's a powerful example of an attention-grabbing narrative hook. This first sentence injects a bit of mystery into the story that readers want to solve. What is the nature of this "nasty little feud"? Who is the villain? Who is the hero? By introducing a character and setting up a conflict in the opening line, Judge Newsom's words evoke

[1] *Autauga Quality Cotton Ass'n v. Crosby*, 893 F.3d 1276, 1277 (11th Cir. 2018) (internal citations omitted).

a provocative image, introduce a character, and describe a conflict—key attributes of a good story.

Another key attribute of a good story is its power to engage readers. Stories engage readers because they depict universal human experiences such as conflict, love, and redemption. Because good stories convey themes or lessons about universally shared human experiences, they're powerful persuasive tools.

WHY STORIES ENGAGE READERS

Storytelling means different things to different people. However, at its core, storytelling is written communication whose power depends on its ability to engage the audience's reason and emotion and to communicate universally held values, accumulated wisdom, and social norms.[2] Most stories (1) have at least one character, (2) depict a conflict between characters, and (3) transmit a message from a unique point of view.

Another attribute of a good story is its streamlined way of transmitting new and often complex information.[3] Stories "connect us with our humanness and link past, present, and future by teaching us to anticipate the possible consequences of our actions."[4] Put another way, stories help people put new experiences in context.[5] Because stories engage audiences with a compelling combination of reason and emotion, they're powerful persuasive tools. As you might've guessed, important differences exist between storytelling in the literary world and storytelling in the legal world. Storytelling lawyers reconstruct past events to further the client's interests. Furthermore, unlike nonlegal storytellers, "[L]awyers are ethical and truthful storytellers; [whose] imagination is informed, shaped, and limited by evidence."[6] The next section further defines legal storytelling.

LEGAL STORYTELLING DEFINED

Despite its almost universal appeal in the nonlegal context, legal storytelling has not always been embraced by the legal writing community.[7] Rhetoricians—scholars who study the art of persuasion—recognize the importance of **logos**,

[2] *See generally* Julia Chaitin, *Stories, Narratives and Storytelling,* July 2003, http://www.beyondintractability.org/bi-essay/narratives; *What is Storytelling?*, ELDRBERRY.NET, http://www.eldrbarry.net/roos/st_defn.htm (last visited Oct. 20, 2023) (discussing definition proposed by the National Storytelling Association in 1997).

[3] *See* Jennifer Sheppard, *Once Upon a Time, Happily Ever After, and in a Galaxy Far, Far Away: Using Narrative to Fill the Cognitive Gap Left by Overreliance on Pure Logic in Appellate Briefs and Motion Memoranda*, 43 WILLAMETTE L. REV. 255, 257 (2009).

[4] *What is Storytelling?*, *supra* note 2.

[5] *See* Sheppard, *supra* note 3, at 257.

[6] Phillip Meyer, *Storytelling for Lawyers* 2 (OXFORD UNIVERSITY PRESS 2014).

[7] *See* Kenneth D. Chestek *Judging by the Numbers: An Empirical Study of the Power of Story*, 7 J. ASS'N LEGAL WRITING DIRECTORS 2-7 (2010). *See generally* Sheppard, *supra* note 3.

persuading through logic and reason; **pathos**, persuading through appeals to the audience's emotions; and **ethos**, persuading through an audience's instinctive respect for authority and character or persuading through organization and reader friendly attributes.[8] Legal writers have traditionally been trained to view logos and its emphasis on logic and reason as more persuasive than pathos and ethos.[9]

Under this traditional view of legal writing, legal storytelling's emphasis on pathos and ethos has been viewed by some scholars as unpersuasive, unprofessional, and unscientific.[10] Ironically, this traditional aversion to legal storytelling is at odds with the conventional wisdom of others in the legal community. Trial lawyers have always understood that logos, pathos, and ethos are powerful tools for persuading juries.[11] Given the almost universal acceptance of storytelling in the litigation context, legal writing scholars began questioning the taboo traditionally associated with storytelling in persuasive legal writing.[12] Furthermore, a growing body of empirical data suggests that judges find storytelling briefs—ones that combine logos, pathos, and ethos to tell cohesive stories—more persuasive than those that rely only on logos.[13]

This book equips you to harness the power of legal stories. As a legal storyteller, you'll create arguments that elevate the client's dilemma beyond a stilted recitation of the law. You must prove how the facts and the law *justify* a decision in the client's favor (i.e., the logos aspect of the case) and *motivate* the judge to rule in your client's favor (i.e., the pathos and ethos aspects of the case). Although legal storytelling has many definitions, for our purposes, legal storytelling is an approach to persuasive writing that embraces three important principles:

1. Effective legal stories reflect core societal values. **Core societal values** are things, ideas, or concepts that a society believes to be so important that they justify legal protection.
2. Effective written advocacy uses core societal values embedded in legal rules, statutes, regulations, local regulations, or other primary sources as the foundation of powerful logos, pathos, and ethos arguments that explain why the client should prevail.
3. Effective written advocacy embraces principles of visual rhetoric and features memorable, engaging theories and themes reflected in every part of the brief via an eclectic mix of persuasive techniques.

[8] LitCharts, *Ethos,* available at https://www.litcharts.com/literary-devices-and-terms/ethos (last visited February 24, 2023).
[9] Chestek, *supra* note 6.
[10] *Id.*
[11] *See Generally* Judge Mark W. Bennett, *Eight Traits of Great Trial Lawyers: A Federal Judge's View on How to Shed the Moniker "I Am A Litigator,"* 33 Rev. Litig. 1 (2014).
[12] *Chestek, supra* note 6, at 3, 32-35.
[13] *Id.*

PROCESSING, PACKAGING, AND REVISING: A THREE-STEP APPROACH TO LEGAL STORYTELLING

Your mind is undoubtedly racing with thoughts about the best way to tell your client's story. The diagram summarizes this book's three-step approach for creating legal stories: processing, packaging, and revising.

① Processing	② Packaging	③ Revising
• **Ch. 2:** Transitioning from Objective Writing to Legal Storytelling • **Ch. 3:** Brainstorming Legal Arguments • **Ch. 4:** Developing a Theory and Theme	• **Ch. 5:** Persuading Through Document Design • **Ch. 6:** Showcasing the Theory and Theme: Drafting Effective Introductions and Conclusions • **Ch.7:** Harnessing the Power of Suggestion: Drafting the Statement of Facts • **Ch. 8**: Substantiating the Client's Desired Conflict Resolution • **Ch. 9:** Storytelling at the Appellate Level	• **Ch. 10:** Delivering a Cohesive Story Through Strong Editing

During **processing,** the legal storyteller creates the story's foundation by extracting core societal values embedded in legal rules; scrutinizing the facts of the client's case; and using those facts to brainstorm arguments and to create a unifying theory and theme. But before engaging in these essential processing tasks, you must make the transition from objective writing to legal storytelling. Chapters 2 through 4 explore the processing phase.

During **packaging**, the legal storyteller infuses the brief with ethos and pathos generating navigational and design tools and utilizes an eclectic mix of hard- and soft-sell persuasive techniques to showcase the client's theory, theme, and arguments. Chapters 5 through 8 explore the packaging phase. Although some formatting and procedural differences exist, the process of packaging legal stories for trial and appellate briefs is virtually identical. Chapter 9 explores key distinctions between trial and appellate briefs.

After completing the processing and packaging phases, you'll have a complete legal story. But your story is incomplete without the polishing and reflection that occur during the revision phase. Revision encompasses more than reviewing your document for spelling errors and grammatical mistakes; it includes developing the meta-cognitive skills to refine your legal story and maximize its persuasive impact.

Part III of the book is the Bonus Material. We've included extras that we hope will be useful to you in law school and beyond. In these chapters, you'll develop a familiarity with concepts that facilitate legal storytelling. Chapter 10 explores the revision phase. Chapter 11 is a step-by-step guide to transforming your legal story into a compelling oral argument, Chapter 12 introduces you to time management basics, and Chapter 13 introduces you to persuasive writing in the workplace.

With this brief introduction to legal storytelling, you're ready to begin processing, packaging, and revising your own legal stories.

Chapter 2

Transitioning from Objective Writing to Legal Storytelling

"Just when I finally felt comfortable writing objectively, my professor switched gears, and I had to learn persuasive writing. I didn't know where to begin."—1L Student

As you learn to write persuasive legal stories, you'll most likely experience some trepidation about crossing a bridge into new territory and feel the same bewilderment expressed by the student in the above quote. These feelings reflect all the blood, sweat, and tears that you've put into learning to write objectively. You've achieved a level of comfort objectively predicting the outcome of the client's case. Now you must venture into new territory. Your new focus will be dramatically different: tell the judge a persuasive legal story. You'll find the client's story in legal rules from cases or statutes or in nonlegal sources such as public policies, traditions, and customs. Then, you'll develop a theory and theme and use a mix of legally and emotionally relevant facts to showcase that story. All these story elements—the rules, public policies, traditions, customs, theory, theme, facts—are preparatory. The story reaches its crescendo in the argument section where you'll demonstrate why the client is entitled to relief.

The good news is that the analytical skills necessary for objective writing will transfer to legal storytelling. Your challenge will be reconceptualizing those analytical skills so that you're able to tell an engaging legal story. But with a bit of practice and a shift in mindset, you'll quickly adapt. In objective writing, your relationship with the client is analogous to that of the fortune teller looking into a crystal ball: The client is your audience, and you are tasked with offering a neutral, objective prediction about the outcome of the client's legal dilemma.

But in legal storytelling, the rules are very different. The shift to legal storytelling requires you to do five things: (1) adopt a new persona, (2) embrace the client's unique point of view, (3) craft compelling arguments, (4) rethink commonly used mnemonic devices such as CREAC or IRAC, and (5) persuade with visual rhetoric. The transition from objective writing to legal storytelling also requires that you learn a new vocabulary. Key words and concepts are highlighted in bold text and defined in Part VII of this book which contains a comprehensive glossary.

ADOPT A NEW PERSONA

Just as Clark Kent transforms himself from an innocuous reporter passively observing injustice to Superman, an active participant in the fight against injustice, you must transform yourself from a counselor to an advocate. Counselors are observers who predict the outcome of a legal dilemma, but advocates are proactive. They urge judges or groups of judges to resolve a legal dilemma in a way that benefits their clients. The conversations below illustrate some dramatic differences between counselors and advocates. Can you identify some of the differences?

Conversation #1

Counselor. (gesturing to a document) The objective analysis in this memo predicts that you have a 50 percent likelihood of success on an intentional infliction of emotional distress claim.

Client. Why 50 percent?

Counselor. A cause of action for the intentional infliction of emotional distress requires the plaintiff to prove the existence of four elements. One of those elements is whether the defendant's conduct was extreme and outrageous. I've begun my analysis with that element because it's typically the most difficult to prove.

Client. I see.

Counselor. Extreme and outrageous conduct is typically reserved for situations involving the death of a loved one under circumstances where the defendant is aware of the plaintiff's susceptibility to emotional distress.

Client. (furrowing his brow) Okay . . .

Counselor. A judge could conclude that the family's decision to conceal the actual time of your boyfriend's funeral disregarded their awareness of your susceptibility to emotional distress. However, the judge could just as easily conclude that the family's decision was the permissible exercise of a legal right to control who attended the funeral. That's why I'm predicting a 50 percent likelihood of success.

Client. (sighing deeply) I'll need to carefully read the analysis in your memo before I can make any decisions.

Counselor. Of course. I'll look forward to hearing from you.

Conversation #2

Judge. (to the court reporter) We're here on the defendants' motion to dismiss. They allege that the complaint does not state a case of action for the intentional infliction of emotional distress because the facts as alleged don't sufficiently allege extreme and outrageous conduct. The plaintiff filed a brief opposing the motion. Have I accurately described the motion and the opposition to the motion?

Advocate. Yes, your honor. The defendants' conduct was extreme and outrageous. They impermissibly exercised their legal rights as the deceased's next-of-kin.

Judge. How so? Get to the point, counsel. I haven't got all day.

Advocate. (nervously glancing at the brief) Your honor, this case is about prejudice masquerading as permissibility. Excluding the plaintiff from the funeral of a man with whom he'd been in a six-year committed relationship disregarded his susceptibility to emotional distress and is at odds with the core societal value of protecting vulnerable people from psychological distress.

The plaintiff was three days away from becoming the deceased's fiancé. The deceased purchased a $30,000 engagement ring and told his mother, someone who disapproved of his lifestyle, about his intent to propose to the plaintiff.

These facts—all of which must be presumed true for the purposes of this motion—support the conclusion that the defendants exercised a legal right in an impermissible way by disregarding their awareness of the plaintiff's susceptibility to emotional distress.

Opposing counsel. (jumping to her feet) Your honor, the defendants' actions were permissible, and we vehemently disagree with these factual characterizations . . .

Judge. (nodding to opposing counsel) I bet they do. I'll read both parties' briefs and take the motion under advisement. Court is adjourned.

Notice how each conversation is shaped by each attorney's radically different persona and target audience. The primary audience for a **memo**, the document memorializing the counselor's prediction, is the client, and the primary audience for a

brief, the document memorializing the client's story, is the judge. The counselor adopts the persona of a neutral observer to predict the outcome of the client's legal dilemma. So, the counselor's conversation with the client reflects the memo's predictive purpose: The focus is on percentages, the likelihood of success, and potential counterarguments.

In stark contrast, the advocate adopts the persona of a biased promoter of the client's interests to persuade an extremely busy judge or group of judges that the client's story is the one that's most consistent with the law or the core societal values underpinning the law. Consequently, the advocate's conversation with the judge reflects the brief's persuasive purpose: telling the client's story. It's the advocate's duty to tell the client's story, even if the advocate thinks that the client has only a 50 percent likelihood of success or even if the advocate must address emotionally charged issues such as homophobia and discrimination. To tell the client's story, effective advocates use story elements—a theory, a theme, and evocative language that subtly highlights the theory and theme—to transform objective legal rules about extreme and outrageous conduct into a story. The following graphic highlights these key story elements:

Story Element #1: Theory	**Story Element #2: Theme**	**Story Element #3: Evocative Language**
"Excluding the plaintiff from the funeral of a man with whom he'd been in a six-year committed relationship disregarded his susceptibility to emotional distress and is at odds with the core societal value of protecting vulnerable people from psychological distress."	"Prejudice Masquerading as Permissibility"	"The plaintiff was **three days away** from becoming the deceased's fiancé. The deceased purchased a **$30,000 engagement ring** and told his mother—**someone who disapproved of his lifestyle**—about his **intent to propose** to the plaintiff."

A **theory** is short articulation of the central idea or thesis that unifies the advocate's argument. The theory of the case is like an elevator pitch. Entrepreneurs use elevator pitches to pique an investor's interest and generate capital for a new business venture.[1] Effective theories are short, meaning that you should be able to introduce your client, identify a few key facts, and explain why, given the applicable law or policy considerations, those key facts entitle your client to the requested relief—all in the time that you'd spend in a thirty second elevator ride. To jumpstart their creativity,

[1] Will Kenton, Investopedia, *What Is an Elevator Pitch? Definition and How They're Used*, Dec. 22, 2022, https://tinyurl.com/yc4dc3dj (last visited September 22, 2023).

some advocates use a writing prompt such as "This case is about XYZ" when generating a theory or theme. The advocate's theory satisfies this criterion. In forty-one words, the advocate introduces the client as someone who's been excluded because of his sexual orientation and then demonstrates that the motion should be denied because the defendants impermissibly exercised their legal right during a time when the plaintiff was susceptible to emotional distress and in a manner inconsistent with the core societal values embedded in the law.

The **theme** is even shorter than the theory. Think of the theme as the pathos or emotional component of the client's story. It's the "juice" that motivates the court to rule in the client's favor. The advocate's theme, "prejudice masquerading as permissibility," is a four word memorable phrase that repeats core components of the theory. As the advocate's conversation illustrates, a judge isn't a kindly grandparent prone to indulgences in the form of long-winded introductory statements. An effective theme helps the advocate succinctly distill the theory into its most important component parts. Notice the relationship between the theory and the theme; they complement each other, permitting the advocate to introduce, summarize, and move seamlessly between arguments.

Theories and themes are examples of hard-sell persuasive techniques. **Hard-sell persuasive techniques** overtly tell the judge why the client is entitled to relief. In stark contrast, **soft-sell persuasive techniques** subtly reference the client's theory, theme, and arguments. Chapter 4 discusses strategies for developing effective theories and themes.

EMBRACE THE CLIENT'S UNIQUE POINT OF VIEW

Effective advocates articulate legal rules, core societal values, and legally relevant facts in ways that subtly highlight the client's unique point of view. Consider the following sentences:

The man shot the woman.

Pushing the elderly bystander out of harm's way, the man shot the armed attacker.

The first sentence doesn't have a story. It identifies the facts with neutral, objective language; it's the kind of purely objective factual statement that would appear in a memo. In stark contrast, the second sentence isn't neutral or objective, but tells a story from the client's unique point of view: The client isn't a cold-blooded murderer but a hero protecting an elderly bystander from an armed attacker. With just one sentence, the advocate primes the judge for a favorable reaction to the client's story of justifiable homicide.

Soft-sell persuasive techniques are subliminal methods of priming the judge for a favorable response to the client's story. The previous section alluded to the interplay of hard and soft persuasive techniques as a defining feature of legal storytelling. Let's explore a real-world example of that interplay. Imagine that you're on a blind date. Your date greets you with an intense, wide-eyed gaze and says: "Hi. I'm your soulmate, the person you've been waiting all your life to meet. So, let's skip the preliminaries and head straight for the altar."

After that introduction, you'd most likely be looking for an escape route, not anticipating a second date. Your date's memorable introduction is a hard-sell persuasive technique. In the world of legal storytelling, hard-sell persuasive techniques are argumentative. They overtly reference the theory and theme, telling the judge why the client is entitled to relief. Contrast the suitor's hard-sell persuasive technique with a soft-sell persuasive technique where the suitor skips the overt declaration but appears well groomed, is charming, and asks questions about your interests—subtle behaviors that make a second date more likely.

Let's return to Conversation #2 between the advocate and the judge to further illustrate the distinction between hard and soft sell persuasive techniques. The advocate's evocative language utilizes soft-sell persuasive techniques such as word choice and detail to prime the judge for a favorable response to the client's theory, theme, and arguments. Notice that the counselor's description of the plaintiff's relationship with the deceased is radically different from the advocate's description. The counselor describes the deceased as the plaintiff's boyfriend. But the advocate's language emphasizes the quasi-marital nature of the relationship with details about timing—the client was three days away from becoming the deceased's fiancé—about cost—the engagement ring costs $30,000—and about the nature of the relationship—the client and the deceased were long-term partners who'd been together in a six-year committed relationship.

The subtlety of the advocate's language primes the judge for a favorable response to the argument that the defendants impermissibly exercised their legal right to control funeral attendance in a way that not only violates the rule of law but in a way that's inconsistent with the core societal value of protecting vulnerable people from psychological distress embedded in the rule. To the untrained eye, these distinctions may seem subtle. But effective legal storytellers are masters of subtlety, using soft-sell persuasive techniques to prime the judge for a favorable response to the client's argument. Chapters 7 and 8 explore soft-sell persuasive techniques in greater detail.

CRAFT COMPELLING ARGUMENTS

Persuasive writing is argumentative. The theory, theme, and hard-and-soft persuasive techniques prepare the judge for the main event: the argument. An **argument** is "a group of ideas arranged logically to convince a reader or listener to do a particular thing or to adopt a particular belief."[2] Advocates use **point headings**, a reader friendly formatting feature, to announce their arguments. A brief about a relatively straightforward legal issue might have only one point heading announcing one argument.

[2] Richard K. Neumann, Jr., Legal Reasoning and Legal Writing: Structure, Strategy, and Style (5th ed. 2005).

However, a more complex legal issue will typically have multiple point headings. Chapter 8.1 explores techniques for drafting persuasive point headings.

The three basic types of legal arguments roughly correspond to the three classic argument types recognized by rhetoricians: logos, pathos, and ethos. Logos arguments are arguments about law—how the facts of the client's case should apply to the clearly established law, what the law should be, or how the law should be interpreted. In a logos argument, the advocate urges the decision-maker to resolve legal issues by examining rules embedded in cases, statutes, constitutions, or other primary legal authorities.[3] Law students are generally more comfortable with logos arguments because they're accustomed to applying legal rules to a factual scenario on an exam or to a hypothetical client's dilemma when writing a memo.

But the shift to legal storytelling requires that you expand your horizons beyond rule-based logos arguments and embrace the persuasive power of pathos and ethos arguments. Pathos and ethos arguments, also known as policy arguments, aren't arguments about legal rules but arguments about the core societal values at the root of those rules and the real-world concerns implicated by those core societal values. Ethos arguments are the analytical cousins of pathos arguments; they appeal to a narrow subset of core societal values related to tradition and custom while pathos arguments appeal to a broader set of core societal values and typically ask the judge to consider how the core societal values at the root of a legal rule impact the court system, society, or future litigants. Don't let the novelty of pathos and ethos policy arguments intimidate you. Chapter 3 explores the relationship between core societal values and logos, pathos, and ethos arguments in more detail.

Logos, pathos, and ethos arguments are packaged in **motion briefs** or **appellate briefs**. Arguments in motion briefs, sometimes referred to as trial memoranda or trial briefs, are presented to one judge. A **motion** is the advocate's request, one that corresponds to the various procedural rules, for a desired ruling.[4] Given its focus on the case's **procedural posture**, the case's stage in the legal process, an advocate filing a motion brief crafts arguments about why the client is entitled to relief on various pre- and post-trial motions such as motions to dismiss, motions for summary judgment, motions to compel, and motions in limine.

In stark contrast, arguments in appellate briefs are presented to a group of judges. Instead of focusing exclusively on a procedural rule, the advocate's argument focuses on the validity of a lower court's ruling on an issue related to procedure, substance, or a combination of both. Because an appellate brief either affirms or questions another court's ruling, advocates crafting arguments in an appellate brief must include the **standard of review**. The standard of review tells the appellate court how much deference to give to the lower court's ruling. Consequently, arguments in motion and

[3] Many techniques and strategies referenced in this handout have either been inspired by or adapted from materials in the following textbooks: Wilson Huhn, The Five Basic Types of Legal Arguments (2d ed. Carolina Academic Press 2008); Mary Beth Beazley, A Practical Guide to Appellate Advocacy (2d ed. 2006); Linda H. Edwards, Legal Writing: Process, Analysis, & Organization (1999).

[4] LLI, Legal Information Institute, Cornell Law School, https://www.law.cornell.edu/wex/motion (last visited Feb. 12, 2023).

appellate briefs will have a substantive component corresponding to the relevant legal issue and a procedural component corresponding to the case's procedural posture.

Although the audience for and the content of motion and appellate briefs differ, advocates use the same kinds of persuasive techniques when crafting compelling arguments. So the good news is that the primary difference between motion and appellate briefs relates more to structure than to content. Because of their similarity, this book uses the word "brief" as a general reference encompassing motion and appellate briefs. Chapter 9 explores key differences between these two types of briefs.

RETHINK COMMONLY USED MNEMONIC DEVICES

The shift to legal storytelling also demands that you change how you think of mnemonic devices such as CREAC or IRAC. **Mnemonic devices** are memory enhancing tools that use "a pattern of letters, numbers, or other relatable associations"[5] to help students remember important concepts. The pattern of letters in CREAC—Conclusion, Rule, Explanation, Application, and Conclusion—and the pattern of letters in IRAC—Issue, Rule, Application, and Conclusion—remind novice legal writers to substantiate their objective predictive analysis by identifying, explaining, and applying a rule to the legally relevant facts of the client's case. The rule-centric nature of CREAC and IRAC explains why memos are organized around legal rules.

In legal storytelling, the *argument type*—logos, pathos, or ethos—determines how advocates organize and substantiate arguments. Let's explore the impact of this paradigm shift with an example. Recall Conversation #1 between the counselor and the client. That conversation focused on the likelihood of success on an intentional infliction of emotional distress cause of action, one where the client has the burden of proving all four elements. Given this rule structure, the counselor would organize the memo around those four elements and predict the client's likelihood of success on each element. But Conversation #2 between the advocate and the judge focused on two arguments about why the defendants' motion to dismiss should be denied. Instead of a scattershot approach focusing on all four elements, the advocate will organize the brief around two arguments related to only one element.

The first argument is quintessentially logos, and the advocate would use a modified version of CREAC, IRAC, or a similar mnemonic device to identify the applicable rule (conduct is extreme and outrageous when the defendant is aware of the plaintiff's susceptibility to emotional distress), use cases to clarify any ambiguities in the rule, and use rule-based reasoning, analogical reasoning, or a combination of both, to substantiate the assertion that the defendants' were aware of the plaintiff's susceptibility to emotional distress because of his six-year relationship with the deceased and the deceased's recent purchase of a $30,000 engagement ring.

[5] Literary Terms, https://literaryterms.net/mnemonic/ (last visited February 22, 2023).

The second argument is quintessentially pathos—the defendants' conduct is at odds with the core societal value of protecting vulnerable, susceptible people. However, the advocate would encounter a conundrum when attempting to substantiate the pathos policy argument using CREAC or IRAC; the rule-centric focus of these mnemonic devices isn't appropriate for pathos and ethos arguments based on core societal values embedded in rules. To avoid this kind of conundrum, advocates use another memory enhancing technique that reminds them to focus on the relationship between arguments and legal storytelling. Because arguments are a series of micro stories that reflect the client's theory and theme, advocates build arguments in a way that mimic the plot of a story. The progression of the client's story is its plot. According to acclaimed writer Margaret Atwood, "A strong plot is centered on one moment—an interruption of a pattern, a turning point, or an action—that raises a dramatic question, which must be answered throughout the course of a story."[6]

In a storytelling brief, the interrupted pattern is the status quo. The **status quo** is the first component of the argument. Arguments must be substantiated with evidence, reasons, examples, and details. And consequently, the status quo identifies and if necessary, explains the sources that form the foundation of the argument. In a logos argument, the status quo component is comprised of rules embedded in cases or statutes, and in a pathos or ethos policy argument, the status quo component is comprised of core societal values embedded in legal rules. The phrase "status quo" is more appropriate than the phrase "rule" or "rule explanation" because this rule-centric language isn't applicable to pathos or ethos arguments that are premised on core societal values.

The desired conflict resolution is the second component of the argument. The **desired conflict resolution** is the advocate's proposed solution to the conflict at the heart of the legal issue. It's the most important component because it uses various reasoning tools such as rule-based, analogical, or policy-based reasoning to substantiate the argument. Advocates use **policy-based reasoning** to substantiate pathos and ethos policy arguments premised on core societal values at the root of legal rules instead of the rules themselves. Chapters 8.3 and 8.4 explore these reasoning tools in more detail.

The good news is that this plot-driven approach to building arguments is broad enough to encompass traditional mnemonic devices such as CREAC or IRAC. When building the plot of a logos argument, advocates typically use **persuasive CREAC**, a modified version of the mnemonic device for packaging objective legal analysis, that's more appropriate for legal storytelling. Chapter 8.3 discusses key distinctions between persuasive CREAC and objective CREAC and explores key considerations for advocates building logos arguments. Chapter 8.4 explores the structure of pathos and ethos arguments.

---

[6] MASTERCLASS, How to Write a Story Plot: Tips, Tricks, and Margaret Atwood's Writing Prompts, September 1, 2021, https://tinyurl.com/yc2m8sbm (last visited February 25, 2023).

PERSUADE WITH VISUAL RHETORIC

Persuasion involves more than the written word. Everything about legal storytelling is strategic, meaning that advocates are always looking for verbal and nonverbal ways of communicating the client's theory, theme, and arguments to the judge. Given legal storytelling's emphasis on nonverbal persuasion, another key difference between objective writing and legal storytelling is the prolific use of visual rhetoric. **Visual rhetoric** is a broad term that describes the symbiotic relationship between persuasion and document design.[7]

Visual rhetoric facilitates ethos and pathos. The persuasive power of ethos arguments derives from their organization and reader friendly formatting features. Judges are reading machines whose professional reputations depend on their ability to quickly read and comprehend lots of information.[8] In recognition of the judicial reader's special needs, storytelling briefs contain ethos-generating navigational tools such as tables of contents, introductions, headings, hyperlinks, and bookmarks and pathos-generating design principles such as an easy-to-read and engaging font, white space, bullet points, charts, and graphs. Chapter 5 explores how advocates incorporate ethos-generating organizational principles and pathos design principles into their briefs.

The legal storyteller's emphasis on visual rhetoric also explains the sequence of components in a brief and why those components differ from those in a memo. Each jurisdiction has its own brief formatting rules, but most briefs contain components that don't appear in memos. The graphic below compares the components of a motion brief with the components of a memo. The bolded boxes highlight similar components:

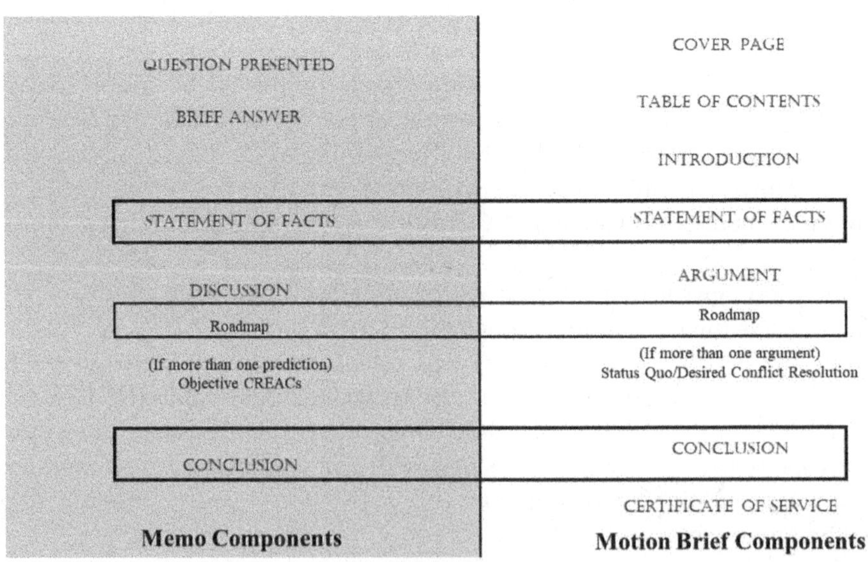

[7] Derek H. Kiernan-Johnson, *Telling Through Type: Typography and Narrative In Legal Briefs*, 7 J. Ass'n Legal Writing Directors 87, 89 (2010); Linda L. Moran, *The Gestalt of Brief-Writing Visual Rhetoric for the Appellate Brief*, 49 No. 7 DRI For Def. 27 (July 2007).

[8] K.K. DuVivier, The Reference Brief, Colo. Law., July 2004, at 71.

The bolded boxes highlight similar components. Notice that the motion brief has three different components: a cover page, table of contents, and an introduction. These reader friendly components help judges see the "big picture" of the client's story. The sequencing of these brief components reflects another maxim of visual rhetoric: **primacy and recency**, the theory that people best remember information that is presented first and last.[9] Consistent with this principle, these big picture components either appear at the beginning or at the end of a typical motion or appellate brief. Chapter 9 explores key formatting differences between appellate briefs and motion briefs.

The cover page identifies the reviewing court and the procedural posture. The Table of Contents succinctly outlines the client's arguments and contains ethos-generating navigational tools such as point headings and plot headings. **Plot headings** are short, nonargumentative phrases in the Statement of Facts that function like a megaphone, directing the judge's attention to the plot of the client's story and foreshadowing arguments. Chapter 7.2 explores techniques for drafting persuasive plot headings. The introduction briefly summarizes the arguments and articulates the theory and the theme. Chapter 6 explores techniques for drafting effective introductions.

Part IV of this book has several sample briefs. Peruse those samples, paying particular attention to each one's cover page, table of contents, introduction, and statement of facts. Try to identify the advocate's legal story. Then, reflect on the Cognitive Corner questions below. Now that you understand some of the major differences between objective writing and legal storytelling, you're ready to process your client's legal story. During processing phase, you'll scrutinize the facts of the client's case, use those facts to brainstorm arguments, and unify those arguments with a compelling theory and theme.

COGNITIVE CORNER

Reflections on the Differences Between Objective and Persuasive Writing

Consider the following questions about making the transition from objective to persuasive writing:

1. Reflect on your experiences with mnemonic devices in objective writing. Were these experiences positive or negative? Explain.
2. What will be your greatest obstacle in the transition from objective to persuasive writing?

[9] David A. Sousa, *Primacy/Recency Effect*, Lancashire Grid for Learning, http://www.lancsngfl.ac.uk/secondary/math/download/file/How%20the%20Brain%20Learns%20by%20David%20Sousa.pdf (last visited Feb. 12, 2023).

Chapter 3

Brainstorming Legal Arguments: Assembling the Story's Building Blocks

"It is impossible to make any legal argument without telling some stories about the facts and about the law."—Philip Meyer, *Storytelling for Lawyers*

"Use soft words and hard arguments."—English Proverb

Legal arguments and stories are inextricable. According to acclaimed jurist and judge Mark Bennett, this relationship exists because "All lawsuits . . . are stories about events gone bad: the breakup of a marriage or business, a devastating physical or emotional injury, the alleged violation of a civil or constitutional right, a stock swindle, a drug deal gone bad."[1] When viewed within this narrative framework, arguments are a series of micro stories reflecting the client's theory and theme about how the judge should rectify the series of disastrous events that's compelled the parties into court. And so, effective arguments spur judicial action.

Because advocates craft arguments for judges, developing arguments that appear reasonable and measured while advancing the client's story—the soft words referenced in the second quote—is strategic. Developing arguments that appear reasonable closely mimics the judge's decision-making process. Judges

[1] Judge Mark W. Bennett, *Eight Traits of Great Trial Lawyers: A Federal Judge's View on How to Shed the Moniker "I Am A Litigator,"* 33 Rev. Litig. 1, 7 (2014).

are like major league referees. They critically evaluate competing legal arguments and then decide which ones should "win" given the law, the core societal values embedded in the law, and the facts. Much like their major league counterparts who work under pressure to make the right call, judges are also under pressure to make the right call when evaluating competing legal arguments. So, they're suspicious of any argument that sounds too extreme or that makes too many concessions.

Understanding the attributes of a compelling argument is relatively easy; but *crafting* an argument can be challenging. You'll undoubtedly encounter a mountain of facts in the client's case file—depositions transcripts, affidavits, and other information such as medical or employment records—and an intricate network of case law, statutes, or regulations governing the conflict at the heart of the client's story. How will you streamline this avalanche of information into a cohesive network of arguments without alienating the judge with overblown emotional appeals, parroting legal rules while ignoring the powerful narratives reflected in the core societal values embedded in those rules, or losing perspective by ignoring the opponent's counter-narrative?

Stay tuned. The remainder of this chapter contains practical advice for overcoming these challenges such as understanding the relationship between the three types of arguments and core societal values and developing strategies and for brainstorming well-rounded arguments that appear reasonable and measured instead of belligerent, pushy or one-sided.

UNDERSTAND THE RELATIONSHIP BETWEEN ARGUMENTS AND CORE SOCIETAL VALUES

Arguments are the building blocks of legal stories. And core societal values are the building blocks of arguments. Recall that core societal values are things, ideas, or concepts that a society believes are so important that they justify legal protection. Consider the following nonlegal arguments; the language evoking core societal values is bolded.

Politician #1: (amid thundering applause) Increasing the minimum wage is sound economic policy. **It's un-American for people who work a 40-hour week to live in poverty.**

Politician #2: (amid thundering applause) Increasing the minimum wage is not sound economic policy. It's un-American to dangle the promise of increased social mobility to low-skilled workers, especially when research shows that businesses would respond by firing the very people the increase is purportedly designed to protect.

As these examples illustrate, each politician appeals to core societal values—the American ideal of hard work, dignity, and social mobility—as the vehicle for arguments for *and* against raising the minimum wage. Politicians understand the rhetorical power of core societal values, and so do legal storytellers. Core societal values are *everywhere*. Sometimes they're explicitly stated in primary sources such as cases, statutes, or regulations and inspire logos arguments. Other times they're implied from dicta, dissenting opinions, and secondary sources such as Restatements and legislative history and inspire pathos and ethos policy arguments.

Grounding arguments in core societal values harnesses the combined rhetorical power of logos, pathos, and ethos. Core societal values are the foundation for logos arguments about legal rules *and* for pathos and ethos arguments about the real-world impact of those values. The previous chapter attempted to calm your fears about moving beyond the comfort zone of rule-based arguments—the grande dame of the first-year law school curriculum—and embracing pathos and ethos policy arguments. Far from being subordinate to logos arguments, pathos and ethos policy arguments are persuasive powerhouses.

To understand the power of pathos and ethos policy arguments, you must understand the symbiotic relationship between logos arguments premised on legal rules and core societal values. One legal writing scholar used a root and branch analogy to explain the relationship between rule-based logos arguments and pathos and ethos policy arguments "Policy is the underground root system; rules are the visible branches."[2] Recall the conversation between the advocate and the judge featured in Chapter 2. The advocate made the following arguments (key terms are bolded for emphasis):

Logos Argument: The defendants' conduct was extreme and outrageous. Excluding the plaintiff from the funeral of a man with whom he'd been in a six-year committed relationship was the **impermissible exercise of a legal right** because it disregarded the defendants' knowledge of the plaintiff's susceptibility to emotional distress.

Pathos Policy Argument: The defendants' conduct was extreme and outrageous. Excluding the plaintiff from the funeral of a man with whom he'd been in a six-year committed relationship **because of homophobia is at odds with the core societal value of protecting vulnerable people from emotional distress**.

Consider these arguments within the context of the following graphic:

[2] Doretta McGinnis, *How to Construct a Policy Argument*, Law School Toolbox, https://lawschooltoolbox.com/11074-2/amp/ (last visited February 20, 2023).

Within this visual framework, logos arguments are "branch" arguments; pathos and ethos policy arguments are "root" arguments. This root and branch analogy also explains why core societal values are the lowest common denominator of all three argument types. So if you can identify core societal values upon which a legal rule is premised, then you can use it to craft compelling pathos and ethos policy arguments. Using core societal values as the inspiration for your logos, pathos, and ethos arguments is a strategy that avoids infusing arguments with so much emotion that the judge begins to question the advocate's credibility.[3] Core societal values are credible because a court, regulatory, or legislative body determined that they were so important that they created civil or criminal sanctions for those who undermine those values. Now that you understand the symbiotic relationship between core societal values and logos, pathos, and ethos arguments, let's further explore these three argument types.

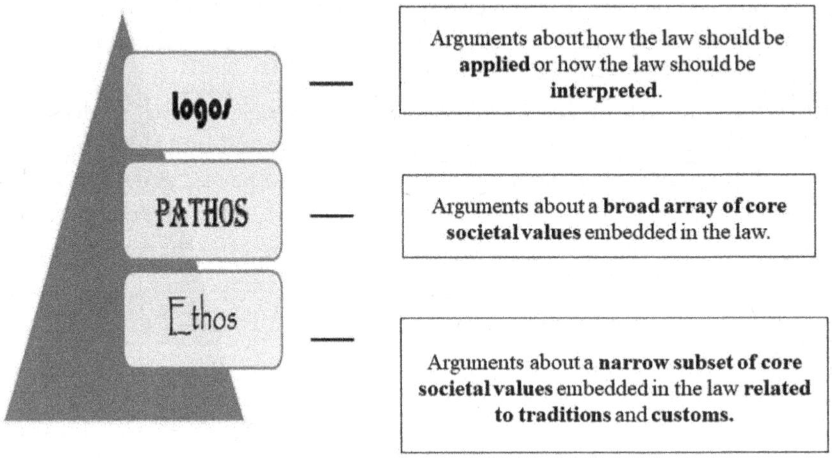

Logos Arguments

The two most common types of logos arguments are fact application and legal interpretation arguments. **Fact application logos arguments** are arguments about how the facts of the client's case should apply to the law. In stark contrast, **legal interpretation logos arguments** are arguments about what the law is (i.e., how the judge should resolve an issue of first impression or a split among the trial or appellate courts) or how the judge should interpret the law (i.e., using the plain language of a statute or looking beyond the statute to other interpretive sources such as legislative intent). Fact application arguments will typically be the kind of logos argument that are the easiest to generate. That's because as a law student you're accustomed to applying rules embedded in cases and statutes to a factual scenario (e.g., the exams in your doctrinal classes or the client's dilemma in your legal writing class). Consider the following examples of a fact application and a legal interpretation logos argument. The bolded language highlights key distinctions between the two types of arguments.

[3] *See* Rebecca Lefler, *Remembering the Human Element, Storytelling in Legal Writing*, For the Defense Newsletter, citing Bryan Garner and Justice Antonin Scalia's admonition that an "overt appeal to emotion is likely to be regarded as an insult."

Fact Application Logos Argument	Legal Interpretation Logos Argument
The **defendant's indefinite, casual remark praising the plaintiff's job performance** is not a clear, unambiguous promise of lifetime employment triggering an exception to the at-will employment doctrine.	To resolve this issue of first impression, the Court should **align itself with appellate courts in neighboring jurisdictions that use a plain language analysis** to abolish exceptions to the at-will employment doctrine.

Notice that the fact application argument doesn't dispute the applicability of the at-will employment doctrine. Instead, the argument is premised on how the facts of the client's case should be applied to the law. Now compare the bolded language in the fact application argument to the bolded language of the legal interpretation argument. The legal interpretation argument is premised on *how* the law should be interpreted, not the facts of the client's case. Also notice that both logos arguments are based on the at-will employment doctrine, which is a legal rule, not the core societal values at the root of that rule.

Pathos and Ethos Policy Arguments

Recall that pathos and ethos policy arguments are analytical cousins; they both rely on core societal values, but pathos policy arguments rely on a broad array of core societal values and their impact on real-world concerns such as how the resolution of the client's case or the application of a statute or rule might impact the court system, society, or future litigants. Ethos policy arguments are premised on a narrower subset of core societal values related to tradition, custom, or precedent. Compare the following arguments. The bolded language highlights key distinctions between the pathos and ethos policy arguments.

Pathos Policy Argument	Ethos Policy Argument
The judicially created exceptions to the at-will employment doctrine should be abolished because they **unduly burden an employer's economic autonomy resulting in a decreased ability to recruit and hire the most qualified workers.**	The judicially created exceptions to the at-will employment doctrine should be abolished because they **unduly burden traditional notions of employer autonomy that facilitate entrepreneurship.**

The pathos policy argument is about the core societal value of autonomy—a bedrock principle at the root of the employment at-will doctrine—and the adverse impact of decreased autonomy on real-world concerns such as employers' ability to hire and recruit. But the ethos policy argument is related to real-world concerns about the impact of decreased autonomy on employers' ability to satisfy their traditional role of encouraging entrepreneurship. Now that you understand the importance of core societal values and their relationship to the three basic types of legal argument, you're ready to begin brainstorming.

BRAINSTORM WELL-ROUNDED ARGUMENTS

Teachers have been touting the importance of outlining and other pre-writing strategies to students since the days of the one-room schoolhouse. But one essential precursor to outlining that is often overlooked is brainstorming. "Brainstorming is when you deliberately try to think up new ideas or solutions to problems."[4] Studies indicate that "writing down your ideas has fascinating neurological effects, including increased attention."[5] Given these neurological benefits, think of brainstorming "as clearing your head to make room for new ideas to move in."[6] In describing the benefits of brainstorming versus "winging it" or coming up with ideas as you write, one writing coach advised that taking "[A] proactive approach to generating ideas tends to not only produce more ideas, but also inspire better quality ones."[7]

A winging it approach to brainstorming also increases the likelihood that you'll lose perspective by overestimating the strength of the client's arguments or ignoring the opponent's counter-narrative. Ignoring the counter-narrative is a rookie mistake. By confronting your opponent's story head-on, you generate the kind of hard arguments referenced in the second quote at the beginning of this chapter. Your arguments must be hard, meaning that they must preempt any "warts" (i.e., adverse legally relevant facts or primary authorities). When you preempt the adversary's arguments, you lessen their impact—hence, the emphasis on the preemptive strategies discussed in Chapter 8.3 and Chapter 8.4.

But the most important benefit of brainstorming is the freedom it gives you to explore ideas without worrying about style, form, or judgment from clients, managing partners, other colleagues working on the case, or (most importantly) you. In short, brainstorming frees you from the tyranny of the blinking curser on a blank computer screen. To brainstorm effectively, find an environment that facilitates creativity, remove all distractions such as cell phones, select an efficient way to memorialize the results of your brainstorming session, and write down all your initial ideas, even if they seem obvious. Once you've done these four things, you're ready to explore the following three brainstorming techniques: (1) developing empathy by stepping into the client's shoes, (2) identifying the core societal values at the root of legal rules, and (3) finding the patterns in primary authorities and legally relevant facts.

---

[4] Matt Ellis, Grammarly Blog, *Brainstorming: How to Generate Ideas and Improve Your Writing*, April 13, 2021, available at https://tinyurl.com/y77ekw9p (last visited Feb. 1, 2023).
[5] *Id.*
[6] *Id*
[7] *Id.*

Develop Empathy

To find the story, begin by setting aside the law.[8] The law governs the legal conflict, but it doesn't explain the actions, inactions, or motives of the client, the opposing party, or other important stakeholders. Being unduly preoccupied with rules at the beginning of the brainstorming process prevents you from seeing the people, places, and things most intimately connected to the client's story. And so, during the initial stages of the brainstorming process, the legal rules are the opening act, not the headliner.

Putting aside the rules facilitates empathy. And empathy is the key to unlocking your client's and your opponent's best arguments. Empathy, colloquially known as "putting yourself in another person's shoes," is the ability to recognize the feelings and reactions of others. One noted author describes empathy as "the willingness of an observer to become part of another's experience, [and] to share the feeling of that experience."[9] In her novel *Mama Day*, author Gloria Naylor describes the connection between empathy, truth, and storytelling: "[E]verybody wants to be right in a world where there ain't no right or wrong. . . . [E]verything got four sides: his side, her side, an outside, and an inside. All of it is the truth."[10] Without empathy, it can be difficult to find the find the four sides of the client's story.

Empathy also helps you brainstorm the client's best arguments, preempt your opponent's arguments, or craft effective counterarguments. But developing empathy can be challenging when you represent a client who differs from you, your family, or your peers because of race, religion, personal affinities, or social and political ideologies. Being empathetic can also be particularly challenging when you over-identify with your client and can't imagine a scenario in which the client isn't entitled to relief or when you over-identify with your opponent's counter-narrative because its more akin to your personal affinities and social and political ideologies.

Empathy visualization exercises help you overcome any psychological obstacles that prevent you from telling the client's story. When working through an empathy visualization exercise, ask yourself a series of questions to find commonalities between your experiences and those of your client, the opposing party, or any other important stakeholders.

The questions you ask yourself will depend on the facts of the case. But the goal is to look for common interests, family backgrounds, educational experiences, and the like. If you look hard enough, you can always find something in common with virtually anyone. Once you've made an emotional connection via common interests, then you're ready to challenge any stereotypes that you, your peer group, or the larger society might have against your client, the opposing party, or other important stakeholders.

---

[8] This information is adapted from Camille Lamar Campbell, *Attorneys for the Damned: Using Legal Storytelling to Facilitate Zealous Representation of Unpopular, Unlikeable, or Infamous Clients*, 20 Second Draft 2, 24 (Fall 2015), http://lwionline.org/uploads/FileUpload/F2015SecondDraftMobile.pdf.

[9] *See* Pamela Hartigan, *Empathy: The Missing Link to Solving the World's Most Pressing Problems*, Huffington Post: The Blog (July 10, 2013, 3:05 PM), http://www.huffingtonpost.com/pamela-hartigan/empathy-the-missing-link-_b_3556404.html (last visited March 4, 2023).

[10] Gloria Naylor, *Mama Day* 230 (Vintage Contemporaries 1993).

Let's use an empathy visualization exercise to brainstorm the client's arguments in the following scenario. You represent a client objecting to her ex-husband's petition to relocate their child to another state. As a litigation associate at a large national law firm, the client works more than 90 hours per week. The client is ambitious. At the initial interview, she tells you that her goal is to become the firm's first female managing partner. Because of her career ambitions, the client voluntarily relinquished custody in exchange for liberal visitation on weekends and holidays. But despite her hectic schedule, the client has never missed a weekend visit with the couple's three-year-old son. Furthermore, the client's weekend visitations frequently involve her parents, siblings, and other family members. The client's ex-husband is a stay-at-home-dad who's financially dependent on his fiancée, a woman he's known for only three months and who's accepted an offer in another state where she'll earn a six-figure salary. As a perk of her employment, the fiancée's employer will pay for the child to attend an elite preschool, one that educates the children of some of that state's richest families.

But despite your best efforts, you find yourself judging the client; you ask yourself questions such as: "What kind of mother puts her career before her child?" "Why won't she just move?" "Why won't she consider petitioning for custody and stopping the relocation?"

If you're blinded by preconceived notions about society's definition of a good mother—a woman willing to sacrifice her career ambitions for her child—you might be able to see only one story: The client is a bad mother who shouldn't prevail in her efforts to prevent the child's relocation. To overcome any psychological obstacles to empathy, begin by finding common ground. The most obvious commonality is the client's profession: You're an aspiring lawyer, and the client is a lawyer. Another more subtle commonality is that you've probably experienced the same difficulty achieving work-life balance. Start by using your law school experiences as a scaffold for empathizing with the client, and then ask yourself the following kinds of questions:

- Are there any limits to what you would do to achieve success as a lawyer? If so, what are they?
- If you were faced with the client's legal dilemma, how would you handle it? Assume that the client was a loved one or close friend. Would that change your answer?
- What would you have to know about the client to help you understand why she voluntarily relinquished custody or why she's not interested in petitioning the court for full custody, even if full custody would prevent a battle over the child's relocation?

Once you've found some common ground, ask yourself questions that examine common stereotypes about motherhood:

- What are some stereotypes about mothers who relinquish custody of their children or who work in traditionally male-dominated professions?
- Do these stereotypes apply to working fathers? Should they? Why or why not?

- Does society have different expectations for male and female attorneys when it comes to work-life balance? If so, what are they?

After completing this kind of empathy visualization exercise, you're more likely to understand the client's reasons for fighting relocation and her unwillingness to petition for custody. Instead of thinking that she's a bad mother, you might begin thinking of her as someone who made a difficult custodial choice that was in her child's best interests, even with the knowledge that others will most likely judge her for a decision that defies common stereotypes about motherhood.

Use the kind of visualization techniques discussed and illustrated in this section when you encounter clients whose representation challenges aspects of your personal beliefs such as religion, race, or political differences; when you over-identify with the client or can't imagine a scenario in which the client isn't entitled to relief; or when you over-identify with your opponent's counter-narrative because its more akin to your personal affinities and social and political ideologies.

Identify Core Societal Values

With the next brainstorming technique, you'll look for core societal values embedded in the rules. By now you should understand the maxim that core societal values are the building blocks of arguments; they're the lowest common denominators of logos, pathos, and ethos arguments, and because they represent values at the root of legal rules, they garner instant credibility from judges. But you can also use core societal values as brainstorming catalysts.

Core societal values contain valuable clues about the people, places, or things at the heart of the legal conflict. Use the same research techniques that you used in objective writing to identify core societal values. Sometimes core societal values will be easily identifiable because they're explicitly stated in rules, statutes, or cases. Other times core societal values will be implicit, meaning that you'll have to synthesize them from primary sources, dicta, dissenting opinions, or from secondary sources such as legislative history and law review articles.

After completing your research, critically evaluate the relevant rule structure. Core societal values can be *complementary* or *contradictory* things, ideas, or concepts. For example, rules with exceptions and rules that require judges to balance factors or examine the totality of the circumstances typically have *competing* core societal values, while rules that require judges to apply elements typically have a *complementary* relationship. Once you know the rule structure governing the client's legal dilemma, ask the following types of questions:

- What's the rule's purpose?
- Who're the people, places, or things that are within the rule's protection?
- Can you identify a conflict between any key ideas, concepts, or values?
- What's the underlying message in those key ideas, concepts, or values?

Your answers to these questions provide important clues about how potential arguments may proceed. As an illustration of this brainstorming process, let's return to the relocation example. Your research reveals the following information about a relocation cause of action:

Relocation decisions are based on a factors-based balancing test	Excerpts from Primary and Secondary Sources
Courts weigh statutory factors to determine if relocation is in the child's best interest.	Relocation disputes present courts with a unique challenge: to promote the best interest of the child while affording protection equally between the relocating parent's right to travel and the non-relocating parent's right to parent. When evaluating a petition to relocate, courts must focus on the best interest of the child, not the economic interests of the relocating parent. When evaluating a petition to relocate, courts must consider whether the relationship between the non-relocating parent and the child can be preserved.

This rule structure yields a treasure trove of information such as a potential cast of characters, core societal values, and the messages transmitted by those core societal values:

Characters	Core Societal Values	Core Value Message
The Relocating Parent	The Right to Travel	Divorced custodial parents have freedom to travel without fear of automatically losing custody.
The Non-Relocating Parent	The Right to Parent	Divorced noncustodial parents have an interest in the care, upbringing, and protection of their minor children.
The Minor Child	Stability	The minor child's interest trumps the interest of either divorced parent.

Notice that the core societal values tell a story about conflict—the inherent tension between the relocating parent's right to travel, the non-relocating parent's right to parent, and the minor child's right to be reared in a stable familial environment that fosters the child's best interest. The core societal values and the facts of the client's case are useful brainstorming tools. Evaluate some of the advocates' potential arguments.

Summary judgment is inappropriate, and relocation isn't in the child's best interest because:

FACT APPLICATION LOGOS ARGUMENTS

- Any nominal, material benefits from attending a preschool for affluent children are outweighed by the daily contact that would become financially and professionally infeasible for the non-relocating parent.
- It would require the child to endure physically and mentally exhausting interstate travel.
- It would prevent the child from bonding with the non-relocating parent and that parent's extended family members.

PATHOS AND ETHOS POLICY ARGUMENTS

- Relocations predicated on the relocating parent's desire for wealth and status are at odds with the core societal values of facilitating stable familial relationships and recognizing the non-relocating parent's right to parent.
- Upholding the constitutionality of the relocation statute avoids circumventing the tradition of *stare decisis* and jeopardizing the best interests of minor children.

Simply by identifying the core societal values at the root of the rules governing parental relocation the advocate has generated five arguments that *could* be included in a brief. We emphasize the word "could" so you don't assume that every argument that you brainstorm will be included in a brief. Factors such as geopolitical influences, which are beliefs, assumptions, or values shared by persons of a particular region, city, state, or country,[11] or the unique facts of the client's case will ultimately determine which arguments you include in the brief.

During the packaging phase of legal storytelling outlined in Chapter 8 you'll streamline the arguments that you brainstormed, memorialize the remaining arguments in point headings, reader-friendly formatting features that announce the advocate's best arguments, and substantiate those arguments using rule-based, analogical, or policy-based reasoning.

[11] *See generally* CFA Institute, *Introduction to Geopolitics,* available at https://tinyurl.com/49ybvsv6 (last visited March 5, 2023).

Find the Patterns

Renowned trial lawyer and legal storytelling virtuoso Gerry Spence observed that "The evidence sends me looking for a good story with which to support it, but the evidence does not create the story on its own."[12] To find the story in the mountain of evidence in the minutiae of the client's file, you must find the pattern. And to find the pattern you must move beyond the micro level of the story—individual cases, statutes, regulations, and evidence such as a depositions and affidavits. These individual components of the client's story are like squares of fabric in a multi-patterned quilt. You must transcend the individual squares of fabric to see the macro story or the overarching patterns; the client's story is in the patterns, not the individual squares. The process of moving from the micro story to the macro story is synthesis, a concept that you encountered when writing a memo. According to legal writing expert Richard Neumann, synthesis is a process of finding and explaining collective meaning that's not immediately apparent from the individual cases themselves.[13] We'll call documents, charts, and other pattern-finding tools synthesis documents.

One popular synthesis document is an annotated outline. As its name implies, an annotated outline is a snapshot of the rules governing the issue at the heart of the client's case followed by annotations or brief descriptions of cases or other primary or secondary authority. The structure of an annotated outline mimics the rule structure of the cause of action at issue in the client's case. Organizing the case law and other primary authority thematically around rules makes it easier to spot patterns.

When you spot a pattern, ask yourself the following questions to brainstorm potential arguments:

- Can you distinguish the facts of the client's case from cases where the court applied the pattern in a way that favors the opposing party?
- What reasonable interpretation of the law might lessen the impact of unfavorable legally relevant facts that triggered an adverse ruling?
- Are the facts of the client's case like those cases where the court applied the pattern in a way that favors the client?

Another common synthesis document is a timeline. Recall that legal stories are structured sequentially around a plot or inciting event that created the conflict propelling the parties into court. Timelines are effective because, much like annotated outlines, they help advocates identify factual patterns upon which to build arguments. Because plot-based timelines "suggest a beginning, middle, and end" they allow advocates to not only see patterns but also causal relationships between events, turning points, and other inciting events essential to the client's story.[14] Timelines are also

---

[12] Philip Meyer, *Storytelling for Lawyers* 28 (Oxford University Press 2014).

[13] Richard K. Neumann Jr., Legal Reasoning and Legal Writing: Structure, Strategy and Style 123 (Aspen Law and Business, 2d ed. 1994).

[14] Susan Leigh Noble, WordPress, *Using timelines to organize information for your novel*, November 21, 2019, available at https://susanleighnoble.wordpress.com/2019/11/21/using-timelines-to-organize-information-for-your-novel/ (last visited March 4, 2023).

flexible. Tech savvy advocates can use interactive tools such as spreadsheets, interactive whiteboards, or PowerPoint templates to create timelines while other more tech adverse advocates can sketch their timeline on a piece of paper, a sticky note, or an index card.[15]

Timelines are examples of visual rhetoric, a concept identified in the previous chapter, that help you identify patterns that might not be readily apparent amid the minutiae of the case file. Furthermore, because timelines are visual, you can easily incorporate them into other components of the brief. Chapter 5 explores how advocates incorporate visual elements into briefs and Chapter 7 explores how advocates incorporate visual elements into the statement of facts.

The brainstorming techniques discussed in this chapter are just a few ways of getting your creative juices flowing. Use the strategies and tips outlined in this chapter and any others suggested by your professor to whittle down the mountain of evidence in the client's case file into a series of micro stories reflecting the client's theory and theme. Now, that you have some ideas about how to brainstorm compelling arguments, let's explore the pièce de résistance of the client's story: an engaging theory and theme.

---

[15] Barbi Honeycutt, PhD, *FLIP it with Timelines! 3 Ways to Use Timelines to Engage Students*, Feb. 28, 2017, available at https://www.linkedin.com/pulse/flip-timelines-3-ways-use-engage-students-barbi-honeycutt-ph-d- (last visited March 4, 2023).

Chapter 4

Developing a Theory and Theme: Creating the Story's Framework

"Pick a theme and work it to exhaustion. . . ."—Dorothea Lange

Noted American photojournalist Dorothea Lange is best known for this iconic Depression-era photograph: *Migrant Mother*. With one glance, you can immediately see how Lange uses the photograph to trigger the audience's emotions. The woman's furrowed brow, the dirt on her body and clothes, and the children's hidden faces invite the audience's sympathy. Once "hooked" by sympathy, the audience can "hear" Lange's message about the struggle for dignity amidst the poverty of the Great Depression.

Just as Lange hooked the audience with a visual image so that they could hear the message, legal storytellers must also hook judges so that they can "hear" the messages embedded in their legal arguments. Legal storytellers succinctly communicate arguments via themes and theories. An effective theme engages the judge's emotions (i.e., the pathos aspect of the case), and then, once hooked, the judge can "hear" the advocate's theory about why the client is entitled to relief (i.e., the logos aspect of the case). Consequently, an effective theory and theme complement one another, permitting the advocate to introduce, summarize, and move seamlessly between legal arguments. The remainder of this chapter explores the relationship between arguments, theories, and themes, deconstructs several examples of effective and ineffective theories and themes, and surveys drafting strategies and techniques. The chapter ends with a self-editing checklist.

UNDERSTAND THE RELATIONSHIP AMONG ARGUMENTS, THEORIES, AND THEMES

Arguments are the building blocks of legal stories. But theory and theme are the vehicles for streamlining and succinctly communicating those arguments. Recall that a theory is a succinct articulation—lasting no longer than the duration of a thirty-second elevator ride—of the central idea or thesis that unifies the advocate's arguments. Theories reference the most salient facts of the client's case and resolve the conflict at the heart of the client's story.

A good theory is also a unifier. In a complex case, you might have multiple arguments. Imagine how difficult it would be to remember all these different arguments while fielding questions at a motion hearing or during an appellate argument. And even when you have only one argument, you'll often find that a good theory helps the judge focus on the message implicit in that argument. The unifying power of a good theory is precisely why you have only one theory, although you may have multiple arguments. Lastly, a theory is *explicit*, meaning that it should be clearly stated in core components of the brief such as the introduction in a motion brief or the summary of the argument in an appellate brief.

In stark contrast, a theme is more succinct than a theory and is a memorable phrase that captures the essence of the theory. A theme is a streamlined way of thinking about the case that engages the judge by focusing her attention on favorable aspects of the client's case. An effective theme is also a unifier, so you'll only have one theme. Lastly, unlike a theory, themes can be explicitly or implicitly referenced in core components of the brief, such as the introduction in a motion brief or the summary of the argument in an appellate brief.

It's also important to understand the subtle differences between an argument, a theory, and a theme. An argument is more factually detailed than a theory or theme and is a more comprehensive explanation of why the legal dilemma should be resolved in the client's favor. To illustrate the relationship between arguments, theory, and theme, consider a famous modern example: The O.J. Simpson criminal trial. At the time of the trial, O.J. Simpson was a famous former college and professional football star who was acquitted of murdering Nicole Brown Simpson, his ex-wife, and Ronald Goldman, her friend, in 1995. It was one of the most notorious criminal trials in American history.[1] The prosecution's case against Simpson, an African American

[1] THE INTERNATIONAL LAWYER JOURNAL, *25 years later, how the O.J. Simpson case has reshaped the law*, June 13, 2019, available at https://tinyurl.com/taznhdnu (last visited March 5, 2023).

male, hinged on physical DNA evidence found at the scene of the crime that linked him to the murder. The prosecution also had a motive for the murders (i.e., a contentious divorce) and Simpson's history of domestic violence against his ex-wife.

The team of trial lawyers representing Simpson were dubbed "The Dream Team" by the media.[2] Lead trial counsel Johnnie Cochran was a masterful litigator who knew that his best shot at winning would be to give the jury a story. Cochran used the Los Angeles Police Department's (LAPD) history of police brutality and racial discrimination, including its notorious practice of falsely accusing African Americans of crimes, to streamline his arguments into a compelling theory and memorable theme supporting his story of Simpson's innocence.[3]

Using the LAPD's history of corruption and racially discriminatory police practices, Cochran's argument emphasized facts that were averse to the prosecution—including the testimony of a key police witness who conducted a warrantless entry onto Simpson's property and who lied about making racist remarks—to craft his theory of the case.[4] According to Cochran, the LAPD's history of racially discriminatory police practices meant that the jurors couldn't trust the messenger (i.e., the police), and therefore shouldn't believe the prosecutor's message about Simpson's guilt, which hinged on physical DNA evidence collected by police officers at the crime scene.[5]

Notice that Cochran's arguments, theory, and theme were premised on the core societal value of credibility, and, more specifically, that the criminal justice system's legitimacy is premised on the credibility of law enforcement officers. The theory's emphasis on credibility and on distrusting the messenger made it easy for jurors to dismiss the testimony of police officers, criminalists, and other prosecution witnesses who presented physical evidence of Simson's guilt.[6]

But Cochran's pièce de resistance was his theme: a short, memorable phrase that summarized his theory about not trusting the messenger heralding Simpson's guilt. In his closing arguments, Cochran famously uttered the phrase, "If it doesn't fit, you must acquit," alluding to the fact that the glove that prosecutors alleged Simpson wore during the murders didn't fit Simpson's hand.[7] This simple theme summarized Cochran's theory about not trusting the messenger and the LAPD's history of racially discriminatory police practices to convey a powerful message that the prosecution didn't prove Simpson's guilt beyond a reasonable doubt. Consider the following visual depiction of Cochran's argument, theory, and theme, organized from the narrowest component to the broadest one:

---

[2] *Id.*

[3] Pennsylvania State University, Words and More: Thoughts about rhetoric and persuasion in our World, *The Trial of O.J. Simpson: How Johnnie Cochran Dominated the Court,* September 14, 2018, available at https://tinyurl.com/2pucs687 (last visited March 5, 2023).

[4] *Id.*

[5] *Id.*

[6] *Id.*

[7] *Id.*

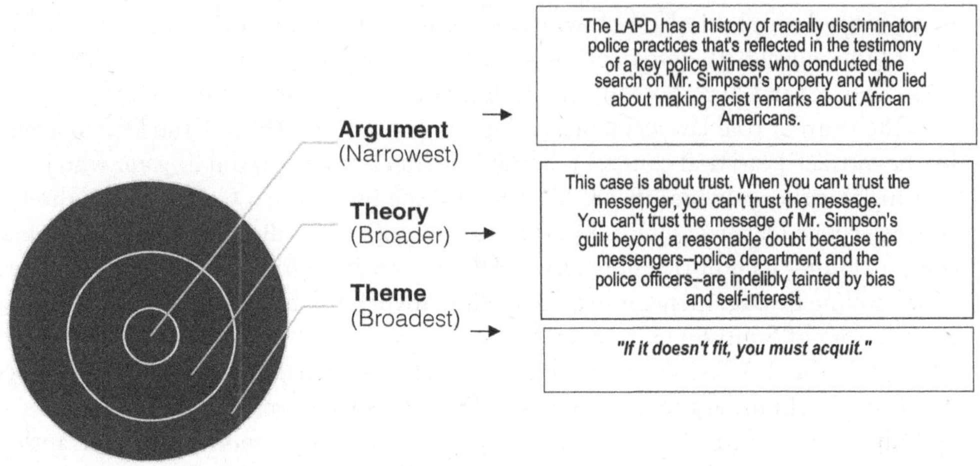

Cochran's mastery of the building blocks of legal storytelling—arguments, theory, and theme—resulted in Simpson's acquittal after only four hours of jury deliberation during a trial that had lasted almost eight months and featured the testimony of approximately 150 witnesses.[8] The speed of the jury's verdict underscores the power of legal storytelling: it isn't always the logic or facts that lead to a verdict; it's also the narrative that convinces the jury to choose one side over the other. The next section tackles the million-dollar question: How do you transform the client's arguments into an effective theory and theme?

STRATEGIES FOR DRAFTING EFFECTIVE THEORIES AND THEMES

This section explores the attributes of effective theories and themes and illustrates several drafting strategies and techniques. The judge reading your brief is likely doing so under severe time constraints. According to statistics from the Administrative Office of the Federal Courts, case filings in the United States district courts increased 6 percent to 390,555, civil case filings rose 5 percent to 297,877, and criminal defendant filings grew 6 percent to 92,678 in 2019.[9] Increased filings translate into judges reading more briefs. Couple these statistics with recent data indicating that the average adult reader has an attention span of about *eight seconds*.[10] These statistics underscore why you must capture the busy judge's attention with engaging theories and themes.

---

[8] *See generally*, The History Channel, *O.J. Simpson Acquitted*, available at https://www.history.com/this-day-in-history/o-j-simpson-acquitted.

[9] *See* U.S. District Courts: *Judicial Business*, 2019, U.S. Courts, available at https://tinyurl.com/2r78vnsz (last visited March 6, 2023). These statistics represent the workload of federal judges prior to the coronavirus pandemic in March 2020, an unprecedented event in the nation's history, which resulted in a marked decrease in case filings. Because of this anomaly, we've used statistics from 2019. Nate Raymond, Reuters, *New federal lawsuits, appeals fell in 2021 amid pandemic-judiciary*, March 15, 2022, available at https://tinyurl.com/2p8hb3tb (last visited March 6, 2023).

[10] Judah Schiller, *Average Human Attention Span by Age: 31 Statistics*, Dec. 7, 2022, available at https://tinyurl.com/5xcdrxrs (last visited Jan. 6, 2023).

Drafting an Effective Theory: Examples and Strategies

Crafting an effective theory is a challenging task that requires you to adopt the same flexible, nonjudgmental mindset that you used to brainstorm arguments. There's no magic formula for developing an effective theory, but with a bit of practice, you can develop the analytical skills needed to recognize an effective theory when you see one. To acquire these analytical skills, you'll need to refine your understanding of the attributes of an effective theory and study examples of effective and ineffective theories. The following graphic summarizes four attributes of an effective legal theory that we've highlighted in various portions of this book:

Attributes of an Effective Theory

- Succinctly targets the weakest aspect of the case
- Highlights the relevant legal standards or core societal values
- Highlights favorable facts using vivid, evocative language
- Unifies disparate arguments

Strategies for drafting effective theories correspond to the attributes referenced in the graphic. The first drafting strategy, one that specialist Dr. Ken Broda-Bahm describes as "focusing on the faults," corresponds to the first attribute of a good theory: targeting the weakest aspect of the client's case.[11] He encourages advocates to focus on the case's weaknesses by asking questions such as: How would you persuade your toughest critic, someone who's inclined to favor the other side? What are the facts that, if left unaddressed, would result in the client losing the case?[12] These kinds of questions not only help you brainstorm an effective theory, but they help you avoid misrepresenting or failing to disclose legally relevant facts about the client's case to the judge. Advocates have a duty of candor to the judge that requires them to present the facts accurately and forthrightly.[13] And any theory that misrepresents the law or facts

---

[11] *See* Ken Broda-Bahm, *Invent Your Trial Theme: Seven Ways*, The Persuasive Litigator, July 20, 2020, PDF on file with author.

[12] *Id.*

[13] *See* Model R. Prof'l Conduct R. 3.3(a)(1)-(2) (Am. Bar Ass'n 2016); *see also* Long v. AvMed Inc., 14 So. 3d 1264, 1266 (Fla. Dist. Ct. App. 2009).

will jeopardize the advocate's or the client's credibility and put the advocate at risk for ethical sanctions.[14]

Let's explore the Focus on the Facts drafting strategy with a nonlegal example. Assume that you're a third-year law student who's applied for a position as an entry-level associate at a local law firm. You're currently ranked in the top 25 percent of your class and received the high-grade award in Legal Research and Writing I, Legal Research and Writing II, and Trial Advocacy. During your 1L year you interned with a local non-profit organization and during your 2L year, you worked as a litigation associate at a national law firm. Before coming to law school, you worked as a beat reporter investigating public corruption and fraud at a major metropolitan newspaper. The following graphic outlines the firm's hiring criteria:

All entry-level associates must have the potential to become excellent attorneys.

Although the firm considers various factors in accessing a candidate's potential for excellence, entry-level associates are typically ranked in the top 5% of their law school class.

However, factors such as a candidate's ability to handle complex legal work with little or no supervision and a demonstrated commitment to social justice issues may be considered when determining a candidate's potential for excellence.

To prepare for your upcoming interview, you crafted the following theories about why the firm should hire you:

Option #1: I'm the best candidate for the position. The hiring criteria are based on the totality of the circumstances rather than on one factor being more important than another.
Option #2: I'm the best candidate for the position. I'm ranked in the top 25 percent of the class and received the high-grade award in Legal Research and Writing I, Legal Writing II, and Trial Advocacy.
Option #3: I'm the best candidate for the position. Evaluating applicants using a variety of factors unrelated to class standing—such as diverse work experiences in the non-profit and private sectors and the ability to handle complex, controversial topics related to public corruption and similar issues with limited supervision—is the most reliable predictor of my potential to become an excellent attorney.

[14] *See, e.g.*, Joseph P. Mastrosimone, *Don't Act Like an Ostrich: How to Not Run Afoul of the Duty of Candor*, J. KAN. B. ASS'N, May 2013, at 14-15.

We'll use the attributes of an effective theory to select the best option. The first theory isn't the best option; it's too vague, meaning that it doesn't highlight such favorable facts in your resume as your diverse experiences in a variety of disciplines (i.e., your work experiences in the non-profit and private sectors and your work as a journalist) or foreshadow your arguments; it merely restates the rule codified in the firm's hiring criteria.

The second option is also problematic. Although it's more factually detailed than the first option and highlights favorable facts about your academic accomplishments, it ignores adverse facts about your class standing and doesn't target the weakest aspect of your case: the firm's concern that you might be ill-equipped to handle the intellectual rigors of working as an entry-level associate at a national law firm. The third option is the best choice. It strikes an appropriate balance between targeting the weakest aspect of your candidacy, such as your class rank, while highlighting favorable facts about your credentials and favorable aspects of the firm's hiring criteria (e.g., a favorable factors-based totality of the circumstances test instead of a less favorable element-based test requiring that *all* successful candidates be ranked in the top 5 percent of the class).

You can also use the Facts Beyond Change Test and the Plausibility Test to evaluate the viability of any theories that you generate.[15] To use the Facts beyond Change Test, ask yourself whether the theory is consistent with the facts beyond change. If any facts are inconsistent with your theory, then choose a different theory. In stark contrast, to use the Plausibility Test, you ask yourself the following kinds of questions: Is the theory plausible? Is the theory internally consistent? Does the theory sound like the truth? If more than one theory passes both tests, choose the theory that you think would best appeal to the judge's worldview. For example, if the judge has a police background, then a theory that a police officer made a mistake is a better choice than a theory suggesting that the police office is lying.[16]

The next drafting strategy uses core societal values embedded in legal rules to generate theories. Just as you used core societal values to brainstorm logos, pathos, and ethos arguments, you can also use core societal values to build effective theories. Notably, this drafting strategy corresponds to the three remaining attributes of a good theory: highlighting core societal values, highlighting favorable facts using vivid, evocative language, and unifying disparate arguments. Let's revisit the arguments that we brainstormed from the relocation example featured in Chapter 3 to generate an effective theory.

FACT APPLICATION LOGOS ARGUMENTS

- Any nominal, material benefits from attending a preschool for affluent children are outweighed by the daily contact that would become financially and professionally infeasible for the non-relocating parent.

[15] *See Theory of the Case*, IBJ: Criminal Defense Wiki, http://defensewiki.ibj.org/index.php/Theory_of_the_Case#Benefits_of_the_Theory_of_the_Case (last visited March 5, 2023).
[16] *Id.*

- Relocation would require the child to endure physically and mentally exhausting interstate travel.
- Relocation would prevent the child from bonding with the non-relocating parent and that parent's extended family.

PATHOS AND ETHOS POLICY ARGUMENTS

- Relocations predicated on the relocating parent's desire for wealth and status are at odds with the core societal values of facilitating stable familial relationships and recognizing the non-relocating parent's right to parent.
- Upholding the constitutionality of the relocation statute avoids circumventing the tradition of *stare decisis* and jeopardizing the best interests of minor children.

The lowest common denominator in each argument is a core societal value embedded in the best interest of the child standard: stability. So, the advocate's theory about why the non-relocating parent is entitled to relief should highlight the relationship between stability and the child's best interest. An effective theory—one that satisfies the Facts Beyond Change Test, the Plausibility Test, and reflects all the attributes of an effective theory—appears below. The advocate for the non-relocating parent uses vivid, evocative language that explicitly and implicitly references stability; key terms are bolded for emphasis.

THE NON-RELOCATING PARENT'S THEORY

If the petition to relocate is granted, a **three-year-old child** will be **uprooted** from the community where he was born and where he has the most extensive network of extended family members to a place **where he has no extended family** and **no feasible way of maintaining the emotional bond**, even with extended periods of summer visitation, that he has with his mother. When relocation would **jeopardize the stability** of such a young child, **the child's interest in stability** trumps the relocating parent's right to travel.

Now, evaluate the theory drafted by the advocate representing the relocating parent. Can you see how that advocate uses the same kind of vivid, evocative language that explicitly and implicitly references stability? Key terms are bolded for emphasis.

THE RELOCATING PARENT'S THEORY

This case is about a good parent making a difficult decision, one that will alter some aspects of the current visitation schedule, to give his **three-year-old child economic, emotional,** and **educational stability**—two of his responsibilities as a **primary caregiver**—that will enable the child to **reap the benefits** of an education at an elite private school. When relocation is in the doesn't **jeopardize** the child's **stability,** relocation child's best interest.

As these examples illustrate, each advocate appeals to the core societal value of stability as the foundation of powerful theories for *and* against relocation. Notice that each advocate's theory is a simple one-paragraph statement that use vivid, evocative language (e.g., "uprooting" a "three-year-old child" versus providing a "three-year-old child" with "economic, emotional, and educational stability") to justify the desired legal outcome and motivate the judge to adopt each advocate's desired resolution.

Drafting a theory is challenging. However, putting in the time and effort to overcome the drafting challenges referenced in this section will save valuable time during the packaging stage. For example, having an effective theory that you can reference will help generate point headings and make it easier for you to showcase the client's theory in the introduction. In short, a good theory functions much like a Global Positioning System (GPS); it keeps you from getting lost in the minutiae of your arguments.

Drafting an Effective Theme: Examples and Strategies

If a good theory functions like a GPS, then a good theme functions like the chorus of a catchy song. The catchy phrase makes the song memorable. Because the song is memorable, you catch yourself singing it absentmindedly under your breath. Because you catch yourself absentmindedly singing it under your breath, you decide to purchase the song. Because you and millions of people like you purchase the song, the songwriter and the artist achieve fame and fortune! In short, the catchiness of the chorus creates a chain reaction that communicates the song's message to its ultimate audience. The legal storyteller uses the "catchiness" of a theme to succinctly communicate the message embodied in the theory. According to one commentator, "When you find the right theme, you will know it—the whole case comes swiftly together and falls neatly into place. . . . [I]t suddenly becomes clear that your point of view regarding the case dispute is the right one and [that] the other side's is wrong."[17] The following graphic summarizes three attributes of an effective theme that we've highlighted in various portions of this book:

Attributes of an Effective Theme

It's memorable

It's simple and immediately understandable

It subtly targets the weakest aspect of the case

[17] Neil Vidmar & Shari Seidman Diamond, *Juries and Expert Evidence*, 66 Brook. L. Rev. 1121, 1160 (2001).

As noted in Chapter 2, storytellers use a variety of mnemonic devices to create memorable themes.[18] Perhaps the most well-known mnemonic device in legal education is IRAC. This mnemonic device, which stands for **I**ssue, **R**ule, **A**nalysis, and **C**onclusion, helps students remember key components of objective predictive legal analysis. Effective legal storytellers also use mnemonic devices to create memorable themes. The list below illustrates some common mnemonic devices that you can use to distinguish your client's case from the sea of legal briefs cluttering the judge's desk.[19]

A word of caution: Don't use a mnemonic device when it results in a theme that sounds too contrived or gimmicky. A subtle approach is often more effective.[20]

Themes should also be simple. In legal storytelling, simplicity means two distinct tasks: conveying an immediately understandable message and word economy. You've successfully completed your first task when, after reading your theme, the judge nods her head in recognition of the irrefutable truth of the theme's message. However, if the judge doesn't understand the theme or isn't sure how it relates to the case, then you've unwittingly created another theme: confusion. Let's explore the immediately understandable aspect of simplicity with the following example.

Mnemonic Device	Definition	Theme
Alliteration	A pattern of similar consonant sounds in a group of words	**B**reaking the **b**ond **b**reaks the child.
Assonance	A pattern of similar vowel sounds in a group of words	No p**ai**n, no g**ai**n.
Metaphor	A comparison between dissimilar things	Asking the jury to ignore prejudicial hearsay evidence is **like** asking the jury to ignore an elephant in the middle of the courtroom.
Rhyme	A similarity in the sound of words	If it doesn't **fit**, you must **acquit**.
Maxim	A succinct saying that captures a universally accepted truth	It takes a village to raise a child.

[18] *See* Dennis Congos, *Nine Types of Mnemonics for Better Memory*, U. Cent. Fla., The Learning Ctr. Exch. (Jan. 2006), http://www.learningassistance.com/2006/january/mnemonics.html.

[19] *See Alliteration—Theme*, Quizlet, http://quizlet.com/15013490/alliteration-theme-flash-cards/ (last visited March 5, 2023).

[20] *See* Ken Broda-Bahm, *Getting Beyond the Catchy Phrase and Creating a Trial Theme That Truly Works*, Jury Expert: The Art and Science of Litigation Advocacy, July 1, 2008, at 5, http://www.thejuryexpert.com/2008/07/getting-beyond-the-catchy-phrase-and-creating-a-trial-theme-that-truly-works/; Rebecca Lefler, *Remembering the Human Element: Storytelling in Legal Writing*, For the Defense (DRI, Chicago, Ill.), May 2012, at 66 (citing Bryan Garner and Justice Antonin Scalia's admonition that an "overt appeal to emotion is likely to be regarded as an insult.").

Core Societal Values	Theory	Theme
Deterrence Protection from Hackers	The Computer Fraud and Abuse Act's enumerated purpose of deterring hackers would be undermined by broadening its scope to garden-variety employment disputes unrelated to unauthorized Internet access.	Narrow and less traveled makes all the difference.

The theme passes the word economy test of simplicity but fails the immediately understandable test. The advocate assumes that the judge is familiar with the theme, a famous Robert Frost quote, and that the judge agrees with the virtues of the road less traveled. Furthermore, even if the judge is familiar with the quote and agrees with its endorsement of the road less traveled, she won't *immediately* understand how the theme relates to the theory. The key word is "immediacy." No judge has the time to decipher the meaning of a theme. And a confused judge won't remember your theme.

Another attribute of a good theme is that it functions like a magnifying glass, focusing the judge's attention on the favorable aspects of your case while subtly targeting its weakest aspects. Psychologists refer to this phenomenon as a cognitive schema.[21] A cognitive schema is a mental funnel that helps the judge process competing and contradictory facts.[22] Consider the following example of a more appropriate theme that properly focuses the judge's attention on the client's theory:

Core Societal Values	Theory	Theme
Employer Autonomy **Legitimate Employee Expectations**	Requiring an employer to permanently retain an unqualified worker like the plaintiff based solely on a compliment jeopardizes the autonomy at the core of the at-will employment doctrine.	A compliment isn't a promise of forever.

[21] *Id.*

[22] Vidmar & Diamond, *supra* note 17.

The theme, "A compliment isn't a promise of forever," captures the essence of the core societal values reflected in the legal theory. The word "compliment" highlights facts that are at odds with the core societal value of legitimate employee expectations, while the phrase "promise of forever" highlights facts that are at odds with the core societal value of employer autonomy. Lastly, a theme should be holistic, meaning that it focuses the judge's attention on the strongest aspects of the case while subtly targeting its weakest aspects. To illustrate this attribute of an effective theme, let's revisit the job search scenario featured at the beginning of this chapter. To prepare for your upcoming interview, you chose the following theory about why the firm should hire you:

> I'm the best candidate for the position. Evaluating applicants using a variety of factors unrelated to class standing—such as diverse work experiences in the non-profit and private sectors and the ability to handle complex, controversial topics related to issues such as public corruption with limited supervision—is the most reliable predictor of my potential to become an excellent attorney.

Use the three attributes of an effective theme to identify the theme that best compliments your theory.

Option 1: Experience
Option 2: Grades aren't everything.
Option 3: Better than all the rest
Option 4: Real world experience, real world results

You guessed it! The fourth option is the best one. The first option is not the best because, although it's simple, it's too vague to clearly summarize the theory and thus, wouldn't be immediately recognizable by the decision-maker. Similarly, the second answer choice isn't the best option because it focuses attention on negative aspects of your credentials that you want to de-emphasize, not highlight in a theme.

Lastly, the third option is incorrect for the same reasons that the first answer choice is incorrect. The more fact-intensive and complex the case, the more challenging it will be to distill its essence in a simple, easy to understand theme. If you're not careful, you'll use these challenges as an excuse to procrastinate as you frantically search for a perfect theme. Notice the "theme" of this sentence: the quest for perfection is counterproductive. Instead of dwelling on the challenges, consider the three theme generating strategies depicted in the following graphic:

Theme Generating Strategies

Quotes

Six Words Stories

Focus Groups

Quotes

Quotes are good sources of themes because they usually speak to universal conflicts and beliefs that are immediately understandable in a particular culture or society. But perhaps most importantly for novice legal storytellers, quotes are perhaps the least labor-intensive method of finding a theme because someone else has already done the hard work for you—quotes are typically catchy, concise, and easily understandable. Movies and other pop culture references are also good sources for quotes with theme-building potential. The Internet also contains a treasure trove of sites that collect quotes about virtually any subject.

Six-Word Stories

As the name suggests, six-word stories are mini-stories that test the storyteller's ability to condense the story's core message. Ernest Hemingway is the author of what is perhaps the most famous six-word story: "For sale: baby shoes, never worn."[23] Other examples of six-word stories include the following.[24]

"Revenge is living well, without you." —Joyce Carol Oates
"All those pages in the fire." —Janet Burroway
"Race masquerading as reasonable suspicion. Again."
"A life betrayed by ordinary dreams."

[23] Sara Roncero-Menendez, *In Six Words These Writers Tell You an Entire Story*, Huffington Post (May 16, 2014), http://www.huffingtonpost.com/2014/05/16/six-word-story_n_5332833.html (last visited March 6, 2023).
[24] The first two six-word stories are from *How Much Can You Say in Six Words? A Tool for VO Practice*, Voice Over Blog, http://blog.edgestudio.com/how-much-can-you-say-in-6-words-a-tool-for-vo-practice (last visited Nov. 7, 2016). The last two were created by coauthor Camille Lamar Campbell.

These six-word stories stimulate powerful emotions and experiences while achieving word economy. Drafting a six-word story is a particularly useful technique for distilling the essence of your theory into a theme, forcing you to prioritize among competing ideas to capture the essence of the theory.

Focus Groups

Another challenge of crafting a good theme is taking off your "law suit" (pun intended) and adopting the persona of a layperson. You adopt the persona of a layperson by thinking like your neighbor across the street or the person next to you at your favorite bar or restaurant. Trial lawyers commonly use focus groups to develop the persona of a layperson. A focus group is a group of people whose responses are solicited to predict a response from a larger group of people.[25] If your goal is to reach the "reasonably prudent person," then the best way to achieve that goal is ask a group of people, preferably with different experiences and backgrounds, to help you develop and evaluate a potential theme.

After recruiting an eclectic mix of people, provide a succinct overview of the material facts and the relevant issues. You might also consider appointing a discussion leader, preferably another student who's familiar with the case, to structure the conversation. The discussion leader should *not* suggest an outcome or a theme but keep the conversation focused on what the members of the focus group consider to be the heart of the case. For example, you might ask questions such as these:[26]

- What is the significance of the case?
- What is the case all about?
- What is its underlying message?
- What word or phrase best describes the case and brings it all together?

Next, listen and synthesize the group's responses. A pattern of responses supplies clues for developing a theme or evaluating the viability of a prospective one. You can also use a focus group to critique an existing theme. One particularly helpful approach is to develop a visual mock-up of your theme and ask focus group members for their reactions and feedback. Consider the following example of a visual theory and theme representation.

---

[25] *Focus Group*, Merriam Webster Dictionary, http://www.merriam-webster.com/dictionary/focus%20group (last visited March 6, 2023).

[26] Vidmar & Diamond, *supra* note 17.

Reprinted with permission from Trinty Bowers.

What feelings does this image evoke?
Can you predict the advocate's theory and theme?

Use the visual representation to ask your focus group the following kinds of questions:

- Is the overall visual depiction clear as opposed to visually cluttered and distracting?
- Is the theme immediately discernable even without verbal explanation?
- Does the theme accurately encompass the advocate's theory?

Focus groups are the most labor-intensive method of developing a theme. However, they typically provide the legal storyteller with the most accurate predictor of a theme's viability.

We've worked through several examples of ineffective and effective theories and themes. The information below reproduces some of these examples; refer to them as a guide when drafting your client's theory and theme:

THE JOB CANDIDATE'S THEORY AND THEME

Theme: Real world experience, real world results.

Theory: I'm the best candidate for the position. **Evaluating applicants using a variety of factors** unrelated to class standing—such as **diverse work experiences in the non-profit and private sectors** and the ability to handle **complex, controversial topics related to issues such as public corruption with limited supervision**—is the most reliable predictor of my potential to become an excellent attorney.

THE NON-RELOCATING PARENT'S THEORY AND THEME

Theme: Breaking the bond breaks the child.

Theory: If the petition to relocate is granted, a **three- year-old child** will be **uprooted** from the community where he was born and where he has the most extensive network of extended family members to a place **where he has no extended family** and **no feasible way of maintaining the emotional bond**, even with extended periods of summer visitation, that he has with his mother. When relocation would **jeopardize the stability** of such a young child, **the child's interest in stability** trumps the relocating parent's right to travel.

THE RELOCATING PARENT'S THEORY AND THEME

Theme: What's best for the child is what's best for his primary caregiver.

Theory: This case is about a good parent making a difficult decision, one that will alter some aspects of the current visitation schedule, to give his **three-year-old child economic, emotional, and educational stability**—two of his responsibilities as a **primary caregiver**—that will enable the child to **reap the benefits** of an education at an elite private school. When relocation doesn't jeopardize the child's **stability**, relocation is in the child's best interest.

Once you've scrutinized these examples, use the following checklist to evaluate your work. Consider modifying it to include any additional considerations suggested by your professor.

☑ Is your theory simple (i.e., no more than a paragraph) easily understandable statement? Is your theme simple (i.e., no more than one sentence or phrase)?

☑ Does your theory and theme target the weakest aspect of the client's case?

☑ Does your theory highlight the relevant legal standards or core societal values at the root of the legal standard?

☑ Does your theory use vivid, evocative language to highlight favorable facts?

☑ Does your theory avoid pitfalls such as merely re-stating arguments, rules, or core societal values?

☑ Does your theme effectively use mnemonic devices such as alliteration, assonance, metaphor, rhyme, or maxims?

Congratulations! You've successfully processed your client's legal story. You've brainstormed arguments and developed a theory and a theme. Now what? We'll move from the processing phase to the packaging phase of legal storytelling. During packaging, the legal storyteller infuses the brief with pathos and ethos generating navigational and design tools and utilizes an eclectic mix of hard-and-soft sell persuasive techniques to showcase the client's theory, theme, and arguments.

Part II

Packaging the Story: Advocating for the Client's Point of View

II

Building the Story Architecture for the Client's Point of View

Chapter 5

Persuading Through Document Design

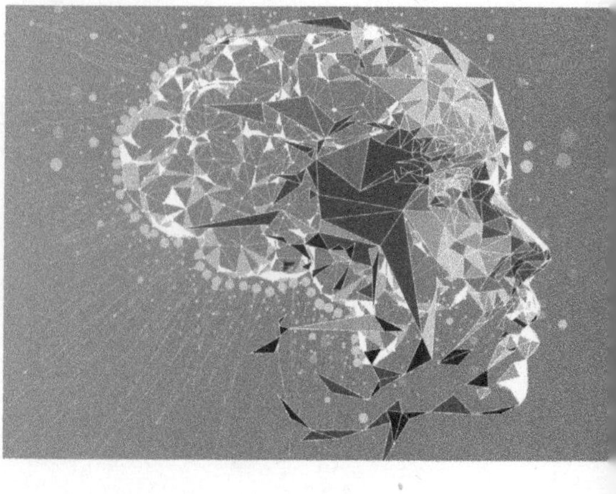

"Technology has handed . . . advocates an array of new tools, inviting creativity and expanding ways to persuade."—Emily Hamm Huseth & Michael F. Rafferty[1]

Though technology has opened the door to a universe of brand-new visual aids that can help you to build a persuasive case for your client's story, the value of visuals is nothing new. In fact, humans are intuitively drawn to visuals and have long used them to persuade and influence others. Science has even confirmed the important role visuals play in drawing our attention to key information.[2] Neuroscience and psychology researchers studying decision-making have found that images can be critical to the deliberative process, especially in persuasion. Many people process the world visually making visual aids especially useful to them. In almost any scenario, text enhanced by an appropriate graphic is more compelling than text alone.

---

[1] Emily Hamm Huseth & Michael F. Rafferty, *A Picture Can Save a Thousand Words: The Case for Using Images in Appellate Briefs*, For Def., Feb. 2019, at 22, 27.

[2] *See* John H. Larsen, *Using Visuals to Better Communicate Logic in Legal Reasoning*, 25 J. Legal Writing Inst. 285 (2021); *see also* Steve Johansen & Ruth Anne Robbins, *Art-iculating the Analysis: Systemizing the Decision to Use Visuals as Legal Reasoning*, 20 J. Legal Writing Inst. 57, 60 (2015) ("Research in neuroscience reveals what we already knew intuitively: visual or graphic representations resonate with readers.")

A simple story about a lost dog can make this point clear. Imagine a child searching for a lost puppy in your neighborhood. To persuade others to help look, the child could describe the missing dog as a small, white, four-year-old Maltipoo named Chewy. While several people might respond to a call for volunteers to aid in the search for the missing dog, don't you think the call for help would be bolstered by featuring the following picture of the missing dog on the flyer?

A simple addition of a single photo advances both the pathos and ethos persuasion threads. First, it taps into the emotional appeal for many people of a "cute and cuddly" animal. Next, it helps bolster credibility, because the picture suggests a deeper link between the human and the missing dog. It also generates ethos by making it easier for the reader to understand what is at stake—it provides a much-needed motivational anchor. When moved from the realm of this simple scenario to a brief written for a judge, the value of a visual can be equally impactful. The addition of a visual improves the document design and strengthens the persuasive force of the brief.

Visuals clear a path for the judge to better understand your arguments, and reinforce arguments made in the text. Effective document design additions can make the dense, thick text in briefs more manageable. Chief Justice John Roberts once compared the arduous task of reading poorly written briefs to "hacking through a jungle with a machete"—spending time trying to cut through dense material to figure out the argument.

> **Reading a poorly written brief is almost like hacking through a jungle with a machete . . . [y]ou spend all your energy trying to figure out what the argument is, as opposed to putting your arms around it and seeing if it works.**
>
> **—Chief Justice John Roberts**

Design principles are reader-focused and free the reader from the task of hacking through a jungle of words in an effort to extract the client's story. They can also be used to bolster ethos and pathos arguments in the brief.

As you work through each step of the processing phase, it's easy to forget about the judge who will eventually read the brief. Briefs that require the judge to brandish a machete are disproportionately logos-centric, meaning that the substantive legal arguments aren't packaged in a way that facilitates ethos or pathos. Facilitating the full span of rheotorical devices requires an understanding of the judicial reader's special needs.

Because most judges have limited time in which to read and understand briefs, the judge reading your brief must work efficiently and will be well served by what legal storytellers call a reference brief[3] that both judges and their busy law clerks can rely on. Reference briefs have the following attributes:

- They strictly adhere to all federal, state, or local rules about format, structure, and organization.
- They incorporate ethos-generating navigational tools such as tables of contents, questions presented, headings, hyperlinks, and roadmaps.
- They effectively use design principles such as font, white space, and visual elements such as charts, graphs, and photographs. Such document principles can generate ethos and pathos, thereby improving the persuasive value of your story.

This chapter introduces you to the most common document design tools and explores some fundamental design principles.

ETHOS-GENERATING NAVIGATIONAL TOOLS

As professional readers, judges must be efficient. And for judicial readers, a key aspect of efficiency is autonomy. Ethos-generating navigational tools give judges maximum autonomy: the ability to quickly locate and seamlessly move between the different sections of the brief. In the absence of the kind of navigational tools covered in this section, judges are forced to hack through the entire brief to find the information they need. Imagine the goodwill that you'll create with busy judges and their law clerks by including a table of contents outlining the brief's large-scale organization. Furthermore, incorporating navigational tools into the overall design of your brief—even if

[3] *See generally* K.K. DuVivier, *The Reference Brief*, Colo. Law., July 2004, at 71.

they're not required by federal, state, or local rules—will score *major* ethos points with judges because you've made their jobs easier.

Making judges' jobs easier won't necessarily win cases, but the navigational tools described in this section increase the likelihood that judges will read your briefs,[4] that they will be empowered to read the briefs in whatever way best meets their needs, and that they won't have to brandish a machete to understand the clients' stories. In addition, today's judges are more likely to read briefs on digital devices. Because the dominant medium for reading text has shifted to electronic screens—even for many judges[5]—document design should reflect the interactive nature of how people read and experience text. For more than a decade, some U.S. Supreme Court Justices have been reading briefs on digital devices.[6] Ethos-generating navigational tools exploit the advantages of digital functionality and bolster our credibility by facilitating reader-focused format judges can traverse with ease.

The diagram that follows depicts some of the most common ethos-generating navigational tools.

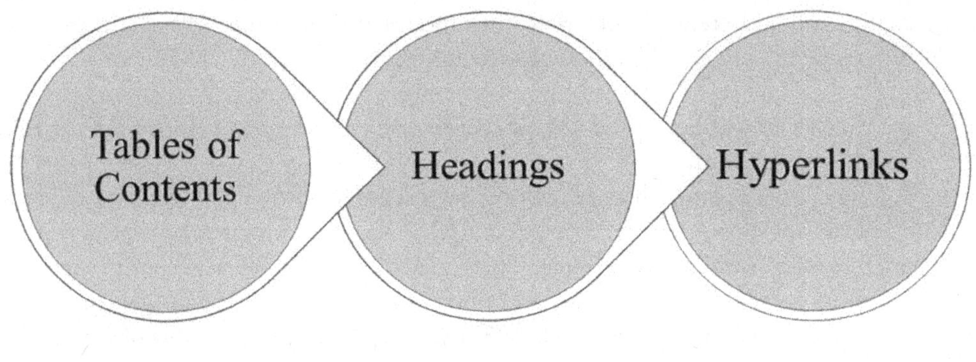

Tables of Contents

An effective table of contents combines hard and soft persuasive techniques to preview the client's story. With just a quick glance at the table of contents, the judge should have a good grasp of the client's theory, theme, and emerging story. Let's explore the power of a good table of contents with a nonlegal example. Compare the two lists that follow. Which one is easier to read?

The list on the right is easier to read than the one on the left because it does what learning theorists call chunking. Chunking is a memory-enhancing packaging tool.[7]

---

[4] *See* Margaret Oertling Cupples, *Appellate Briefing: Some Thoughts on Writing Briefs That Can Clear a Path through the Jungle*, 30 Miss. C. L. Rev. 1, 49 (2011).
[5] *See* Ellie Margolis, *Is Medium the Message? Unleashing the Power of E-Communication in the Twenty-First Century*, 12. J. ALWD 1, 12, (2015); Elizabth G. Porter, *Taking Images Seriously*, 114 Colum. L. Rev. 1687 (2014).
[6] Joseph A. Rosenberg, *Why Lawyers Should Write for the Digital Reader*, 27 Legal Writing 111, 113 (2023).
[7] *See* Shailini Jandial George, *The Cure for the Distracted Mind: Why Law Schools Should Teach Mindfulness*, 53 Duq. L. Rev. 215, n. 20 (2015); Connie Malmud, *Chunking Information for Instructional Design*, http://theelearningcoach.com/elearning_design/chunking-information/ (last visited Nov. 2, 2016).

Apple	Fruit
Grapes	A. Nontropical Fruit
Pineapple	1. Apple
Peaches	2. Grapes
Passion fruit	3. Peaches
Coconut	B. Tropical Fruit
	1. Pineapple
	2. Passion fruit
	3. Coconut

By grouping related bits of information into general categories (i.e., nontropical versus tropical fruits), the advocate creates a built-in organizational structure for judges to better understand the relationship between important concepts.

Savvy legal storytellers understand how chunking information in a table of contents clarifies the relationship between arguments. Include a table of contents in any brief that's more than six pages or whenever you have multiple arguments. Consider the following table of contents.

TABLE OF CONTENTS

Introduction 1

Statement of Facts 2

[Plot Headings]

An Interrupted Climb Up the Corporate Ladder 2
Behavior Continues Despite Notice and Response 4
A Lawsuit to Restore Workplace Harmony 5

Argument 6

[Main Point Heading]

I. Summary Judgment Is Improper Because Genuine Issues of Material Fact Exist About Whether Mr. Simms's Gender Made Him a Target for Sexual Harassment and Because a Liberal Interpretation of Causation Is Consistent with Congress's Intent 8

[Subpoint Headings]

A. Had He Been Female, Mr. Simms Would Not Have Been Victimized by a Supervisor Who Pinched His Buttocks Every Other Day and Who Sent Twelve E-mails Soliciting Sexual Activity.

B. The *Brown* Test for Imputing Liability to Bisexual Harassers Is Most Consistent with Congressional Intent to Eliminate All Types of Sexual Harassment.

[Page numbers maximize navigational autonomy]

II. This Court Should Adhere to the Supreme Court's Version of the *Ellerth/Faragher* Affirmative Defense, Not a Modified Version from an Unpublished Case with No Precedential Value 13

Conclusion 15

The table of contents provides the judge with a comprehensive snapshot of the advocate's story and uses a combination of hard- and soft-sell persuasive techniques such as:

- **Plot headings** to outline the plot of the client's story and foreshadow arguments. Plot headings are a soft-sell persuasive technique that we'll explore in Chapter 7.2.
- **Point headings** to announce the advocate's best arguments via distinctive formatting features (i.e., bold typeface and underlining). Point headings are hard-sell persuasive techniques whose purpose and function we'll explore in Chapter 8.1.
- **An easy-to-read font** and **page numbers** to maximize navigational autonomy, enabling the judge to efficiently read the brief. Font is a soft-sell persuasive technique that is discussed in the second part of this chapter.

Simplify the process of creating a table of contents by using templates that are standard in many word-processing systems. These standardized templates automatically update the table of contents to reflect changes in the body of the brief. Taking a few seconds to activate your computer's table of contents function is an easy, relatively painless way of creating a judge-friendly brief.

Although these templates will automatically update the table of contents, your word processor won't detect the kinds of proofreading errors discussed in Chapter 10. So, make sure that each section of the brief is identified, that the plot and point headings identified in the table of contents are identical to the ones contained in the body of the brief, and that the page numbers in the table of contents match the page numbers in the brief. Taking a few seconds to activate your computer's table of contents function is an easy, relatively painless way to help the judge navigate the client's story.

Headings

Judges love headings;[8] they help judges process the client's story by providing visual relief in a sea of text. So, it's not surprising that headings are featured in some of the most important sections of the brief such as the table of contents, the statement of facts, and the argument section. Take a quick glance at the following menus. They illustrate the power of strategically placed headings. Which one is easier to read and to remember?

Each menu contains identical offerings, but the headings make the menu on the left easier to read. The enhanced readability of the menu with headings is another example of the memory-enhancing power of chunking. Grouping related bits of information—pancakes, Belgian waffles, and biscuits—into the general category of breakfast gives the customer a frame of reference for remembering individual menu items. Now that you understand the power of strategically placed headings, we'll explore some basic heading types with an emphasis on impact headings, the most fluid kind of heading.

[8] *See* Andrew M. Low, *Tips from the Judges*, Colo. Law., Mar. 2013, at 49; Gerald Lebovits, *Do's, Don'ts, and Maybes: Legal Writing Do's—Part I*, N.Y. St. B.J., May 2007, at 64.

Caitlyn's Roaring Twenties Grill

Breakfast Classics

Two Buttermilk Pancakes served with Bacon or Sausage
Belgian Waffle topped with Seasonal Fruit
Biscuits and Red Eye Gravy served with Ham and Eggs

Brunch Specials

Strawberries and Crème Crepe topped with Powdered Sugar
Not Your Mama's Meatloaf topped with Mushrooms
Eggs Benedict topped with Hollandaise Sauce

Caitlyn's Roaring Twenties Grill

Two Buttermilk Pancakes served with Bacon or Sausage
Belgian Waffle topped with Seasonal Fruit
Biscuits and Red Eye Gravy served with Ham and Eggs

Strawberries and Crème Crepe topped with Powdered Sugar
Not Your Mama's Meatloaf topped with Mushrooms
Eggs Benedict topped with Hollandaise Sauce

Basic Heading Types

Savvy legal storytellers use a potpourri of headings, sprinkling them anywhere the judge will likely need visual relief. The diagram at the beginning of this chapter identifies three basic types of headings: impact headings, plot headings, and point headings. Because of their complexity, plot and point headings are discussed in Chapters 7.2 and 8.1. The chart that follows summarizes some key differences between these three heading types.

	Impact Headings	**Plot Headings**	**Point Headings**
Location	Argument Section	• Table of Contents • Statement of Facts	• Table of Contents • Argument Section
Purpose	To reinforce a core component of a point heading	To outline the plot of the client's story	To announce arguments
Key Feature	Argumentative phrases written in bold, italicized typeface	Nonargumentative phrases written in bold typeface	Argumentative sentences written in distinctive typefaces and typically preceded by a Roman numeral, letter, or number

Impact Headings

Impact headings are hard-sell persuasive techniques that break up the wall of words created by paragraph after paragraph of dense text. In a nonstorytelling brief, point headings might be the judge's only source of visual relief in the argument section. But in the storytelling brief, the advocate uses impact headings to visually reinforce core point heading components. Consider the following example. Notice how the impact headings create visual relief while reenforcing core components of the point heading.[9]

Subpoint Heading →

A. Had He Been Female, Mr. Simms Would Not Have Been Victimized by a Supervisor Who [**] ***Pinched His Buttocks Every Other Day*** and Who *[**]* ***Sent Twelve E-mails Soliciting Sexual Activity.***

[Three Pages Later]

Targeted for Unwanted Sexual Groping ←

Impact heading #1 reenforces bolded, italicized portion of the point heading after the first set of asterisks.

The supervisor targeted Mr. Simms for sexually aggressive conduct by touching him in a more physically intrusive manner than she did his female coworker, Ms. Serena Askew. The difference between the way the supervisor treated Mr. Simms and Ms. Askew—the difference between a full-body pat-down versus an innocent workplace flirtation akin to a crush—creates a reasonable inference of gender-based sexual harassment. (Simms Dep. 3:97.) On a daily basis, Mr. Simms's supervisor groped him in a sexually suggestive way. For example, she would (1) massage his neck and shoulders, (2) tightly hug Mr. Simms while moving her breasts against his chest in a circular motion, and (3) rub her hands up and down Mr. Simms's back and tightly squeeze his buttocks. (Id.)

In stark contrast, the supervisor's behavior toward Ms. Askew was definitively nonsexual. For example, the supervisor never rubbed Ms. Askew's back or gave her a massage. She never pressed her breasts against Ms. Askew's chest and never groped Ms. Askew's buttocks. On those rare occasions when the supervisor touched Ms. Askew, the supervisor's conduct was more restrained and platonic, not an unrelenting sexually aggressive pursuit. For example, the supervisor once sat in Ms. Askew's lap (DuBois Dep. 6:238), and on another occasion, she played with her hair (id. at 5:228). This undisputed evidence of gender-based differential treatment suggests that the trial court erred in its application of the summary judgment standard and that a reasonable juror could have concluded that Mr. Simms was targeted because of his gender.

[9] This hypothetical scenario is based on a legal writing problem created by Professor David Cleveland and revised by Professor Kathryn Webber.

Targeted for Unwelcome Sexually Suggestive E-mails →

Impact heading #2 reenforces bolded, italicized portion of the point heading after the second set of asterisks.

A reasonable juror could have also concluded that Mr. Simms was targeted for sexually aggressive treatment because of the sexually suggestive gender-specific language contained in e-mails. In the Second Circuit, gender-specific words expressing sexual desire can support an inference of gender-based discrimination in violation of Title VII. See, e.g., Puchino v. Verizon Wireless Commc'n Inc., 618 F.3d 112, 116 (2d Cir. 2010). Applying this rule to the facts of this case suggests that the supervisor's gender-specific language was an expression of sexual desire for Mr. Simms because of his gender. Two reasons support this assertion. First, Mr. Simms's supervisor admitted that she sent him 10 to 12 e-mails containing pictures of nude women. Dubose Dep., Ex. 10 (Simms Dep. 4:153). In these e-mails, the supervisor referred to Mr. Simms as a "delicious piece of beefcake." (Simms Dep. 3:133.) The word "beefcake" is a gendered nickname describing "a photographic display of muscular male physiques or a man featured in such a display." Beefcake, Merriam-Webster, http://www.merriam-webster.com/dictionary/beefcake (last visited Nov. 17, 2016). This definition coupled with the sexually suggestive invitations for sex suggest that the supervisor's gender-specific language was an expression of sexual desire for Mr. Simms because of his gender.

Second, had Mr. Simms been female, his supervisor would never have subjected him to such intrusive, sexually suggestive workplace e-mails. For example, the supervisor never sent Ms. Askew any e-mails with attachments of nude photographs, never insisted that she come over to her house for "wild and crazy fun," and never gave her a gender-specific nickname expressing a desire for a purely sexual relationship. Instead, the supervisor merely sent Ms. Askew little handwritten notes and letters—fewer than five times in total—complimenting her as a "person" and expressing a wish to socialize outside the office. (Anderson Dep. 2:66-67, 68-69.) These flirtatious, nonsexual notes would tell Ms. Askew that she was "special." (Id. at 2:66.) Comparative evidence of differential treatment and the supervisor's repeated use of the gendered term "beefcake" creates a reasonable inference that Mr. Simms was targeted for sexual aggression because of gender stereotypes that men are more receptive to aggressive sexual advances than women. Thus, the trial court erred when it granted summary judgment on the "because of sex" element.

Without these impact headings, the judge would encounter paragraph after paragraph of text densely packed into an 8 1/2″ x 11″ rectangle without *any* visual relief. Furthermore, because both impact headings are italicized phrases, they don't compete with the subpoint heading.

Impact Heading Drafting Tips

There are no hard and fast rules about where to place impact headings. But the key to drafting effective impact headings is to remember that they're designed to reinforce the point headings, not compete with them. These four drafting tips will reduce the likelihood of distracting competition between your point and impact headings.

Tip #1: Include an impact heading for every three pages of argument.
Tip #2: Don't place impact headings too close to point headings.

Visually Confusing: Point Heading and Impact Heading on the Same Page

Subpoint Heading → A. Had He Been Female, Mr. Simms Would Not Have Been Victimized by a Supervisor Who [**] ***Pinched His Buttocks Every Other Day*** and Who [**] ***Sent Him Twelve E-mails Soliciting Sexual Activity.***

Targeted for Unwanted Sexual Groping ← Impact Heading #1

The supervisor targeted Mr. Simms for sexually aggressive conduct by touching him in a more physically intrusive manner than his female coworker, Ms. Serena Askew. The difference between the way the supervisor treated Mr. Simms and Ms. Askew—the difference between a full-body pat-down versus an innocent workplace flirtation akin to a crush—creates a reasonable inference of gender-based sexual harassment. (Simms Dep. 3:97.) On a daily basis, Mr. Simms's supervisor groped him in a sexually suggestive way. For example, she would (1) massage his neck and shoulders, (2) tightly hug Mr. Simms while moving her breasts against his chest in a circular motion, and (3) rub her hands up and down Mr. Simms's back and tightly squeeze his buttocks. (Id.)

Tip #3: Don't include impact headings in the table of contents.

Impact headings are derivative, meaning that they reenforce core point heading components. Because their role is merely auxiliary, including impact headings in the table of contents creates visual confusion, leaving the judge wondering whether the advocate simply forgot to finish the point headings.

Tip #4: Impact headings are argumentative phrases, not sentences.

The distinction between phrases—a group of words that don't express a complete thought—and sentences is crucial when drafting impact headings. Opting for phrases instead of sentences reenforces their auxiliary nature and prevents the judge from confusing them with your point headings.

Now that you know about the power of impact headings to create visual relief and to reenforce core point heading components, reap their ethos-generating rewards by scattering them all over the argument section.

Hyperlinks

As noted earlier, in a legal world increasingly dominated by technology, ever increasing numbers of judges read briefs electronically.[10] And those judges often depend on hyperlinks. Hyperlinks are highlighted words or phrases that, with just one click, take judges to a case cited in a brief, an exhibit, or in deposition testimony. This ease of access permits unparalleled autonomy; judges are no longer chained to their desks because of the impracticality of lugging around stacks of depositions and exhibits. In discussing his preference for hyperlinked briefs, one well-known federal judge observed that "[f]ew lawyers are providing these links, and I believe they should be standard practice. . . . [They] allow me instant access to record facts and research authorities that are often critical to my decisions."[11]

When appropriately used, hyperlinks can also function as soft-sell persuasive techniques that subtly highlight or emphasize the client's story. The appellate brief featured earlier in this chapter included the following hyperlinks:

- First, Mr. Simms's supervisor admitted that she sent him 10 to 12 e-mails containing pictures of nude women. Dubose Dep., Ex. 10 (Simms Dep. 4:153).
- The word "beefcake" is a gendered nickname describing "a photographic display of muscular male physiques or a man featured in such a display." Beefcake, Merriam-Webster, http://www.merriam-webster.com/dictionary/beefcake (last visited Nov. 17, 2016).

The advocate uses hyperlinks to highlight a deposition exhibit, obviating the need for a detailed textual description and to reiterate the meaning of the word "beefcake," a term that is critical to the client's gender discrimination claim. Your professor may also

---

[10] *See* Ellie Margolis, *Is the Medium the Message? Unleashing the Power of E-Communication in the Twenty-first Century,* 12 JALWD 1, 21-25 (Fall 2015) (noting the trend among federal appellate judges); Ellie Neiberger, *Judge-Friendly Briefs in an Electronic Age,* 89 Fla. B.J. 46, 46 (July 2015) (noting the trend in Florida).

[11] *See* Jonathan Hafen, *Judicial Profile: Hon. David Nuffer Judge, U.S. District Court for the Northern District of Utah,* 62 Fed. Law. 39 (Aug. 2015).

permit you to hyperlink primary authorities available on Westlaw or Lexis or reputable nonlegal Internet sources such as dictionaries. But hyperlinks should *never* replace legal citations and should never be used as a substitute for analysis.

Hyperlinks are now commonplace technology that you are likely to frequently encounter as a practicing lawyer. Further, bookmarks, a type of hyperlink that allows readers to jump from location to location within a document, are typically used in tables of contents and authorities and can be easily inserted into briefs you prepare for your legal writing class.

ETHOS- AND PATHOS-GENERATING DESIGN PRINCIPLES

Creating a brief that's easy for the judge to navigate is just the first step of the ethos- and pathos-generating process. Savvy legal storytellers also understand that a well-designed brief is a soft-sell persuasive technique that facilitates ethos and pathos. Visual rhetoric[12] describes the symbiotic relationship between persuasion and document design. In storytelling briefs, advocates use visual rhetoric to capture the mood and atmosphere of the client's story. As an illustration, let's revisit the menu analogy. Take a quick look at these two menus. Which one is more visually appealing?

Caitlyn's Roaring Twenties Grill

Breakfast Classics

Two Buttermilk Pancakes served with Bacon or Sausage
Belgian Waffle topped with Seasonal Fruit
Biscuits and Red Eye Gravy served with Ham and Eggs

Brunch Specials

Strawberries and Crème Crepe topped with Powdered Sugar
Not Your Mama's Meatloaf topped with Mushrooms
Eggs Benedict topped with Hollandaise Sauce

Caitlyn's Roaring Twenties Grill

Breakfast Classics: Two Buttermilk Pancakes served with Bacon or Sausage Belgian Waffle topped with Seasonal Fruit Biscuits and Red Eye Gravy served with Ham and Eggs

Brunch Specials: Strawberries and Crème Crepe topped with Powdered Sugar, Not Your Mama's Meatloaf topped with Mushrooms, Eggs Benedict topped with Hollandaise Sauce

The menus have the same content, but two things make the menu on the left more visually appealing than the one on the right: font, a collection of related letters that

[12] *See* Derek H. Kiernan-Johnson, *Telling Through Type: Typography and Narrative In Legal Briefs*, 7 J. Ass'n Legal Writing Directors 87, 89 (2010); Linda L. Moran, *The Gestalt of Brief-Writing Visual Rhetoric for the Appellate Brief*, 49 No. 7 DRI For Def. 27 (July 2007).

have a distinct physical or digital manifestation,[13] and white space, the absence of text. The menu on the right is unappealing because it lacks white space. Notice how the different fonts—Harlow Solid Italic for the main heading and PERPETUA for the subheadings—not only make the menu on the left more visually appealing but evoke a mood and atmosphere that visually capture the restaurant's brand.

Choosing a different font for the menu subheadings creates visual interest. The contrasting typefaces help diners differentiate between the restaurant's name and its menu offerings. Harlow Solid Italic injects a bit of pizzazz into the menu; but observe how too much pizzazz leads to visual havoc. Compare these two menus:

Caitlyn's Roaring Twenties Grill

Breakfast Classics

Two Buttermilk Pancakes served with Bacon or Sausage
Belgian Waffle topped with Seasonal Fruit
Biscuits and Red Eye Gravy served with Ham and Eggs

Brunch Specials

Strawberries and Crème Crepe topped with Powdered Sugar
Not Your Mama's Meatloaf topped with Mushrooms
Eggs Benedict topped with Hollandaise Sauce

Caitlyn's Roaring Twenties Grill

Breakfast Classics

Two Buttermilk Pancakes served with Bacon or Sausage

Belgian Waffle topped with Seasonal Fruit

Biscuits and Red Eye Gravy served with Ham and Eggs

Brunch Specials

Strawberries and Crème Crepe topped with Powdered Sugar

Not Your Mama's Meatloaf topped with Mushrooms

Eggs Benedict topped with Hollandaise Sauce

Using Harlow Solid Italic for the entire menu is visually unappealing and destroys its uniqueness. The menu on the left is the more visually appealing one; changing the font resolves the visual havoc by creating a line of demarcation between the main heading, the subheadings, and the text in a way that emphasizes the distinction between the restaurant's name and its menu offerings.

These menu examples illustrate how legal storytellers use fundamental principles of document design not only to create visually appealing briefs but to visually capture the mood and atmosphere of the client's story. This section introduces you to three particularly effective ethos-generating design principles:

[13] *See Font*, WHATIS.COM, http://whatis.techtarget.com/definition/font (last visited Nov. 17, 2016).

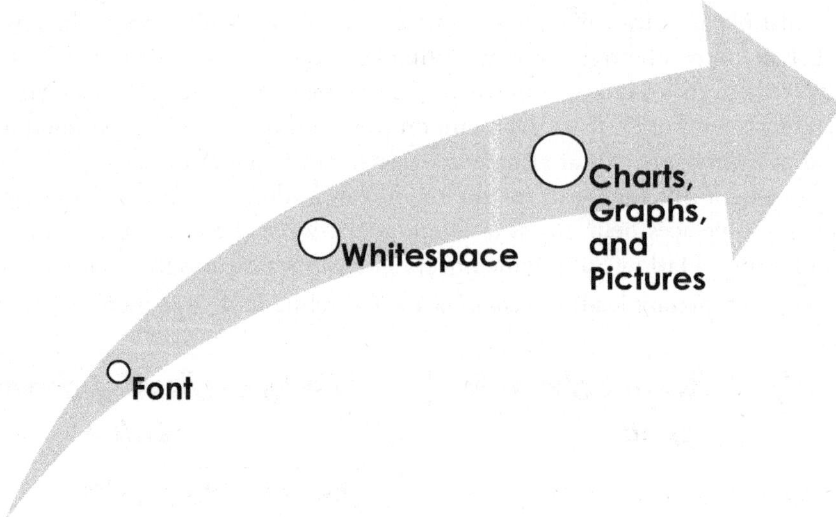

Font

With the advent of sophisticated word-processing software, most legal writers are familiar with the dizzying array of fonts that are just a click away. Because of their ready availability, advocates sometimes overlook the storytelling and ethos and pathos generating power of a distinctive, visually appealing font. Graphic artists typically divide fonts into two families: serif and sans serif fonts.

A serif font has "tails" or small horizontal or vertical strokes at the ends of the lines that mimic handwriting while a sans serif font doesn't have tails, creating a cleaner, more modern appearance. The letter on the left has serifs, and the letter on the right doesn't:

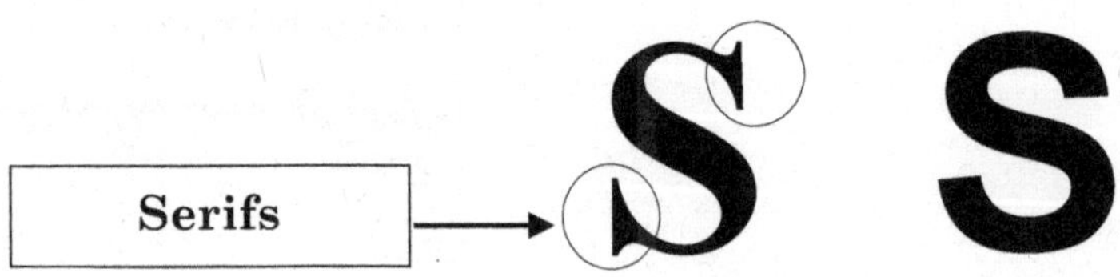

The conventional wisdom among graphic designers and at least one appellate court is that readers can more easily read and process large blocks of text when they're written in serif fonts.[14] Consequently, the typical word-processing software defaults to serif fonts such as Times New Roman, Arial, or Calibri. So, in most instances,

[14] *See* U.S. Court of Appeals for the Seventh Circuit, Practitioner's Handbook for Appeals, Requirements and Suggestions for Typography in Briefs and Other Papers 128 (2014), http://www.ca7.uscourts.gov/rules/type.pdf.

your word-processing system has been programmed so that you "automatically" select a visually engaging font. But some legal writing scholars have questioned the neuroscience supporting the conventional wisdom of the enhanced readability of serif fonts.[15] The debate about the readability of serif versus sans serif font is beyond the scope of this book. But it does underscore one extremely important ethos-generating design principle: savvy legal storytellers make intentional choices about the best font for advancing the client's story instead of mindlessly defaulting to standard fonts such as Times New Roman and Arial selected for them by their word-processing software.

Judges have also joined the movement to be intentional about font selection, criticizing advocates for bad typography in briefs.[16] For example, the Seventh Circuit Court of Appeals has a special section of its rules devoted to typography and font, advising advocates that they "can improve [their] chances [of winning an argument] by making [their] briefs typographically superior."[17] So how does an advocate select a font in an intentional, deliberate way? Understand the audience and the client's theory and theme. First, understand your judicial audience. Scrutinize the local rules and all applicable procedural rules and use them as a guide to font selection. For example, briefs submitted to the United States Supreme Court must use a typeface in the Century family (e.g., Century Expanded, New Century Schoolbook, or Century Schoolbook),[18] and the Seventh Circuit expresses a preference for more traditional fonts, ones with the word "book" in their names or that closely mirror those traditionally used in typesettinug books; examples include Palatino and Bookman Old Style fonts and fonts in the Baskerville family.[19] Most judges are fairly conservative. Avoid any font that is too dramatic or too unconventional; you'll risk alienating the judges and conveying a message that your client shouldn't be taken seriously. Second, if the applicable procedural rules or your professor's formatting instructions permit discretion, allow your theory and theme to lead you to an appropriate font, one that evokes a mood and that visually captures the client's persona.

Consider the following example of intentionality in font selection. Assume that the audience for your brief is a panel of Second Circuit judges whose procedural rules don't require a specific font.[20] Your client's theory and theme are as follows.[21]

---

[15] *See* Ruth Anne Robbins, *Painting with Print: Incorporating Concepts of Typographic and Layout Design into the Text of Legal Documents*, 2 J. Ass'n Legal Writing Directors 119-120 (2004).

[16] *See* Kiernan-Johnson, *supra* note 8, at 115 (discussing Judge Frank Easterbrook's aversion to bad typography and his contempt for Times New Roman font).

[17] *See* Practitioner's Handbook for Appeals, *supra* note 10, at 3.

[18] U.S. Sup. Ct. R. 33.

[19] *See* Practitioner's Handbook for Appeals, *supra* note 10, at 3.

[20] *See* U.S. Court of Appeals for the Second Circuit, *Brief and Appendix*, http://www.ca2.uscourts.gov/clerk/case_filing/appealing_a_case/civil_case/brief_and_appendix.html (last modified Jan. 31, 2014).

[21] This hypothetical scenario is based on a legal writing problem created by our colleague, Professor Jani Maurer.

Theory:

The deponent is a pioneer in the brave new world of digital news. And the journalist's privilege protects pioneers who use investigatory reporting techniques to police the activities of media gatekeepers.

Theme:

The New News Is Still News

In the emerging story outlined in the theory and summarized in the theme, the client is a pioneer, an Internet journalist who's struggling to be recognized as a legitimate journalist by those who would deny Internet journalists the protection of the privilege. After carefully evaluating the client's theory and theme, the advocate decides to deviate from a more traditional serif font and opt for a font that visually conveys the mood created by the theory and theme.[22] Compare the radically different mood that the employee's attorney creates by simply changing the font from Century Schoolbook to Courier New:

The New News Is Still News.

(Century Schoolbook)

The New News Is Still News.

(Courier New)

Courier New replicates the look of a typewriter and thus evokes the feel of a newspaper. The advocate is using a newspaper-style font to subtly suggest that the prestige afforded to traditional journalists should be extended to Internet journalists. Admittedly, in this example it's relatively easy for the advocate to select a visually engaging font that's consistent with the client's story. But sometimes choosing the appropriate font won't be so easy; in this situation, keep it conservative and opt for more traditional serif fonts with the word "book" in their names.

White Space

White space is an often-overlooked aspect of document design. Much like headings, white space provides visual relief in a sea of text and thus facilitates ethos. Use the following tips to create white space in your briefs.

[22] *See Leveraging Stereotypes in Design: Masculine vs. Feminine Typography*, http://designshack.net/articles/typography/leveraging-stereotypes-in-design-masculine-vs-feminine-typography/ (last visited Nov. 2, 2016).

- Break up the wall of words with frequent paragraphs—at least two per page—and use transitional phrases between paragraphs to prevent choppiness.
- Use shorter paragraphs and sentences to increase white space in the body of the text.[23]
- Consider using numbered lists or bullets[24] to streamline the delivery of information.
- Include an extra line between the end of one section of the brief and the beginning of the next section.[25]

Resist the urge to fill up every available square inch of an 8 1/2″ x 11″ page with text. In matters of document design, less is always more.

Charts, Graphs, and Pictures

The last design principle is among the powerful: visual storytelling via charts, diagrams, graphs, and pictures.[26] Graphics are particularly effective communication tools because they grab the judge's attention. At the same time, they also streamline the delivery of information and improve the judge's retention rate.

> **Visual aids—charts, timelines, pictures—help a good writer make it easy for the reader to consume information.**
>
> **—Judge Melanie G. May, Florida's Fourth District Court of Appeal**

Graphics are attention-grabbing space savers. Space is a valuable commodity in a brief. Diagramming a case's complex procedural history, creating a timeline in a factually complex case, or creating a chart of the names and titles of key litigants convey information more efficiently than words.[27] A well-placed graphic can also foreshadow arguments about the case's procedural posture or standard of review. For example, a plaintiff objecting to a motion for summary judgment could incorporate a simple two-column table contrasting the parties' testimony on key issues to demonstrate that factual disputes preclude summary judgment.[28]

Furthermore, charts, graphs, and pictures are a reader-friendly way to increase judges' retention rates. According to one study, readers' retention skyrockets to 50 percent when visuals accompany text, as opposed to a 10 percent retention rate when text is presented without visuals.[29] Including charts, diagrams, graphs, and pictures

[23] *See* Lisa Solomon, *Pixel Persuasion: Appellate Brief-Writing For the 21st Century*, App. F., Jan. 2014, at 2.
[24] *See* Moran, *supra* note 8.
[25] *Id.*
[26] *See generally* Adam L. Rosman, *Visualizing the Law: Using Charts, Diagrams and Other Images to Improve Legal Briefs*, 63 J. Legal Educ. 70 (2014) (encouraging practitioners to incorporate visuals into briefs); Mike Skotnicki, *Suggestions for Emphasizing Facts without Using Emphasis*, Briefly Writing Blog (June 25, 2012), http://brieflywriting.com/2012/06/25/suggestions-for-emphasizing-facts-without-using-emphasis/.
[27] 22. Rosman, *supra* note 21, at 78.
[28] Thomas G. Collins & Karin Marlett, *New Tools Can Enhance Legal Writing*, 75 N.Y. St. B.J., June 2003, at 10, 14.
[29] *Id.* at 11.

in your briefs increases the likelihood that judges and their busy law clerks will retain important information about your clients' cases.

The statement of facts and argument sections are the natural choice for charts, graphs, and pictures. Consider the following two-column list that could easily be inserted into a statement of facts:

Plaintiff Hailey Gideon filed this lawsuit against the First Union Anglican Church of Colorado and several codefendants:

Reverend Aaron Lewis	Chief Executive Officer
Reverend Jonathan Ozeki	Council of Bishops President
Reverend Dominick Vanderbilt	Plaintiff's Immediate Supervisor

Notice how a simple two-column list presents background facts in a space-saving, reader-friendly way. You can also use a graphic to emphasize the passage of time. For example, in lieu of a narrative description in the argument section of the brief, the assistant U.S. attorney in the Sixth Amendment scenario could use a picture of a calendar for visual impact:

The accused waited until the middle of jury selection to fire his attorney—the same attorney that he had met with for five weeks and whom he had observed sleeping during each pretrial meeting. Those pretrial meeting dates are circled below:

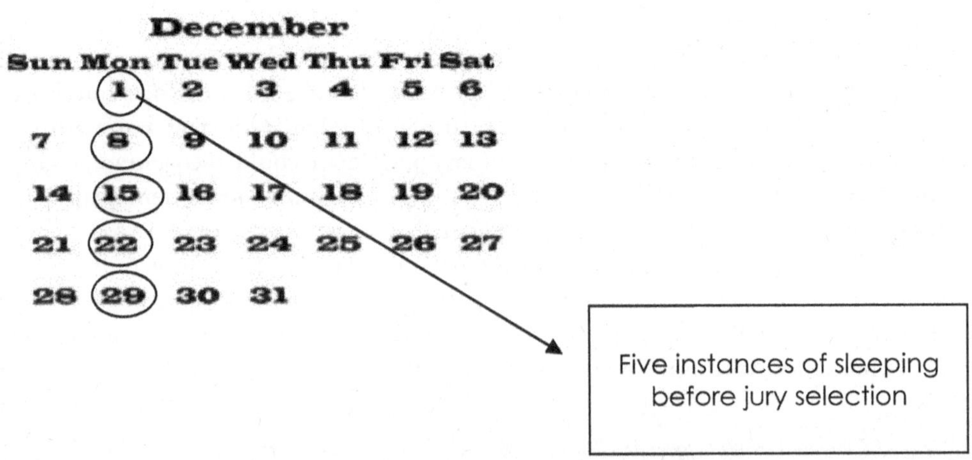

The calendar reinforces the number of opportunities that the defendant had had to seek new counsel prior to trial. With the graphic, the prosecution accentuates its theory: that the motion for a new trial is a delaying tactic that undermines the government's Sixth Amendment interest in expedient and efficient trials.

Graphics can also be used to clarify legal arguments for the judge. Practice using SmartArt[30] on Word for Microsoft 365 to simplify the rule presentation in a manner that advances your client's interest. Organizing the rule through a graphic illustration helps the judge understand the rule through your client's eyes. In the example below an inmate seeking gender affirmation surgery uses a graphic to demonstrate that the surgery is merely one type of medical care extended to inmates under the Eighth Amendment:

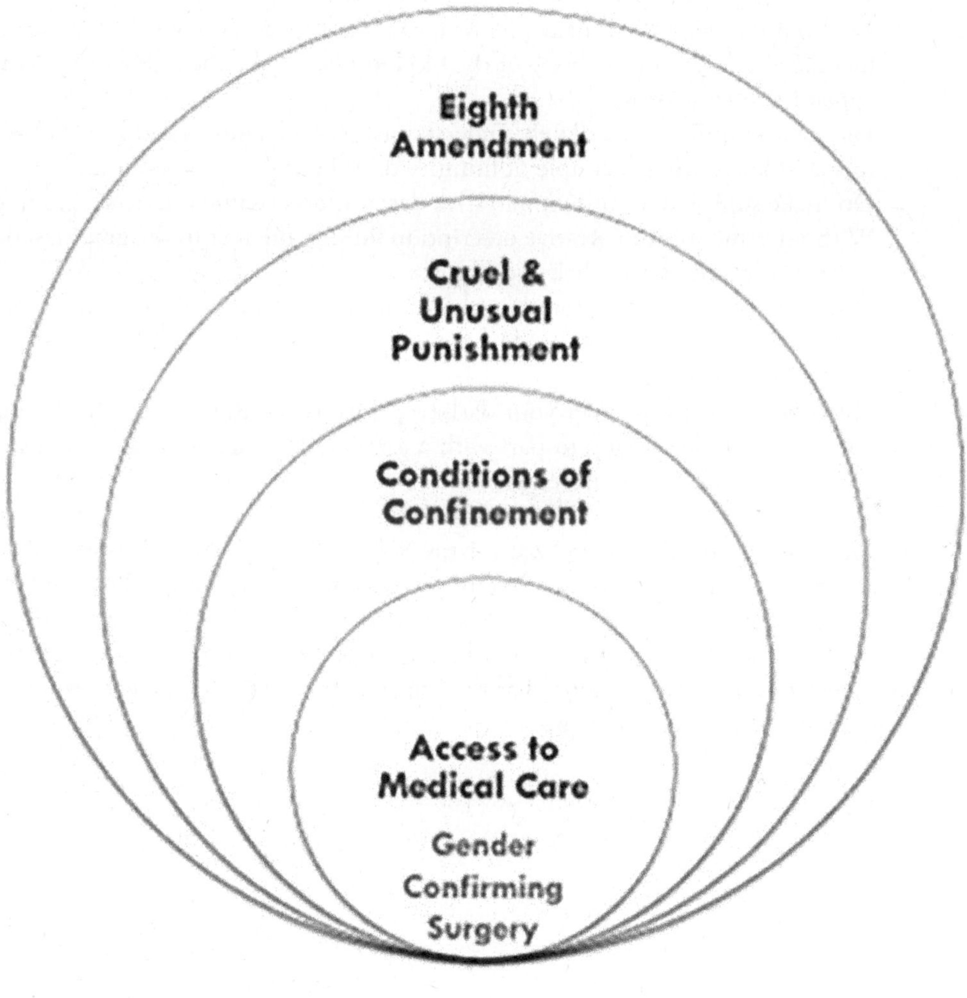

While the graphic alone cannot replace the legal arguments advanced in the text in case law and the Constitution, it can certainly help to prime the judge when placed ahead of the text or to clarify the judge's understanding when placed after the text.

[30] There are several free tutorials online for this easy shortcut to designer illustrations.

Lastly, practice graphical excellence. Graphical excellence means communicating the ideas embodied in the visuals with clarity, precision, and efficiency.[31] Consider the following tips for achieving graphical excellence:

- **Don't** present data in a way that misleads the judge or that misrepresents the facts.
- **Do** know the specific point you want to demonstrate with each graphic. Is your goal to create a visual comparison? To show causation? To summarize? To show the passage of time?
- **Do** keep graphics adjacent to the text you want to accentuate. It is better to include visual aids in the body of the brief; do not make the judge jump to an appendix to view them.
- **Do** make graphics immediately understandable. You'll lose the judge if she has to spend longer than a couple of minutes deciphering your graphics.
- **Do** make sure that an in-text narrative description accompanies each graphic. Without some sort of narrative description linking the text to the graphics, the judge won't understand their significance.
- **Don't** add graphics just for the sake of adding graphics. Be sure that each graphic you include advances your arguments and elevates the ethos or pathos threads of your brief.
- **Don't** be afraid to "murder your darlings." Just as we must ruthlessly edit our copy, we must be willing to part with a graphic if it isn't essential—even if it took significant time to develop.

It's tempting to focus all your energy on the substance of the brief instead of on its packaging. However, the ethos-generating navigational tools and ethos- and pathos-generating design principles discussed in this chapter are important and can make the difference between a mediocre brief and one that is visually pleasing and easy to navigate and doesn't require that the judge hack through a jungle of words in a struggle to extract the client's story.

[31] Collins & Marlett, *supra* note 28, at 12.

Chapter 6

Showcasing the Theory and Theme: Drafting Effective Introductions and Conclusions

"The beginning is the promise of the end."—Henry Ward Beecher

Anyone who has relied on Google maps knows that the directions are only as good as the destination address. An accidental substitution of avenue for street or a single transposed number will disrupt your plans and lead you away from your destination. Given this truism, it's critical to carefully consider the *end* at the *beginning* of your route. Likewise, your brief has a "beginning" and an "end" that must be considered carefully. Because they are the proverbial alpha and omega—the introduction and conclusion are essential to the narrative arc or the story's trajectory.[1] But introductions and conclusions are important for another reason: the principle of primacy and recency discussed in Chapter 2. As the first and last substantive components of the motion brief, their location exponentially increases the likelihood that the busy judge will read them.

[1] MasterClass, *Learn about Narrative Arcs: Definitions, Examples and How to Create a Narrative Arc in Your Writing*, September 8, 2021, https://www.masterclass.com/articles/what-are-the-elements-of-a-narrative-arc-and-how-do-you-create-one-in-writing (last visited February 26, 2023).

Even if the judge stopped reading the brief after your introduction, she should still have an accurate snapshot of the brief's arguments. An effective introduction is a crucial precursor to the statement of facts. As outlined in the next chapter, the statement of facts provides advocates with an extended opportunity to develop the emerging story. Although appellate briefs don't contain introductions, their functional equivalents are the **summary of the argument**. This component succinctly previews the advocate's arguments[2] and explicitly identifies the client's theory and theme. Like the introduction, judges often read the summary of the argument before reading the brief, and thus, it's the place to begin developing the client's persona and shaping the judge's perception of the legal conflict. Chapter 9 explores the summary of the argument component in more detail.

The story's narrative arc ends with the conclusion. The conclusion is the last substantive component of motion and appellate briefs and briefly reiterates the client's requested relief. Resist the urge to give the conclusion short shrift. One storyteller observed that endings "[C]an function as a confused writer's guiding light in figuring out just what the story is about and how to wrangle its unwieldy earlier sections."[3] This astute observation underscores the wisdom of the analogy at the beginning of the chapter; just as you think about your destination when you plug in an address into Google maps, you must consider the conclusion as you draft your introduction. What do you want the client's story to be at the end of the journey? Do the theory, theme, and arguments reflected in earlier components of the brief match the desired relief requested in the conclusion? Once you've clearly answered these questions and understand the promise of the beginning reflected in the introduction, you're ready to draft a conclusion that's headed in the right direction.

The remainder of this chapter explores tips for drafting effective introductions and conclusions, deconstructs several samples, and supplies you with checklists for evaluating your work.

PROVIDE A SNAPSHOT OF THE CLIENT'S STORY

The introduction is the advocate's first opportunity to persuasively frame the client's story for the judge. And given the competing demands on time and attention—even for readers invested in the outcome—it's important to remember that first impressions count. The introduction is the advocate's opportunity to take the harried judge (who is likely reading this brief in a room outside of your presence and without the benefit of a "live narration") by the hand and help her understand the client's needs. The following graphic identifies the core components of an effective introduction:

[2] Fed. R. App. P. 28(a)(8).

[3] K. M. Weiland, *3 Things to Know About the Ending of a Story*, August 9, 2021, available at https://tinyurl.com/89vfe392 (emphasis omitted) (last visited Jan. 6, 2023).

Components of an Effective Introduction

- **Theory** (always explicit) & **Theme** (implied or explicit)
- **Legal Snapshot** (allude to procedural and substantive governing rule; include prayer for relief)
- **Key Operative Facts** (who is the client, how did the client get here, nature of the conflict)

Highlighting these core components while complying with length restrictions—introductions shouldn't be more than a page or a page in a half—will be a challenging but necessary task. Recent studies reveal that the average attention span has drastically diminished in recent years. The constant deluge of information that confronts us from social media, e-mails, and similar emergent technologies is the culprit. In one study, researchers revealed that the average attention span of an adult is approximately eight seconds—notably, considerably shorter that the attention span of a goldfish![4] Yes, you read that right, eight seconds. Although most judges work assiduously to defy this alarming statistic, they're susceptible to the same distractions as everyone else. These statistics demonstrate that introductions must be engaging *and* succinct.

Introduction Drafting Tips

Advocates have a variety of strategies at their disposal for drafting effective introductions; but let's explore two distinct but equally effective options. We'll call the first option "The Whole Nine Yards." It provides the judge with a robust preview of the advocate's theory, theme, and arguments that's akin to an opening statement. An engaging narrative hook is a distinctive feature of The Whole Nine Yards introduction. A narrative hook "captures the attention of the audience and make[s] them interested in finding out what will happen next."[5] One popular way of creating a narrative hook is to begin the introduction with a dramatic version of the inciting event. Consider

[4] Judah Schiller, *Average Human Attention Span by Age: 31 Statistics*, Dec. 7, 2022, available at https://tinyurl.com/5xcdrxrs (last visited Jan. 6, 2023).

[5] G. Wiesen, *What Is a Narrative Hook?*, LANGUAGE.HUMANTIES.ORG, February 9, 2023, available at https://www.languagehumanities.org/what-is-a-narrative-hook.htm (last visited February 10, 2023).

the following introduction from an opinion authored by Supreme Court Justice Neil Gorsuch during his tenue on the Tenth Circuit Court of Appeal:

FILED
United States Court of Appeals
Tenth Circuit

January 23, 2014

Elisabeth A. Shumaker
Clerk of Court

PUBLISH

UNITED STATES COURT OF APPEALS

TENTH CIRCUIT

ANDREW J. YELLOWBEAR, JR., Plaintiff - Appellant, v. ROBERT O. LAMPERT, Director, Wyoming Department of Corrections; STEVE HARGETT, Warden, Wyoming Medium Correctional Institution, individually and in their official capacities, Defendants - Appellees.	No. 12-8048

Appeal from the United States District Court
for the District of Wyoming
(D.C. No. 2:11-CV-00346-ABJ)

> Andrew Yellowbear will probably spend the rest of his life in prison. Time he must serve for murdering his daughter. With that much lying behind and still before him, Mr. Yellowbear has found sustenance in his faith. No one doubts the sincerity of his religious beliefs or that they are the reason he seeks access to his prison's sweat lodge—a house of prayer and meditation the prison has supplied for those who share his Native American religious tradition. Yet the prison refuses to open the doors of that sweat lodge to Mr. Yellowbear alone, and so we have this litigation.

Justice Gorsuch is widely acclaimed for incorporating legal storytelling principles into his opinions.[6] Notice his prolific use of soft-sell persuasive techniques to describe the dramatic, inciting event—strategic use of punctuation (e.g., the em dash), detail (e.g., describing the heinousness of the crime), story words (e.g., the vivid language describing the sincerity of plaintiff's religious beliefs such as "Mr. Yellowbear has found sustenance in his faith," and describing a sweat lodge as a "house of prayer and meditation"), and juxtaposition (e.g., "No one doubts the sincerity of his religious beliefs . . . . Yet the prison refuses to open the doors of that sweat lodge to Mr. Yellowbear alone.")—to prime the reader for the court's adverse ruling against

[6] *See generally* Nina Varsava, *Elements of Judicial Style: A Quantitative Guide to Neil Gorsuch's Opinion Writing*, 93 N.Y.U.L. Rev. 75 (2018).

the prison officials.[7] Another popular technique for creating an engaging narrative hook is beginning the introduction with a quote. Consider the following example:

INTRODUCTION

"Music is among the most valuable of teaching tools. It makes complex concepts more accessible and enjoyable."— Don MacMannis, Ph.D.

At stake in this lawsuit is Defendant Serge Kersaint's ability to use a copyrighted song use as a vehicle for teaching future generations of legal writing students. Professor Kersaint's dedication to improving his students' writing skills inspired him to transform the plaintiffs' song about love created for mass public consumption into a song about writing created for a niche audience of first-year law students.

Summary judgment is appropriate in this case. Under federal law, fair use of a copyrighted work for educational purposes such as teaching is not copyright infringement. Consequently, a reasonable juror could only conclude that Professor Kersaint's publicly beneficial, educational use of the plaintiffs' song is protected by the fair use doctrine because the balance of the statutory factors outlined in 17 U.S.C.A. section 107 weigh in favor of fostering innovative, transformative uses of copyrighted material, not stifling an educator's creativity. Professor Kersaint respectfully requests that this Court grant his motion for summary judgment, deny the plaintiffs' cross-motion for summary judgment, and hold as a matter of law that his creative transformation of the plaintiffs' song into an engaging teaching tool constitutes an equitable fair use of copyrighted material.

The second strategy for drafting effective introductions is the "Short but Sweet" introduction. As suggested by its name, this option uses a more succinct rendition of the client's story without the dramatic flourishes that are the hallmark of The Whole Nine Yards introduction. As in almost everything that you will learn about legal writing, there are different ways to draft effective introductions. Choose the drafting option that's most consistent with your voice, vision, and your professor's stylistic preferences.

[7] *Yellowbear v. Lampert*, 741 F.3d 48 (10th Cir. 2014).

Sample Introductions

With this working knowledge of the purpose and importance of introductions, read the following examples of a Whole Nine Yards introduction and a Short but Sweet introduction.[8] Scrutinize them. Which parts introduce the parties? Which parts identify the parties' needs? Which parts explain the procedural history? Most important, which parts allude to the advocate's theory and theme? Test yourself by answering the questions at the end of this section.

The Whole Nine Yards Introduction

Petitioner Jordan Winslow is among the two million Floridians who lost their jobs during the Great Recession. To give his son economic and emotional stability—two of his responsibilities as Daniel's primary caregiver—Mr. Winslow made the difficult decision to relocate to Boston, Massachusetts.

A reasonable juror evaluating the undisputed evidence could reach only one conclusion: Relocation to Boston—a city with opportunities that do not exist in Florida—is in Daniel's best interest. In Boston, Daniel will reap the benefits of a structured learning environment at a school whose graduates attend some of the best high schools in the nation.

Furthermore, technological advances such as Skype make fostering a meaningful long-distance relationship between Daniel and the respondent feasible, despite the existence of some financial sacrifices that might require minor adjustments to the respondent's lifestyle. Given these facts, this Court should grant the motion for summary judgment and enable Daniel to reap the benefits of a once-in-a-lifetime opportunity for continued growth in Boston.

Short but Sweet Introduction

This matter arises out of Foxler County R-IV School District's ("Foxler County") Motion for Summary Judgment pursuant to Rule 56(c) of the Federal Rules of Civil Procedure. See Fed. R. Civ. P. 56(c). D.C., a 14-year old freshman in Foxler County, seeks relief in the form compensatory, general, and punitive damages under Title IX of the Education Amendment Acts of 1972 ("Title IX"), stemming from the taunts, insults, and physical assaults she suffered from a senior on the basketball team at Foxler County High School. See 20 U.S.C. §§1681-1688 (2006).

This Court should deny Foxler County's Motion for Summary Judgment because school officials violated Title IX when Defendant failed to protect D.C. from repeated exposure to sexual harassment. School officials turned a blind eye to the constant harassment committed by one of its star athletes against a teenage girl.

On June 17, 2011, D.C. filed a Verified Complaint and Demand for a Jury Trial against Foxler County, alleging violation of Title IX. Defendant answered on July 5, 2011, and responded by filing a Motion for Summary Judgment pursuant to Rule 56(c) on January 22, 2012. This brief is written in opposition to Defendant's Motion for Summary Judgment. D.C. is entitled to pursue her education free from the debilitating onslaught of sexual discrimination and harassment, even at the expense of the school basketball program.

Introduction Self-Editing Checklist

Once you've drafted the introduction, use the following checklist to evaluate your work. Use the blank spaces to modify the checklist to include any additional considerations suggested by your professor.

[8] Thanks to Joseph Morgese, who was brave enough to share his sample memo from his first year of law school.

- ☑ Does your introduction generally describe the nature and basis of your party's claim?
- ☑ Does your introduction provide the prayer for relief?
- ☑ Does your introduction contain a *brief* recitation of the procedural facts (i.e., general information about case)?
- ☑ Have you cited only when needed?
- ☑ Is the overall tone of the introduction persuasive?
- ☑ Does the introduction introduce the character, conflict, and allude to a theory and theme?
- ☑ If the judge stopped reading the memo after your introduction, would he or she have an accurate "snapshot" of the client's story?
- ☑ Is your introduction an appropriate length (no more than one or one and a half pages)?

ASK FOR THE CLIENT'S DESIRED RESOLUTION

The conclusion—the final section of the brief—is the advocate's last chance to tell the judge exactly what the client wants. Because advocates constantly reiterate their arguments throughout the brief using an array of hard- and soft-sell persuasive techniques, you need only remind the judge of the client's desired relief. The conclusion should be short and sweet: exactly one sentence.

Conclusion Drafting Tips

Because of its brevity, the conclusion section is likely to be the easiest part of the brief to draft. To jumpstart the writing process, open a blank document. Once you create an appropriate cover page, take a few minutes to write your conclusion. Like that first $20 deposited as a good-faith effort in your savings account, this is a simple, doable task that you can complete at the very start of your journey. Of course, this is only the first formal expression of your written work—your pre-drafting brainstorming precedes the composition of even this draft section.

Sample Conclusions

Below are conclusions corresponding to the sample introductions presented above.

From **The Whole Nine Yards** version:

> For the foregoing reasons, Petitioner Jordan Winslow respectfully asks this Court to grant his Motion for Summary Judgment on his Petition for Relocation.

From **The Short but Sweet** version:

> For the foregoing reasons, Plaintiff D.C. respectfully urges this Court to deny Defendant's Motion for Summary Judgment.

Another option slightly modifies these examples by referencing the advocate's theory and theme. Both approaches incorporate by reference the entire brief. One does so explicitly, while the other does so implicitly.

From **The Whole Nine Yards** version:

> Because relocation affords his child limitless opportunities, Petitioner Jordan Winslow respectfully urges this Court to grant his Motion for Summary Judgement on his Petition for Relocation.

From **The Short but Sweet** version:

> Based on her repeated exposure to sexual harassment, Plaintiff D.C. respectfully urges this Court to deny the Defendant's Motion for Summary Judgment.

Conclusion Self-Editing Checklist

Once you've drafted the conclusion, use the following checklist to evaluate your work. Use the blank spaces to modify the checklist to include any additional considerations suggested by your professor.

- ☑ Does your conclusion offer a clear prayer for relief?
- ☑ Does it incorporate by reference the entire brief?
- ☑ Does it allude to the client's character, the conflict, and the theory and theme?
- ☑ Is it one sentence?
- ☑ Is it free of any cites to cases?
- ☑ Is it persuasive?

COGNITIVE CORNER

Introductions and Conclusions

Consider the following questions about the introduction and conclusion:

1. What is the primary goal of the introduction?
2. Why is it important to build storytelling techniques into the introduction?
3. Why should there be an "ultimate" conclusion when the entire brief has multiple conclusions throughout?

Chapter 7

Harnessing the Power of Suggestion: Drafting the Statement of Facts

"Your case is all head and no heart." —Jack McCoy, Law and Order

Admit it. For many of us, *Law and Order's* Jack McCoy is *the* man: He's a shrewd, methodical, and passionate lawyer. For decades, he captivated audiences on one of television's longest-running courtroom dramas. He's also absolutely right that without a heart your case is doomed. A statement of facts with a head *and* a heart is crucial because, as explained by legal storyteller Ruth Anne Robbins, "[M]ost judges are moved by fairness, common sense, and compassion, not clever legal analysis."[1] Another legal storytelling proponent made a similar observation, reminding advocates that judges "aren't computers that weigh the facts and the applicable case law and then score each brief, so that [the] party with the highest score wins."[2]

The statement of facts is among the most important sections of the brief, the place where the head of the case (i.e., your theory) and the "juice" of the case (i.e., your theme) merge to form a complete rendition of the client's story. According to renowned litigator James McElhaney, "[L]ots of thoughtful judges admit that they

---

[1] Brian J. Foley & Ruth Anne Robbins, *Fiction 101: A Primer for Lawyers on How to Use Fiction Writing Techniques to Write Persuasive Facts Sections*, 32 Rutgers L.J. 459, 462 (2001).
[2] Mike Skotnicki, *Your Brief Should Tell a Story (of Conflict)*, Briefly Writing Blog (May 14, 2012), http://brieflywriting.com/2012/05/14/your-brief-should-tell-a-story-of-conflict/.

start to take sides . . . as soon as they read the statement of facts."[3] The statement of facts is important for another reason: its location. Because it appears fairly early in the brief, the judge forms an impression of you and your client's story when reading it. If you fail the first-impression test by omitting crucial facts, then the judge won't believe your arguments. If your statement of facts is nothing more than a random list of facts, then the judge won't understand how the client's story is consistent with the theory and theme.

In objective writing, the statement of facts is a bipartisan fence-sitter. But in persuasive writing, the statement of facts is a partisan cheerleader with a definite agenda: subtle persuasion via soft-sell persuasive techniques. Subtlety is extremely important in the statement of facts. Recall the discussion in Chapter 3 analogizing judges to referees. A judge, much like a referee, needs the serenity of the statement of facts to begin processing the issues without the distraction of the advocates making arguments, stating their opinions, or characterizing the facts. Soft-sell persuasive techniques strike the appropriate balance between the foreshadowing function described above and providing the judge with the space he or she needs to begin forming an impression of you and your client's story. Consequently, an effective statement of facts uses an array of soft-sell persuasive techniques to arrange, shift, and sort facts so that they subtly foreshadow the client's theory, theme, and arguments. Soft-sell persuasive techniques are generally more persuasive than hard-sell persuasive techniques because most people prefer to reach their own conclusions. Judges are no different.

This chapter is subdivided into two sections. Chapter 7.1 discusses a three-step process for drafting a persuasive statement of facts. Chapter 7.2 shifts from the theoretical to the practical with an in-depth discussion of several soft-sell persuasive techniques and ends with bonus materials intended to help you jump-start your writing process.

[3] James W. McElhaney, *The Art of Persuasive Legal Writing, Briefs Come Alive When Every Word Sings to the Reader*, A.B.A. J., Jan. 1996, at 76, 78.

Chapter 7.1

A Three-Step Process for Crafting the Statement of Facts

"I believe that the writer should tell a story. I believe in plot. I believe in creating characters and suspense." —Ernest Gaines, author

A persuasive statement of facts, also known as the statement of the case, foreshadows upcoming legal arguments. Instead of beating the judge over the head with opinions, conclusions, and characterizations, the legal storyteller arranges the facts to create a story that shows—not tells—the judge why the client's theory and theme appropriately resolve the legal issue. The following visual outlines this persuasive process:

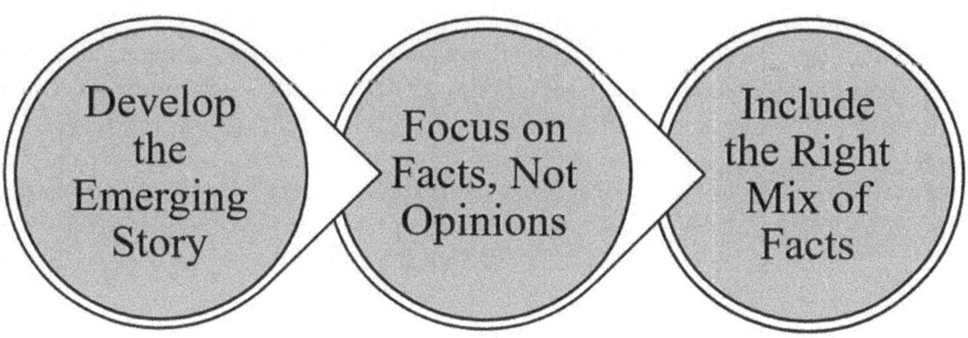

DEVELOP THE EMERGING STORY

You've reviewed the facts, researched the law, and drafted a solid theory and theme. Now what? Help the judge understand your client's legal dilemma by developing the emerging story previewed in the introduction. When the judge finishes the statement of facts, he or she should understand the client's complete story—what journalists call the Five Ws and the One H:[4]

- Who is your client?
- What happened?
- Why did it happen?
- Where, when, and how did it happen?

The answers to these questions are the foundation of your story. A story is an account of how a main character ("who") with a distinct point of view ("where, when, and how") facing a conflict ("what" and "why") ultimately resolves that conflict.[5] In the world of legal storytelling, the client is the main character. The legal storyteller presents the conflict created by the legal issue in a way that supports the client's desired resolution. In legal storytelling, the judge, not the storyteller, supplies the story's resolution in the form of a judicial opinion. Because the judge ultimately decides how the client's story will end, legal stories are always incomplete. The legal storyteller must design the statement of facts to suggest the appropriate resolution.[6]

The good news is that you don't have to reinvent the wheel when designing your client's story. Legal storytellers frequently rely on **stock characters** and **stock stories**. The word "stock" refers to a universally recognized character or story type that is repackaged to match the client's theory and theme. A common stock story describes the plight of star-crossed lovers whose love will ultimately be destroyed by internal or external forces beyond their control.[7] Shakespeare's Romeo and Juliet are the archetypal star-crossed lovers; they loved each other deeply but died tragically because their families condemned the relationship.

Notice that the stock story dictates the characters: The primary characters are the star-crossed lovers (Romeo and Juliet), and the villains/tyrants are their families, who ultimately succeed in keeping the young lovers apart.

Stock characters and stories are incredibly persuasive. Because judges are familiar with these stories and how they end, selecting a stock story and stock characters that correspond with your theory and theme increases the likelihood that the judge will

[4] Jeremy Porter, *Your Brief Should Tell a Story (of Conflict)*, Journalistics Blog (Aug. 5, 2010), http://blog.journalistics.com/2010/five-ws-one-h/.
[5] Foley & Robbins, *supra* note 1, at 466.
[6] *Id.* at 467.
[7] Shamekia Thomas, *Star-Crossed Lovers: Definition, Archetype & Role in Shakespeare*, Education Portal, http://education-portal.com/academy/lesson/star-crossed-lovers-definition-archetype-role-in-shakespeare.html#lesson (last visited Nov. 3, 2016).

identify with your client and, thus, be more receptive to the hard-sell persuasive techniques that you'll use in other sections of the brief.

Another benefit of stock characters and stories is their versatility. Most people know that Romeo and Juliet's story doesn't end well—they perish, and the villains/tyrants win. However, despite knowing the ending, most readers still root for young lovers, perhaps wishing that they had the power to change the ending. Unlike the helpless reader in the Romeo and Juliet example, the legal storyteller is not bound by the stock story's typical ending. A well-written statement of facts can subtly suggest to the judge that he or she can embrace the legal storyteller's theory, using the law as an instrument of reconciliation.

The seminal U.S. Supreme Court case *Loving v. Virginia* is the archetypal story of star-crossed lovers—Mildred Jeter, a 17-year-old African American, and Richard Loving, a 23-year-old white construction worker—against a powerful villain, Virginia's miscegenation laws banning interracial marriage. After marrying in Washington, D.C., and returning to Virginia in 1958, the couple was charged with unlawful cohabitation and jailed.[8] If you were writing a brief in support of the Lovings, you could characterize Virginia's miscegenation law as the tyrant that the judge must overrule to reconcile the star-crossed lovers. The remainder of this section explores the components of a persuasive legal story: character, point of view, and conflict.

Cast the Client's Character

It's obvious that your client is the **protagonist** or main character. However, it might not be so obvious that your client doesn't have to be perfect. Most of us don't identify with perfection because we aren't perfect.

Judges aren't any different. Judges are more likely to empathize with a perfectly imperfect client. Chapter 3 defines empathy as the ability to recognize the feelings and reactions of others. To create empathy, portray your client as a perfectly imperfect person who, although struggling with the conflict created by the legal issue, is entitled to the requested relief.

If your client is a business, nonprofit agency, or similar nonhuman entity, then you'll need to create the client's "brand." Branding refers to the various techniques that marketers use to communicate the values, characteristics, and attributes that create a business's identity.[9] Connect the organization to a key player such as the president, the CEO, or a managerial employee, thereby making that person the "face" of the organization. When creating the organizational client's brand, focus on presenting facts that facilitate empathy, such as:

---

[8] *Loving v. Virginia: The Case Over Inter-racial Marriage*, ACLU, https://www.aclu.org/racial-justice/loving-v-virginia-case-over-interracial-marriage (last visited Nov. 3, 2016).

[9] James Heaton, *The Difference between Marketing and Branding*, Tronvig Group Blog, http://www.tronvig group.com/the-difference-between-marketing-and-branding/ (last visited Nov. 3, 2016).

- Details about the organization's mission and notable achievements
- The organization's motivation for taking the action at issue in the lawsuit
- Potential consequences that the organization would face if the judge denies its requested relief

Begin the process of casting the client's character by picking the stock character type or combination of types that best fits your theory and theme. What follows is a non-exclusive list of stock characters with illustrative examples.[10]

Stock Protagonists	Illustrative Example
Warrior	Prototypical Hollywood hero such as Luke Skywalker from *Star Wars*
Creator	Writer or artist struggling to succeed
Caregiver/Martyr	Mother or father taking care of family against the odds; religious icons or leaders such as Jesus, Moses, or Buddha
Outlaw/Destroyer	Robin Hood
Sage/Scholar	Wise advisor; Obi Wan Kenobi from *Star Wars*
Magician	Merlin; Gandalf from *Lord of the Rings*
Ruler	King Arthur
Lover	Romeo and Juliet
Jester/Fool	Many lead roles in comedies; Kramer or George from *Seinfeld*
Innocent	Dorothy from *Wizard of Oz*

Consider the following example. Assume you've been hired to file a motion for a new trial on behalf of a client convicted of violating a federal money laundering statute.[11] The client claims that the trial judge's denial of his oral motion to represent himself violated his Sixth Amendment rights under the U.S. Constitution. The core societal values and your arguments, theory, and theme are as follows.

[10] Ruth Anne Robbins, *Harry Potter, Ruby Slippers and Merlin: Telling the Client's Story Using the Characters and Paradigm of the Archetypal Hero's Journey*, 29 Seattle U. L. Rev. 767, 778-779 (2006) (adapting the work of Dr. Carol Pearson).

[11] This hypothetical is based on a problem initially created by Professor Linda Barris and updated and revised by our colleague, Professor Heather Baxter.

Core Societal Values:

Self-preservation
Dignity
An expedient and efficient judicial system

Argument

A criminal defendant has an absolute right to self-representation if the request is asserted before the beginning of meaningful trial proceedings, especially when the potential prejudice of a jury selection tainted by sleeping counsel outweighs any minimal trial disruption.

Theory:

Delaying the beginning of meaningful trial proceedings until after jury selection minimizes damage to the integrity of the trial process while respecting the defendant's autonomy to select a jury of his peers.

Theme:

"Jurors are the guardians of justice."

The emerging story outlined in the theory and summarized in the theme is one where all the interests align and weigh in favor of the defendant's self-representation. The client is an underdog, someone with a legitimate motivation, not a savvy criminal manipulating the court and undermining the judicial system. Armed with this information, you're ready to develop your client's character. The key words of this emerging story are "underdog," "legitimate motivation," and "guardians of justice."

One option is to cast the client in the role of the innocent, someone with no previous criminal record, who is at the mercy of his sleeping trial lawyer. Casting the client in the role of the innocent would explain why the client waited so late in the jury selection process to assert his rights and why he disregarded the trial attorney's sleeping during pretrial meetings. Another alternative would be to cast the client as a jester/fool who, although foolishly disregarding the warning signs of a sleeping attorney at pretrial meetings, mistakenly thought that the attorney's sleeping would end once trial began. Pick a stock character type that is consistent with your theme. Implicit in your theme ("Jurors are the guardians of justice") is that your client deserves a new trial with competent representation. Casting the client in the role of the outlaw/destroyer or in the role of the explorer/wanderer/seeker undermines your theme. No judge would feel empathy for an outlaw, wanderer, or seeker, people who might disrespect the judicial process.

Apply the same process of scrutinizing the theory and theme when casting the character of an organizational client. Assume that your client, a nonprofit religious organization, fired a popular youth counselor because she had a child out of wedlock, an activity that violated the organization's religious teachings. The youth counselor filed suit for wrongful discharge, alleging that the employee handbook and the employer's disciplinary practices created an implied employment contract that modified the presumption of at-will employment.[12] The core societal value and your arguments, theory, and theme are as follows.

Core Societal Value:

Employer autonomy

Arguments

An interpretation of the implied contract exception that would invalidate a clear and conspicuous at-will employment disclaimer would subject the Church to civil liability for ending its relationship with an employee whose lifestyle jeopardizes its ability to rescue troubled children.

This Court should align itself with appellate courts in neighboring jurisdictions and abolish any exception to at-will employment that unduly burdens the Church's autonomy to fulfill its organizational mission.

Theory:

The deference afforded to an employer's personnel decisions enshrined in the at-will employment doctrine safeguards the Church's autonomy to protect its mission of community service.

Theme:

"Protection, not perfection."

The emerging story outlined in the theory and summarized in the theme is all about employer autonomy. The key concepts are deference, autonomy, and preserving and protecting the client's mission of community service. Given these key concepts, the caregiver/martyr stock character fits nicely with the arguments, theory, and theme. Notice how the core societal value of employer autonomy and the theory and theme work in tandem to create a plausible explanation about why the client should prevail.

The client's decision to fire a popular employee is primarily about protecting its vulnerable clientele, not its religious teachings. Shifting the focus from religion to

[12] In an at-will employment relationship, the employer can terminate an employee at any time for any reason, except an illegal one, or for no reason at all, without incurring legal liability. *See The At-Will Presumption and Exceptions to the Rule*, Nat'l Conference of State Legislatures, http://www.ncsl.org/research/labor-and-employment/at-will-employment-overview.aspx (last visited Nov. 17, 2016).

the client's secular organizational mission fosters empathy for a client whose religious teachings might be at odds with modern views of sexuality—namely, that age and maturity level, not marital status, are more relevant criteria for evaluating the propriety of sexual activity.

Cast Secondary Characters

Every legal story has at least one secondary character. Typically, the primary secondary character is the **antagonist**, the person or entity who opposes the client. However, depending on the facts of the case, there may be other nonprimary secondary characters who you need to fully develop the client's story. **Nonprimary secondary characters** might include a witness who bolsters your theory and theme or a witness whom you can't ignore because that person bolsters opposing counsel's theory and theme.

A word of caution: Include only those nonprimary secondary characters who are necessary to fully develop the emerging story. Your client is the focal point. Everyone and everything else is secondary. What follows below is a nonexclusive list of antagonists and nonprimary secondary stock characters with a brief description of their functions.[13]

Secondary Stock Characters	Type	Function
Villain/Tyrant	Antagonist	Displays characteristics of pure evil whose primary function is to prevent the client from achieving the desired resolution.[14]
Shape Shifter	Antagonist	Displays characteristics of good and evil. Because of their duality, these characters can either be a catalyst for change or a distraction.
Threshold Guardian	Secondary	A potentially neutral character who tests the client's ability to handle the conflict at the heart of the legal issue.
Mentor	Secondary	A wise person who teaches/helps client to overcome obstacles.
Companion/Ally	Secondary	Humanizes the client, adding extra dimensions to the client's personality or challenging client to be more open and balanced.[15]

[13] Robbins, *supra* note 10, at 775.
[14] Jeremiah Burt, *What Traits Would an Archetypal Character Have?* CLASSROOM, SCHOOL SUBJECTS, http://classroom.synonym.com/traits-would-archetypal-character-have-4946.html (last visited Nov. 3, 2016).
[15] Rosie Dub, *Juggling Archetypes: Heroes, Villains, and Shapeshifters*, WRITE ON THE FRINGES BLOG (May 27, 2012), http://writeonthefringes.blogspot.com/2012/05/juggling-archetypes-heroes-villains-and.html.

Furthermore, don't automatically cast the antagonist as the villain. A villain has *no* redeeming qualities. When you automatically cast the antagonist as the villain, you risk losing credibility with the judge. As a keen observer of human nature, the judge knows that people typically aren't entirely good or bad. When you automatically cast the antagonist as the villain, the judge will think that you're unreasonable at best or naïve at worst.

Instead, characterize the antagonist as a redeemable person whose actions have created or substantially contributed to the legal conflict. How you describe the antagonist should subtly suggest to the judge that the antagonist can be redeemed *only* by a resolution that favors the client. Furthermore, keep your focus on the antagonist's actions and the consequences of those actions; stay away from character assignation. By focusing on the person's or entity's actions, you essentially depersonalize your opponent without sounding too argumentative.

Let's cast the secondary characters in the Sixth Amendment right to self-representation scenario. To fully develop the theory, you'll need to cast the following nonprimary secondary characters: the trial judge who denied the client's motion, the sleeping trial lawyer, and the prosecutor. Think strategically when casting the role of antagonist. Quash any thoughts of casting the trial judge as the villain. Motions for new trial are typically filed with the judge who presided at trial. You *absolutely* want to avoid alienating the decision maker. Instead, cast the trial judge as a mentor, someone who, with the benefit of hindsight and the full development of the facts, can restore integrity to the judicial process via granting the motion for new trial.

Cast the sleeping trial attorney as the antagonist, a shape shifter whose erratic behavior during jury selection provides the trial judge with the opportunity to reconsider the denial of the client's motion. Another option is to cast an external force as the antagonist. For example, you could subtly suggest to the judge that the entire criminal justice system, one where the quality of representation too often depends on the defendant's financial resources, is the quintessential shape shifter who the judge has the power to neutralize by granting the client's motion for new trial. Your last option is to cast the prosecutor as the antagonist in the form of a threshold guardian. A threshold guardian is a neutral character who's merely a symptom of a larger problem—the unequal distribution of resources between government-funded prosecutors and privately funded criminal defense attorneys—or as someone simply doing his job with no real power to protect the client from his sleeping attorney.

Select a Point of View and Characterize the Conflict

Every good storyteller knows that a story has two sides. The perspective from which you tell the story is called point of view. Your goal is to tell the story from a point of view favorable to the client. Create a favorable point of view by telling the story from the client's perspective.

In the Sixth Amendment scenario, you wouldn't begin with a discussion of the indictment but with the client's nonexistent criminal history and inexperience with the criminal justice system, information that squarely positions your client as the archetypal innocent or jester/fool. Similarly, you'd end with information about the length of the prison sentence and other negative consequences of the judge's denial of the motion for new trial.

Telling the story from a favorable point of view could mean telling the story from the point of view of someone *other than* the client. For example, in the at-will employment scenario, you might begin the story with details about the client's motivation for ending the employment of such a popular employee or from the perspective of the plaintiff's immediate supervisor. By shifting the point of view from the institutional employer to a key supervisory employee, you brand the institutional client and facilitate empathy.

You should also characterize the conflict favorably. Conflict is at the heart of all good stories. Lawsuits make great stories because they are *full* of conflict. In legal storytelling, the conflict is the legal issue that the judge must resolve. Conflicts can be internal (e.g., the client battling drug addiction to regain custody) or external (e.g., the client suing a former employer to regain a job).

A stock story is a prepackaged story "template" with universally recognized conflicts.[16] For example, the stock story of the star-crossed lovers has a prepackaged conflict: *person versus person* (e.g., Romeo and Juliet versus their families) or *person versus society* (e.g., the Lovings versus Virginia's law prohibiting interracial marriage). Other examples of the kinds of conflict that you might see in stock stories include *person versus self* (e.g., the client battling drug addiction to regain custody of a child) and *person versus nature* (e.g., the client seeking to restore property damaged in a hurricane).

How you define the conflict determines how the judge will want to resolve it.[17] In the *Loving v. Virginia* example, describing the conflict as person versus person (i.e., Richard and Mildred Loving versus the prosecuting attorney) would have likely alienated the Supreme Court Justices. However, by describing the conflict as the Lovings versus Virginia's laws prohibiting interracial marriage, a quintessential person versus society conflict, you won't alienate the judge with an ad hominem personal attack. Perhaps more important, describing the conflict as person versus society harnesses the power of suggestion: The judge, like the people rooting for Romeo and Juliet, recognizes the stock story type and thus is predisposed to resolving the conflict in a way that reunites the young lovers by declaring Virginia's miscegenation laws unconstitutional.

What follows are examples of stock story types, pop-culture portrayal of stock stories, the conflict type triggered by the stock story, and general suggestions about the kinds of cases that match a particular stock story type.

---

[16] Mike Skotnicki, *Several Types of "Stock Stories" Can be Used in Persuasive Brief Writing*, Briefly Writing Blog (May 29, 2012), http://brieflywriting.com/2012/05/29/several-types-of-stock-stories-can-be-used-in-persuasive-brief writing/; Mike Skotnicki, *Weaving the Facts of Your Case into an Innately Familiar "Stock Story" Can Influence the Reader of Your Brief*, Briefly Writing Blog (May 21, 2012), http://brieflywriting.com/2012/05/21/weaving-the -facts-of-your-case-into-an-innately-familiar-stock-story-can-influence-the-reader-of-your-brief/ (discussing the work of Professor Jennifer Shephard).

[17] Foley & Robbins, *supra* note 1, at 470.

Stock Story Types	Popular Culture Examples	Conflict Types	Case Type
The Witch-hunt/Falsely Accused[18]	• *Minority Report* • *Gone Girl* • *The Fugitive*	• Person v. Person • Person v. Society/Institution	Most civil or criminal cases
Underdog and Whistleblowers	• *Rocky* • *Creed* • *Dark Waters*	Person v. Society/Institution	• Employment Discrimination • Labor Law • Civil Rights
The Metamorphosis	• *Breaking Bad* • *Dr. Strange*	• Person v. Self • Person v. Person • Person v. Society/Institution	Most civil or criminal cases
The Quest[19]	• *Lord of the Rings* • *The Mandalorian* • *Everything Everywhere All at Once*	• Person v. Person • Person v. Self • Person v. Society/Institution	• Family Law • Property Law • Contracts • Intentional Torts & Negligence

Now that you have the information to develop the emerging story, you're ready to begin building your credibility. In the context of the statement of facts, building credibility means focusing on facts, not opinions, and including the right mix of facts.

FOCUS ON FACTS, NOT OPINIONS

> When you start interpreting the facts . . . you have stopped guiding [the judge] through the thicket of the lawsuit. Instead, you have popped out the legs on your traveling sales case and wound up a dozen or so of your little walking dolls, hoping sales will be brisk.

To be persuasive, your statement of facts must be more than a bullet list of disjointed, unconnected facts. However, novice legal storytellers sometimes think that characterizing or offering opinions about the facts is persuasive. *Nothing* could be further from the truth. When your statement of facts contains opinions, you cross the line from soft-sell persuasive techniques that facilitate persuasion to hard-sell persuasive techniques that trigger the judge's skepticism. Litigator James McElhaney succinctly describes the credibility-damaging effect of hard-sell persuasive techniques.[20]

[18] Skotnicki, *Several Types of "Stock Stories," supra* note 17.
[19] Skotnicki, *Weaving the Facts, supra* note 17.
[20] McElhaney, *supra* note 3, at 78.

Think of the image of a traveling salesperson hawking goods on the street corner as a poignant reminder to focus on the facts. To avoid credibility-damaging opinions and characterizations, understand the distinction between fact and opinion.

A fact is information that is *indisputably* the case—something that opposing counsel could not object to because it's contained in the pleadings, depositions, or the record on appeal. Facts are the raw material of your argument, not the argument itself. Information doesn't become a fact simply because it supports your argument or simply because you believe it to be true. Litigants often use the same set of facts to make wildly divergent arguments about the interpretation of those facts.

In stark contrast, an opinion cannot be indisputably proven and reflects the advocate's beliefs, feelings, or judgments about facts or about their significance. Commentary about what the facts mean or about their significance belong in the argument section of the brief, not the statement of facts. Consider the following examples.

Fact	Opinion
During her decade-long employment, Ms. Gideon was either nominated for or won "counselor of the year" for nine of those ten years.	Ms. Gideon was an extremely effective youth counselor and a hard worker.
Trial counsel's ten-word opening statement was two minutes long.	The motion for new trial is based on an incompetent trial attorney who, as evidence of his incompetence, gave an opening statement that was constitutionally inadequate.

The information in the right column contains opinions. The phrases "extremely effective" and "hard worker" reflect the advocate's judgment about the client's value to the employer. The writer interprets the counselor of the year designation as evidence of the employee's effectiveness and hard work. But the client's work history doesn't *indisputably* prove her effectiveness or hard work. Another equally plausible interpretation is that the counselor of the year designation is a popularity contest unrelated to an employee's actual work performance. Similarly, the writer's statements about the client's "incompetent trial attorney" who gave a "constitutionally inadequate" opening statement is a judgment about trial counsel's performance, not facts that can be indisputably proven.

The information in the left column contains information that can be indisputably proven with evidence garnered during pretrial discovery or from the record on appeal. Purely factual statements give the judge the freedom to make his or her own conclusions about the relative merit of the client's workplace accomplishments or about the effectiveness of the trial attorney's opening statement. Notice how the writer's use of soft-sell persuasive techniques—the use of vivid, detailed language and words with favorable connotations—subtly suggests that the client was a diligent, loyal, and effective employee.

A persuasive statement of facts doesn't hit the judge over the head with opinions or factual characterizations but effectively uses soft-sell persuasive techniques that develop the client's story and foreshadow upcoming legal arguments. The difference between hard-sell and soft-sell persuasive techniques is a subtle but extremely important distinction that often makes the difference between a statement of facts that builds credibility and one that fails the first-impression test.

Another important distinction between facts and opinions is that facts can be cited while opinions cannot. If the information is not a direct quote or paraphrase from the litigation documents or record on appeal, then the information is most likely an opinion. Most judges require a citation to every fact that appears in the statement of facts. The failure to properly cite can lead to embarrassing rebukes from the judge.[21] The inclusion of a citation assures the judge that the information is a fact, builds the advocate's credibility, and ensures that the statement of facts is free of opinions and characterizations.

INCLUDE THE RIGHT MIX OF FACTS

A persuasive statement of facts has the right mix of facts. You've got a lot to do in the statement of facts—cast the client's character and any secondary characters, portray the conflict from the client's point of view, develop the theory and theme, and foreshadow the legal arguments. The right factual mix efficiently accomplishes these tasks. To incorporate the right mix of facts, you must have a thorough understanding of the three types of facts:

- Legally relevant facts
- Emotionally relevant facts
- Background and procedurally relevant facts

Each fact type corresponds to a specific part of the rhetorical triangle:

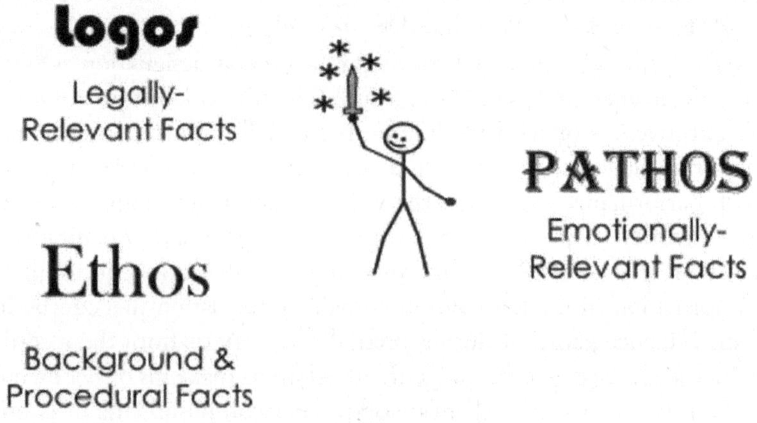

[21] *See* Wes Hendrix, *From Good to Great: The Four Stages of Effective Self-Editing*, 14 J. App. Prac. & Process 267, 269 (2013) (discussing a First Circuit Court of Appeals case dismissing an appeal because the appellant's brief did not cite to the record).

Legally relevant facts support your logos arguments. Because of their importance, legally relevant facts dominate the statement of facts. Professional gamblers have a saying: Never leave money sitting on the table. In the statement of facts, legally relevant facts are like money—*never* leave any sitting on the table. You leave facts sitting on the table by omitting legally relevant facts or by describing them with an insufficient amount of detail. Detail is an important soft-sell persuasive technique discussed in Chapter 7.2. The bonus materials section of Chapter 7.2 contains tips to ensure that you don't omit legally relevant facts.

Omitting adverse legally relevant facts can lead to sanctions. The Model Rules of Professional Conduct promulgated by the American Bar Association[22] and the rules of professionalism promulgated by state bar associations typically require that advocates disclose all the legally relevant facts, even those that are adverse to the client. Although professionalism rules require disclosure, *nothing* requires that you use a verbal mega-phone to direct the judge's attention to these adverse facts. Chapter 7.2 will discuss soft-sell persuasive techniques for minimizing the effect of adverse legally relevant facts.

Emotionally relevant or pathos facts are what distinguish the statement of facts in a brief from the statement of facts in an objective memo. Emotionally relevant facts make the statement of facts come alive, providing the emotional "heart" that transforms an otherwise dry recitation of legally relevant facts into a story that ignites the judge's interest. U. S. Supreme Court Justice Antonin Scalia said one quality of a first-rate statement of facts is that it provides context and human interest "to get across all the elements of the case that would make the judge sympathetic to your cause, without being obvious about it. . . ."[23]

Justice Scalia's cautionary comments are particularly instructive: don't cross the line from drama to melodrama. Further, if you include too many emotionally relevant facts, you run the risk of making the statement of facts too long. The statement of facts should read like a short story, not a novel. How does the legal storyteller balance the need for brevity with the need for heart? A definitive answer isn't possible. However, a good rule of thumb is to include emotional facts strategically, placing them at points in the story where they're absolutely essential to develop the theme and to provide context about characters and the nature of the conflict.

Background and procedurally relevant facts are also integral components of the statement of facts. Background and procedural facts are ethos facts that facilitate credibility. These facts help the judge understand the "big picture" of the lawsuit, describe the litigants' path to the court, or identify key evidentiary rulings. Legal storytellers typically place background and procedural facts at the beginning or end of the statement of facts.

When you include the right mix of legally relevant, emotionally relevant, background and procedurally relevant facts, you maximize persuasiveness by connecting all three parts of the rhetorical triangle in the most important part of the brief. Although

---

[22] Model Rules of Prof'l Conduct R. 3.3(a)(1) and 3.3(a)(2).

[23] Interview by Bryan A. Garner with Antonin Scalia, U.S. Supreme Court Justice (Oct. 2, 2006), *reproduced in* 13 Scribes J. Legal Writing 51 (2010).

the precise mix depends on the characters, conflict, and point of view of your emerging story, the legally relevant facts should dominate. Use the emotionally relevant facts as gap fillers, providing context and background for the theory and theme, and then include just a dash of background or procedural facts for context.

With this magical mix, you have the recipe for a persuasive statement of facts. Now that you're familiar with the three-step process for crafting a persuasive statement of facts, you're ready to begin exploring the soft-sell persuasive techniques outlined in Chapter 7.2.

Chapter 7.2

Soft-Sell Persuasive Techniques in the Statement of Facts

"Talk softly and carry a big stick."—Theodore Roosevelt

Soft-sell persuasive techniques harness the power of suggestion by subtly highlighting the client's theory and theme without resorting to hard-sell persuasive techniques. This chapter explores several strategies for seamlessly integrating soft-sell persuasive techniques into the statement of facts.[24] All of the persuasive techniques discussed in this chapter can be used independently or in combination with one another to harness the power of suggestion *without* sacrificing credibility. Four particularly effective soft-sell persuasive techniques are shown next:

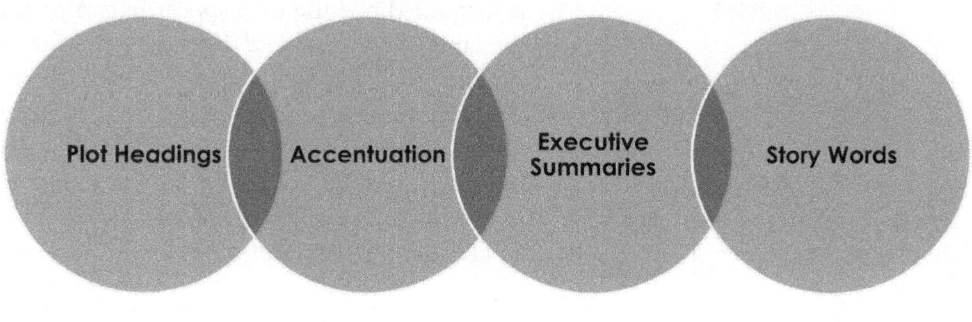

[24] Many of techniques and strategies in this chapter have either been inspired by or adapted from materials in the following textbooks: Mary Beth Beazley, A Practical Guide to Appellate Advocacy (2d ed. 2006); Linda H. Edwards, Legal Writing: Process, Analysis, & Organization (1999); Laurel Currie Oates et al., The Legal Writing Handbook—Analysis, Research, and Writing (2d ed. 1998); Robin Wellford Slocum, Legal Reasoning, Writing, and Other Lawyering Skills (3d ed. 2009).

PLOT HEADINGS

In storytelling briefs, plot headings outline the story presented in the statement of facts. Recall the chart from Chapter 5 summarizing the different types of headings. Plot headings are short, nonargumentative phrases written in bold type that function like a megaphone, directing the judge's attention to the story's plot and foreshadowing the arguments. The story's progression—from beginning, to middle, to end—is called its plot.

All good stories have a plot. Let's revisit the story of *Romeo and Juliet.* Shakespeare doesn't begin his story by jumping head first into the conflict (i.e., the plot to separate the lovers). Instead, he introduces the main characters and the story's context: the origins of Romeo and Juliet's romance and their membership in feuding families. Only after providing a bit of context does Shakespeare transition to the story's conflict and ultimate resolution.

The statement of facts also has a plot. In legal storytelling, the beginning of the story is called the status quo. The **status quo** is a snapshot of the client's life before the conflict. Your portrayal of the status quo will consist primarily of emotionally relevant or background facts. Then, you'll transition to the story's conflict. Your portrayal of the conflict will be dominated by legally relevant facts.

The statement of facts typically ends with procedural facts describing the client's journey to court. Legal storytellers can't dictate the story's end or resolution; instead, they use soft-sell persuasive techniques to subtly suggest the client's *desired* resolution. The plot structure of a legal story looks like a pyramid:

Appropriately drafted plot headings are persuasive for two reasons. First, plot headings hit all three points of the rhetorical triangle: logos, pathos, and ethos. Second, the logos, pathos, and ethos-generating power of good plot headings is magnified because they appear in two places: the table of contents *and* the statement of facts. Because plot headings appear in two places, they harness the power of suggestion via repetition, a soft-sell persuasive technique discussed later in this chapter. Create plot headings by scrutinizing your cast of characters, the conflict, and the emerging story reflected in the theory and theme. Use the following criteria to evaluate plot headings:

- Can the judge immediately understand the headings (i.e., are they concrete and specific)?
- Are the headings free of legal conclusions and opinions?
- Have you included a plot heading for each pivotal point in the plot (i.e., the status quo, conflict, and desired resolution)?

As an illustration, let's work through the process of drafting plot headings for at-will employment scenario referenced in Chapter 7.1. Recall the emerging story.

Core Societal Value:

Employer autonomy

Arguments

An interpretation of the implied contract exception that would invalidate a clear and conspicuous at-will employment disclaimer would subject the Church to civil liability for ending its relationship with an employee whose lifestyle jeopardizes its ability to rescue troubled children.

This Court should align itself with appellate courts in neighboring jurisdictions and abolish any exception to at-will employment that unduly burdens the Church's autonomy to fulfill its organizational mission.

Theory:

The deference afforded to an employer's personnel decisions enshrined in the at-will employment doctrine safeguards the Church's autonomy to protect its mission of community service.

Theme:

"Protection, not perfection."

Stock Character Types:

Client (protagonist) = Caregiver/Martyr
Key supervisory employees (secondary character) = Caregiver/Martyr
Plaintiff (secondary character) = Threshold Guardian

Conflict/Stock Story Type:

The Quest

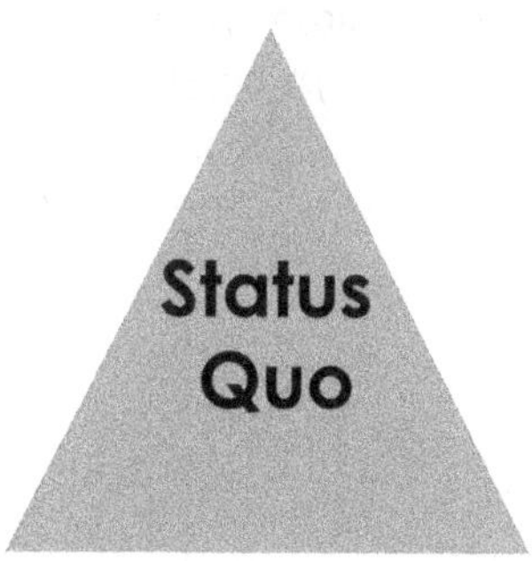

Now use these story elements as a guide for drafting plot headings. Start with the status quo plot heading. You've cast the client in the role of the caregiver/martyr. Your theme is that the community will suffer if the client can't release employees whose lifestyle choices jeopardize its mission of rescuing troubled children. In the ideal pre-lawsuit world, the client had the autonomy to make personnel decisions that benefited the community. Which emotionally relevant facts evoke this ideal pre-lawsuit world? Which emotionally relevant facts evoke the image of the client as caregiver or depict its organizational goals? Consider the following status quo plot heading:

Status Quo	Conflict	Desired Resolution
Hired as a Role Model for Homeless Children	?	?

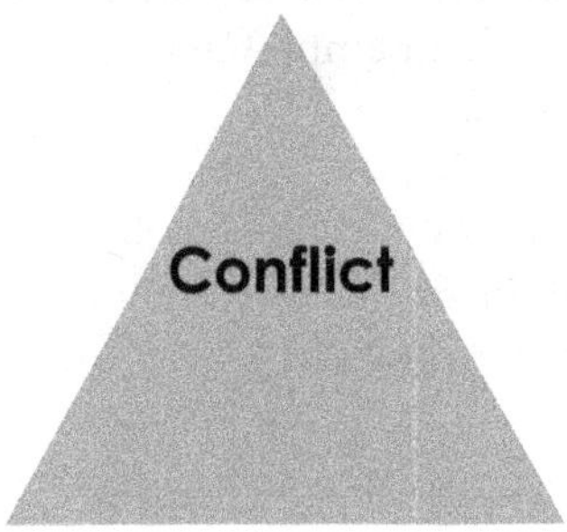

Next, draft the conflict plot heading. The conflict plot heading should frame the conflict in a way that foreshadows the client's arguments. In the at-will employment scenario, the conflict revolves around three provisions contained in an employee handbook: (1) a clause prohibiting employees from engaging in premarital sex, (2) a comprehensive progressive discipline policy with a detailed procedure for requesting a pretermination administrative hearing, and (3) an at-will disclaimer advising employees that the handbook doesn't alter the common law presumption of at-will employment. The presumption of at-will employment permits an employer to fire an employee for any nondiscriminatory reason (i.e., conduct that violates the client's religious teachings).

The plaintiff will argue that she was wrongfully terminated because the client voluntarily created a comprehensive progressive discipline policy with a detailed procedure for requesting a pretermination hearing. According to the plaintiff, the client's inclusion of such a detailed progressive discipline policy alters the presumption of at-will employment, invalidates the at-will employment disclaimer, and triggers the implied contract exception to at-will employment. By summarily firing her, the plaintiff will argue that the client breached its implied contract, depriving her of the opportunity to defend her lifestyle choices at a pretermination hearing.

In stark contrast, your client will argue that the pretermination hearings are limited to genuine workplace disputes, not philosophical debates about the appropriateness of its religious teachings. Consequently, the plaintiff's admission that she violated the morals clause by engaging in premarital sex is the key to the client's argument.

Consider the following conflict plot heading:

Status Quo	Conflict	Desired Resolution
Hired as a Role Model for Homeless Children	**An Admitted Violation of the Morals Clause**	**?**

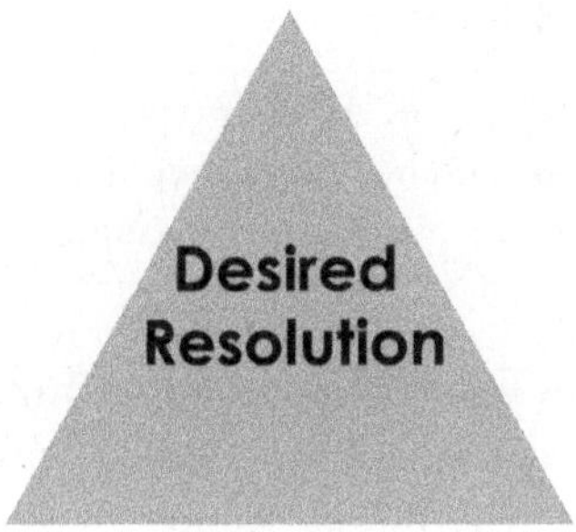

The last heading is the desired resolution plot heading. The desired resolution plot heading showcases legally relevant facts that subtly suggest the client's desired resolution. In this example, the resolution depends on the judge's decision about the relationship between the three handbook provisions at the center of the legal conflict. The client's primary argument is that its clear and conspicuous at-will employment disclaimer demonstrated its intent to maintain the presumption of at-will employment and conditioned the availability of a pretermination hearing to employees embroiled in genuine workplace disputes, not religious ones. Consider the following desired resolution plot heading:

Status Quo	Conflict	Desired Resolution
Hired as a Role Model for Homeless Children	**An Admitted Violation of the Morals Clause**	**An At-Will Employment Disclaimer Below the Plaintiff's Signature**

Notice how the phrase "below the Plaintiff's signature" subtly foreshadows the client's desired resolution without resorting to overt argument. When read together, these plot headings trigger all three parts of the rhetorical triangle: logos by foreshadowing the upcoming legal arguments, pathos by establishing the client's character, and ethos by breaking up the statement of facts into reader-friendly chunks that provide the judge with visual relief in a sea of text. Now let's explore an example of what *not* to do when drafting plot headings using the criteria mentioned at the beginning of this section:

- Can the judge immediately understand the headings (i.e., are they concrete and specific)?
- Are the headings free of legal conclusions and opinions?
- Have you included a plot heading for each pivotal point in the plot?

Using this criteria, can you see why the plot headings in the first row are more persuasive than the ones in the second and third rows?

Status Quo	Conflict	Desired Resolution
Hired as a Role Model for Homeless Children	**An Admitted Violation of the Morals Clause**	**An At-Will Employment Disclaimer Below the Plaintiff's Signature**
Role Models	**The Pregnant Plaintiff**	**The At-Will Employment Disclaimer**
Dedicated Role Model for Homeless Children	**An Immoral Plaintiff**	**A Prominent At-Will Employment Disclaimer Compels Summary Judgment**

The plot headings on the second row are too vague to foreshadow the upcoming legal arguments. Similarly, the plot headings on the third row are too riddled with opinions and factual characterizations to trigger pathos. The bonus section of this chapter contains tips for drafting effective plot headings.

ACCENTUATION

Every legal story has two sides. According to learning theorists, people remember and place the most emphasis on things read first and last.[25] This phenomenon is called the primacy-recency effect. Effective legal storytellers use the memory-enhancing power of the primacy-recency effect to accentuate favorable facts by placing them in positions of emphasis (e.g., at the *beginning* or *end* of sentences or paragraphs) or to downplay unfavorable facts by placing them in positions where they are deemphasized (e.g., in the *middle* of sentences or paragraphs).

Students sometimes worry that these types of placement strategies are manipulative. Nothing could be further from the truth. The professionalism rules referenced in Chapter 7.1 require that you disclose adverse legally relevant facts in the statement of facts, but nothing in those rules requires that you accentuate adverse legally relevant facts. Judges expect advocacy, so they aren't critical of lawyers who use persuasive techniques to minimize the negative impact of adverse legally relevant facts.[26]

Understanding the distinction between inclusion and accentuation is the key to drafting a persuasive fact statement. Consider a real-world example: In most states, driving without a license is a misdemeanor traffic offense. Assume that, in your rush

[25] David A. Sousa, *Primacy/Recency Effect*, Lancashire Grid for Learning, http://www.lancsngfl.ac.uk/secondary/math/download/file/How%20the%20Brain%20Learns%20by%20David%20Sousa.pdf (last visited Nov. 19, 2016).

[26] K. K. DuVivier, *The Reference Brief*, Colo. Law., July 2004, at 71.

to get to class, you forgot your driver's license. You discover that you're driving without a license halfway into your journey. Would you flag down a police officer and disclose that you are driving without a license? Would you consider yourself a criminal for not turning yourself in? Of course not.

Instead, you'd accentuate the positive by driving the speed limit and following the traffic rules. Only if stopped by the police would you disclose that you're driving without a license. Adopt a similar mindset when drafting the statement of facts. Your goal is to disclose legally relevant adverse facts without accentuating them. What follows are five techniques for accentuating favorable facts and downplaying unfavorable ones.

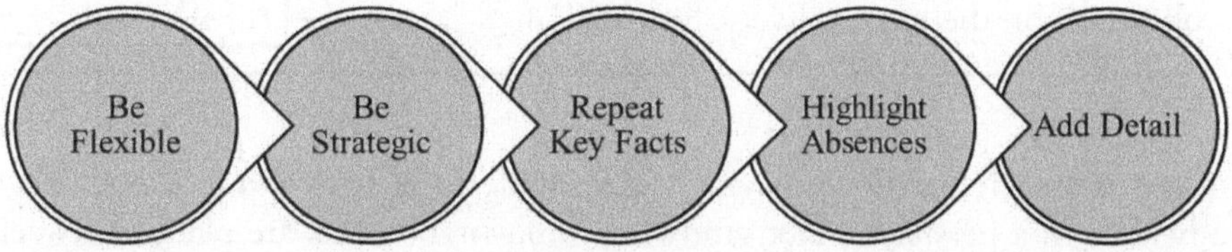

Be Flexible

With just a bit of flexible thinking, you can often neutralize unfavorable facts. Children are masters of flexible thinking. Consider the following exchange between a child and her mother:

Mother: You get dessert only if you eat all of your vegetables.
Child: Should I have chocolate cake or ice cream for dessert?

The child takes a negative fact—dessert is reserved for those occasions when the child eats all of her vegetables—and transforms it into a favorable one simply by assuming that she will be entitled to dessert. Channel your inner child, and transform unfavorable facts into more favorable ones. Consider the following examples.

Unfavorable Fact	Unfavorable Fact Transformed/Neutralized
The Beacon Hill Nursery School **does not have a year-round soccer program.**	The Beacon Hill Nursery School **has a summer soccer program.**
When the client asked to represent himself, he had **been represented by counsel for five weeks**.	When the client asked to represent himself, he had **only been represented by counsel for five weeks** and **did not have the opportunity to observe counsel's courtroom demeanor**.

The bolded phrases demonstrate how the writer has either neutralized or transformed an unfavorable fact with flexible thinking. Notice that the transformation happens without misrepresenting the fact's original meaning. Thinking flexibly is an integral component of legal storytelling.

Be Strategic

Effective legal storytellers strategically use sentence structure to harness the power of suggestion. Use short stand-alone sentences to accentuate favorable facts and longer sentences to downplay unfavorable ones. Consider the following example.

Whenever Mr. Dewey observed his lawyer sitting motionless and with his eyes closed, he voiced his objection on the record. Every. Single. Time. ← *A short, stand-alone sentence accentuates favorable facts.*

Another technique for downplaying unfavorable facts is to create a persuasive fact "sandwich." In a persuasive fact sandwich, unfavorable facts are placed between two sentences with favorable facts. Consider the following excerpt from the defendant's statement of facts in the Sixth Amendment scenario.

Favorable fact → During jury selection, Mr. Dewey noticed that his lawyer was sitting motionless with his eyes closed. The lawyer remained in this position for ten minutes. Mr. Dewey had a few pretrial meetings with his attorney where he observed his lawyer sitting motionless with his eyes closed for two or three minutes. ← *Unfavorable fact*

However, jury selection was Mr. Dewey's first opportunity to observe his lawyer's trial skills. Seconds after observing his lawyer sleeping, Mr. Dewey jumped to his feet, begging to represent himself. Mr. Dewey's request was denied. After a brief recess, opening statements began. ← *Favorable fact*

Another technique for accentuating positive facts and downplaying negative ones is the strategic use of dependent clauses and phrases. Dependent clauses and phrases aren't complete sentences. Because dependent clauses and phrases are incomplete, the judge's attention shifts to another part of the sentence. Downplay unfavorable facts by placing them in dependent clauses in the middle of the sentences and accentuate favorable facts by placing them in dependent clauses at the beginning or end of sentences. Consider the following examples.

Although the jury had not been sworn, this Court ruled that Mr. Dewey's oral motion was untimely.	Dependent clause at the beginning of the sentence emphasizes a favorable fact.
Before the jury was sworn, but after all the jurors had been selected, this Court ruled that Mr. Dewey's oral motion was untimely.	Dependent clause in the middle of the sentence downplays an unfavorable fact.

Effective legal storytellers also use active and passive voice strategically. A sentence is written in the active voice when the person or thing doing the action is explicitly identified in the sentence. In contrast, a sentence is written in passive voice when the person or thing doing the action is identified implicitly. When the identity of the sentence's subject is implicit, you divert the judge's attention from the subject of the sentence. The passive voice is particularly effective for deemphasizing unfavorable facts. Consider the following sentences.

This Court denied Mr. Dewey's oral motion as untimely.	Active voice. The Court is explicitly identified as the subject of the sentence.
Mr. Dewey's oral motion was denied as untimely.	Passive voice. The Court is not explicitly identified as the subject of the sentence.

The prosecutor will use the active voice to subtly suggest to the judge that Mr. Dewey's motion for new trial should be denied for the same reasons that his oral motion was denied. However, Mr. Dewey's attorney will use the passive voice to de-emphasize the importance of the judge's prior ruling, subtly suggesting that the motion for new trial is an opportunity for the judge to reevaluate his or her prior ruling.

Repeat Key Facts

Because the statement of facts is a foreshadowing tool, it's a bridge to the argument section of the brief. Consequently, any legally or emotionally relevant fact included in the statement of facts must also be repeated in the argument section with the same degree of specificity. The repetition between the two sections is a visual reminder of the importance of those facts.

Consider the following real-world example of the communicative power of repetition. Imagine the havoc that a purple stop sign would cause. Drivers would be confused because every stop sign in the United States is red. The color red is a visual medium telling drivers to stop. Just as you would be confused by a purple stop sign, judges reading your statement of facts will be confused if they don't see facts in the argument section that are presented with the same degree of specificity as they are in the statement of facts. The repetition of facts—first in the statement of facts and then in the argument section—communicates the importance of these facts to your readers.

Use a distinctive pattern of words to introduce favorable facts. Repeated use of identical word patterns is the verbal equivalent of a highlighter accentuating favorable facts. Consider the following excerpts from a statement of facts in the at-will employment scenario.

→ No one discussed any of the handbook provisions with Ms. Gideon. No one directed her attention to the disclaimer. No one even referenced a disclaimer until Ms. Gideon filed this lawsuit.

→ Ms. Gideon's supervisor did not (1) provide written notice of the reasons for termination, (2) mention the defendant's progressive discipline policy, or (3) advise her of the pretermination hearing procedures outlined in that policy.

A word of caution: Limit the use of this technique to avoid lessening its impact.

Highlight Absences

The absence of a fact *is* a fact. Accentuate the absence of key facts by explicitly noting their absence. Consider the following example from the plaintiff's statement of facts in the at-will employment scenario.

The progressive discipline policy mandates that the defendant "shall discharge its fact-finding mission at a pretermination administrative hearing where the employee . . . shall have an opportunity to present evidence." The policy has no exceptions. →

The writer highlights a highly favorable factual absence with a short, stand-alone sentence.

Add Detail

Accentuate favorable facts by describing them in detail and downplay unfavorable facts by describing them generically. Think of this interplay between detailed and generic factual descriptions as the difference between a far-sighted student reading with his glasses on and that same student reading with his glasses off: when the student wears glasses, the positive aspects of the student's surroundings are accentuated and when the student's glasses are off, those very same positive aspects blend into the background. These same principles apply in the statement of facts. When you describe favorable facts generically, you dilute their persuasive power. However, detail grabs the judge's attention.

Because detail grabs the judge's attention, be thoughtful about where to include them. For example, if the date of a particular event or a person's name or position aren't legally, emotionally, or procedurally relevant facts, then a generic description is appropriate. Consider the following examples.

Mr. Dewey's trial attorney was inattentive during portions of the trial.	The prosecutor's brief downplays unfavorable legally relevant facts by describing them generically.
In a fourteen-day trial, Mr. Dewey's trial attorney slept during twelve of those fourteen days.	Defense counsel's brief accentuates legally relevant favorable facts by describing them in detail.
Appellant Greg Grusendorf was fired.	A generic factual description downplays facts that the advocate doesn't want to emphasize.
Appellant Greg Grusendorf was fired after taking three puffs from a cigarette while on a lunch break.	A more detailed factual description accentuates facts that the advocate wants to emphasize.

EXECUTIVE SUMMARIES

An **executive summary** is a short paragraph at the beginning of the statement of facts that succinctly captures the most compelling legally and emotionally relevant facts embodied in the theory and theme. Because the statement of facts is the place where the judge begins taking sides and forming crucial first impressions about you and about your client, it *must* be memorable.

Recall the primacy-recency effect discussed earlier in this chapter. Because the executive summary is likely to be what the judge remembers most from the statement of facts, it should function like a good movie trailer: capturing just enough facts so that the judge is motivated to read the entire statement of facts. Just in case the judge doesn't read another word of the statement of facts, your executive summary should hit all the important highlights.

Judges find executive summaries particularly persuasive because they often use this same soft-sell technique in writing court opinions. Consider the following example of an effective executive summary from a Tenth Circuit Court of Appeal case.[27]

Executive Summary

On December 14, 1984, appellant Greg Grusendorf took three puffs from a cigarette while on a lunch break from his job as a firefighter trainee with the Oklahoma City Fire Department. He was fired that afternoon by his supervisor on the grounds that he had violated the terms of an agreement he signed as a precondition of employment that he would not smoke a cigarette, either on or off duty, for a period of one year from the time he began work.

You don't need to read any further to "see" the judge's disdain for the city's employment practices.[28] The judge's vivid, detailed language (i.e., "three puffs from a cigarette," "while on a lunch break," "fired that afternoon") creates a verbal snapshot of a plaintiff who has been victimized by an obtrusive employer. The court's language sets the scene for the conflict and foreshadows the court's ultimate resolution of the legal issues. Consider two executive summaries written by the plaintiff's attorney in the at-will employment example.

The second executive summary is the classic example of what *not* to do: cross the line from subtle persuasion to overt argument. The primary difference between the two executive summaries is the degree of subtlety. The first executive summary uses numbered lists; vivid, detailed language ("summoned to her immediate supervisor's office," "interrogated about rumors that she was pregnant," and "then terminated") to summarize the most compelling legally and emotionally relevant facts. The first executive summary is more persuasive because it leads the judge to the argument via soft-sell persuasive techniques.

[27] Grusendorf v. City of Oklahoma, 816 F.2d 539, 539 (10th Cir. 1987).
[28] *Id.*

Executive Summary 1	Executive Summary 2
In the minutes following her arrival to work on February 14, 2014, Plaintiff Hailey Gideon was summoned to her immediate supervisor's office, interrogated about rumors that she was pregnant, and then terminated.	Plaintiff Hailey Gideon was fired from her job as a youth counselor because she decided to raise her unborn child as a single mother.
Ms. Gideon's supervisor did not (1) provide written notice of the reasons for termination, (2) mention the defendant's progressive discipline policy, or (3) reference the pretermination hearing procedures outlined in that policy. All of these procedures are outlined in the employee handbook.	The defendant strategically used promissory language in its handbook to lure the most talented job applicants with unconditional promises of a pretermination hearing.

STORY WORDS

"A picture is worth a thousand words." This well-known adage captures the essence of what effective legal storytellers do in the statement of facts: ignite the judge's interest by creating verbal snapshots that foreshadow legal arguments. What follows are some suggestions for painting a pretty picture in the statement of facts.

Depict the Client's Character

Good legal storytellers help the judge see their client's character. If the judge finishes the statement of facts without a clear picture of your client's persona or without an understanding of the context of the legal conflict, then you've failed the first-impression test of the statement of facts. Use vivid, emotionally laden words to breathe life into the persona embodied in the client's stock character type. For example, if you've cast the clients in the role of the star-crossed lovers, then you'll need to select the appropriate words to convey that persona.

Legal storytellers are "word gurus," meaning that they use the pathos-inducing power of certain words to create a client persona that triggers the judge's empathy. The connection between words and emotion is a powerful one. Words with the same meaning often evoke completely different emotional responses. For example, the phrase "pit bull" is more likely to convey an image of power, strength, and aggression than the word "poodle." Connotation refers to a word's emotional meaning as opposed to its literal one. The charts below contain examples of key words with radically different connotations that the litigants in the Sixth Amendment and at-will employment scenarios might use in their statement of facts.

The Prosecutor's Words	Defense Counsel's Words
Inattentive	Sleeping/Sitting motionless
The accused/The defendant	Mr. Dewey/Bill
Asked	Begged
Stated	Voiced
Pro se	Self-representation

The Employer's Words	The Employee's Words
Invited	Summoned
Asked	Interrogated
Released from Employment	Terminated/Fired
Homeless children	Homeless teenagers
Morals clause	Conduct clause

Sometimes students shrug off the pathos-inducing power of vivid, image-provoking words, thinking that their value lies only in their ability to demonstrate an impressive vocabulary. Nothing could be further from the truth. Aside from their ability to create the client's persona, words can also influence readers' behavior.

Social psychologists refer to the synergy between words, emotion, and behavior as priming. Priming occurs when readers' behavior is directly influenced by what they read.[29] For example, one study on priming found that even subliminal exposure to competitive words led to an increase in competitive behavior among attorneys negotiating a settlement.[30] Effective legal storytellers use this synergy between words, emotion, and behavior to prime the judge for a favorable response to their client's story.

Consider the following excerpt from defense counsel's statement of facts in the Sixth Amendment scenario. Pay attention to the cumulative effect of the writer's vivid, image-provoking bolded words and the effective use of soft-sell persuasive techniques. Notice how the combination of these elements prime the judge for a favorable response.

Statement of Facts

Seconds after observing his lawyer sleeping, Mr. Dewey jumped to his feet, begging to represent himself. Although the jury had not been sworn, Mr. Dewey's motion was denied as untimely. After a brief recess, opening statements began.

In the minutes before the jury reconvened to hear opening statements, this Court reminded the attorneys of their duty of zealous representation.

[29] Carrie Sperling, *Priming Legal Negotiations through Written Demands*, 60 CATH. U. L. REV. 107, 136 (2010).
[30] *Id.*

Seconds later Mr. Dewey's lawyer gave a two-minute opening statement. Afterwards, whenever Mr. Dewey observed his lawyer sitting motionless with his eyes closed, he voiced his objection on the record. Every. Single. Time. In a fourteen-day trial, Mr. Dewey's trial attorney slept during twelve of those fourteen days. During each of those twelve days, Mr. Dewey continued to **voice** his objection on the record.

In just two paragraphs, the writer develops the client's persona with emotionally relevant facts. The client is an innocent at the mercy of a sleeping trial attorney whose incompetency undermines the integrity of the criminal justice system.

The advocate uses the client's name, transforming him from a nameless, faceless criminal defendant to "Mr. Dewey," a person deserving of the judge's empathy. Notice that the writer doesn't identify the sleeping attorney by name, instead referring to him as the "trial attorney." Referring to secondary characters with a generic term or by a party designation focuses the judge's attention on your client's persona. Phrases and words such as "jumping to his feet," "[e]very. [s]ingle. [t]ime," "begged," and "voiced" paint a poignant picture of Mr. Dewey's dilemma and prime the judge for a favorable response to the "Jurors are the guardians of justice theme."

Another highly effective method of developing the client's persona is point of view. Telling the story from the client's point of view helps the judge understand how the client became embroiled in the legal conflict. Establish the client's point of view with an executive summary chock full of emotionally relevant facts and with a status quo plot heading and emotionally relevant facts portraying the client's life before the conflict. Consider the status quo plot heading and excerpt from defense counsel's statement of facts in the Sixth Amendment scenario:

A Defendant with No Criminal History

In January, Bill Dewey was an unemployed mechanic looking for a roommate. A coworker suggested that he advertise on Craigslist. Stacy Peters answered the advertisement. Ms. Peters had references and offered to pay the security deposit in cash. Believing that this woman was a nice person who had been extremely lucky with some recent investments, Mr. Dewey invited her to become his roommate. He did not conduct a background check and did not ask for an employment history. Before losing his job, Mr. Dewey never needed a roommate.

Nothing in the record indicates that Mr. Dewey knew that his new roommate was on parole or that she had a criminal history that included a prior conviction for drug trafficking and a two-year stint in a Virginia prison. Similarly, nothing in the record indicates that Mr. Dewey knew that his roommate had a boyfriend who was a confidential FBI informant. By May—four months after meeting his roommate—Mr. Dewey was transformed from a man whose only previous encounter with law enforcement was a jaywalking ticket to one at the center of an FBI investigation for felony drug trafficking and money laundering.

Notice how the advocate shifts the point of view away from unfavorable legally relevant facts (i.e., that the client is charged with some pretty serious felony offenses) with a detailed description of the client's nonexistent criminal history and lack of experience with the criminal justice system—emotionally relevant facts that develop the client's persona as the archetypal innocent or jester/fool who was the unwitting dupe of his new roommate, a secondary character, cast in the role of the femme fatale.

Show, Don't Tell

Most artists have a vision of what they'd like the audience to see. But instead of telling the audience what to see, artists arrange images on a canvas or manipulate clay to create sculptures that show the message instead of telling it.

In much the same way, legal storytellers arrange the legally relevant, emotionally relevant, and procedurally relevant facts to show (i.e., foreshadow a particular argument) instead of telling (i.e., resort to overt argument). When you show the judge the facts, he or she can visualize what happened to the client and thus understand the client's dilemma on a deeper, more substantive level. Consider the following examples.

Telling Sentence	Showing Sentence
Ms. Gideon was an extremely effective youth counselor and a hard worker.	During her decade-long employment, Ms. Gideon was either nominated for or won "Counselor of the Year" for nine of those ten years.
Ms. Peters had an extensive criminal history that included a prior conviction for drug trafficking and a two-year stint in a Virginia prison.	Ms. Peters had a prior conviction for drug trafficking and a two-year stint in a Virginia prison.

A word of caution: Avoid intensifiers. Intensifiers are adverbs and adjectives that are added to other words to enhance their meaning.[31] In persuasive writing, intensifiers are often used to disparage an opponent's argument. The easiest-to-spot intensifiers are adverbs that end in *–ly*. In the following examples, the intensifiers are bolded and should be eliminated from the statement of facts.

> Bill Dewey files this motion for new trial to overturn a conviction based entirely on circumstantial evidence in a trial teeming with injustice.

> The Prosecutor clearly ignored Bill Dewey's sleeping counsel, obviously opting for persecution instead of justice.

[31] *Qualifiers*, Writing Center, Univ. of N.C. at Chapel Hill, http://writingcenter.unc.edu/handouts/qualifiers/ (last visited Nov. 3, 2016).

These kinds of words and phrases are red-flag indicators of telling instead of showing. Let the facts supply the "intensity" for which intensifiers are a poor substitute.[32] Avoid intensifiers for another reason: They most always signal either a lack of confidence in your arguments or a kind of bravado that damages your credibility with the judge. Chapter 10 continues the discussion about the credibility-damaging impact of intensifiers.

Two other particularly effective showing techniques are juxtaposition and the selective use of quotes. **Juxtaposition** is the arrangement of two or more ideas to suggest comparison, contrast, rhetorical effect, suspense, or character development. Consider the following examples.

In the minutes before the jury reconvened to hear opening statements, this Court reminded the attorneys about their duty of zealous representation. Seconds later, Mr. Dewey's lawyer gave a two-minute opening statement.

→ Defense counsel juxtaposes two legally relevant facts to show, not tell, the judge that the client's trial attorney was incompetent.

The conduct clause is a four-line paragraph referencing the importance of avoiding particularly offensive conduct buried within a subsection relating to work rules. But the progressive discipline policy has its own heading and spans two handbook pages.

→ The employee's attorney in the at-will scenario juxtaposes two legally relevant facts to show, not tell, the judge that the more intricate and detailed progressive discipline policy should trump the conduct clause.

Another effective showing technique is the selective use of quotes. If the witnesses' words or the words of a document are helpful, quote them. Using a quote is more memorable than a paraphrase and is less distracting than typographic emphasis such as bold, underline, or italics. Furthermore, the selective use of quotes also facilitates ethos by relieving eye fatigue. Because the overuse of quotes lessens their impact, reserve quotes for only the most compelling facts. Notice how the employer's attorney skillfully uses a direct quote from the deposition transcript coupled with a status quo plot heading to highlight favorable facts:

Hired as a Role Model for Homeless Children

During his deposition, the plaintiff's immediate supervisor discussed the relationship between the Church's fundamental mission of service and its morals clause:

---

[32] Kenneth F. Oettle, *Eschew Exaggerations, Disparagements, and Other Intensifiers,* 11 Scribes J. Legal Writing 125, 127 (2007).

Q. Does the morals clause require perfect employees?
A. Absolutely not. It only requires that counselors deserve a child's respect. →
Q. What happens when a counselor loses a child's respect?
A. You lose them to the streets.

> A strategically placed quote emphasizes the employer's theme: "Protection, not Perfection"

Combining a quote with the typography style used in the actual document is also extremely effective, especially in cases where the outcome of the legal issue turns on the interpretation of a document. Notice how the employer's attorney in the at-will scenario skillfully uses a direct quote from the handbook in conjunction with a conflict plot heading to show, not tell, the judge that the at-will employment disclaimer was prominently displayed:

An At-Will Employment Disclaimer Below the Plaintiff's Signature

The acknowledgment page is the only section of the handbook requiring employees to affirmatively acknowledge compliance with their signatures. Plaintiff signed the handbook on her first day of employment.

A half inch below the plaintiff's signature is the following phrase: "I ACKNOWLEDGE THAT THIS EMPLOYMENT HANDBOOK IS NOT A CONTRACT OF EMPLOYMENT AND THAT MY EMPLOYMENT IS AT-WILL." This language is the only portion of the disclaimer that is written in all capital letters.

By signing, plaintiff acknowledged that: "AT-WILL EMPLOYMENT MEANS THAT A CHURCH EMPLOYEE DOES NOT HAVE AN UNLIMITED CONTRACTUAL RIGHT TO PROGRESSIVE DISCIPLINE PRIOR TO TERMINATION."

By mimicking the all-caps typography that appears in the employee handbook, the writer paints a compelling picture of an employer who went to great lengths to protect the presumption of at-will employment. Which one do you think the court is most likely to remember, a description of the disclaimer or an actual quote from the disclaimer written in the identical typography style?

BONUS MATERIALS: "A LITTLE SOMETHING EXTRA"

Tips to Jump-Start the Writing Process

The first two tips are particularly helpful in the prewriting stage where you begin to organize the raw material of the statement of facts. The next two tips are particularly helpful as you begin drafting the statement of facts, and the last two tips are particularly helpful when editing the statement of facts.

Organize the Facts

Chapter 7.1 discussed the importance of integrating a magical mix of facts—heaping cups of legally relevant facts, mixed with a handful of emotionally relevant facts and a dash of background and procedural facts—into the statement of facts. However, there's more than meets the eye when it comes to creating this magical mix. Even in a relatively straightforward case, you'll often have lots of facts that you need to evaluate and sort into a relevant factual category. Mastery of the facts is indispensable because you *never* want to leave any facts sitting on the table.

Ensure that you don't leave any facts sitting on the table by designing a system for managing, sorting, and organizing them. Be creative here, letting your instincts guide you. For example, if you're a visual learner you might create a timeline, flowchart, spreadsheet, or similar diagram, and use a system of color-coding to designate each kind of fact.

If you're a kinesthetic learner,[33] then you might create a storyboard or wall of sticky notes sorted by type of fact that you place on bulletin or dry-erase board. If you're tech savvy, mapping software is also available to help organize and sort the facts. The bottom line is this: Develop a system for managing the facts and use it.

The benefits of organizing the facts extend beyond drafting the statement of facts. If the judge schedules an oral argument on a motion or if you have to present the case to an appellate court, then you don't have to relearn the facts of the case. You've already got a handy checklist of all the facts organized and sorted by type.

Generate Story Words

Legal storytellers are "word gurus." However, the process of becoming a word guru is less arduous than you might suspect. A perfect score on the verbal portion of the SAT is not a prerequisite. Use a thesaurus to bolster your vocabulary and to improve

[33] Kinesthetic learners thrive in interactive learning environments where they can physically move and practice skills instead of more passive settings such traditional lecture classrooms. Kirin Sinha, *Kinesthetic Learning: Moving Toward a New Model for Education,* Edutopia Blog (July 24, 2014), http://www.edutopia.org/blog/kinesthetic-learning-new-model-education-kirin-sinha.

your ability to select vivid, emotionally laden words that breathe life into the persona embodied in the client's stock character type. A thesaurus is a book that organizes words in groups of synonyms and related concepts. However, with the advent of technology, you're no longer bound by books. A quick online search reveals a plethora of free and fee-based online word-generating tools, including tools that combine mapping technology to help you choose words with the appropriate connotation.

Draft Plot Headings First

Because the plot headings outline the plot of the client's story, they're the natural place to begin the drafting process. Furthermore, the plot structure inherent in each plot heading—from status quo, to conflict, to desired resolution—ensures a well-organized statement of facts.

Recall that your plot headings can't include legal conclusions and opinions. However, students often struggle with drafting conclusion and opinion-free plot headings. Paradoxically, a good tip for writing opinion-free plot headings is to begin by drafting a plot heading that *includes* conclusions or opinions. Next ask yourself: What are the *facts* that support those conclusions and opinions? Then replace the conclusions and opinions with the relevant facts.

Now the only thing left to do is add the factual information that follows each plot heading. Any flowcharts, timelines, or similar documents that you've used to organize the facts will make this step of the drafting process much easier. You can simply cut and paste facts from your organizational tool into the section of the statement of facts that corresponds to the appropriate plot heading.

Avoid Duplicative Party Designations

Duplicative party designations distract the judge and clutter the statement of facts with unnecessary words.

A party designation is duplicative when, immediately after listing each party's full name, the writer immediately follows that initial designation with a quotation to the party's last name enclosed in parenthesis. Consider the following example of a duplicative party designation.

> Plaintiff Hailey Gideon ("Gideon") filed this lawsuit against the First Union Anglican Church of Colorado ("Church") and several codefendants:

Reverend Aaron Lewis ("Lewis")	Chief Executive Officer
Reverend Jonathan Ozeki ("Ozeki")	Council of Bishops President
Reverend Dominick Vanderbilt ("Vanderbilt")	Plaintiff's Immediate Supervisor

Novice legal storytellers often think that these kinds of duplicative party designations are reader-friendly clarifications. But duplicative party designations are akin to

legalese (i.e., statements that the writer uses to sound like a lawyer) that interrupt the natural flow of the statement of facts.[34] Consider the following example of the same information presented without the duplicative party designations.

Plaintiff Hailey Gideon filed this lawsuit against the First Union Anglican Church of Colorado and several codefendants:

Reverend Aaron Lewis	Chief Executive Officer
Reverend Jonathan Ozeki	Council of Bishops President
Reverend Dominick Vanderbilt	Plaintiff's Immediate Supervisor

Notice that the same information presented without the duplicative party designations is much more reader friendly. Also notice that the duplicative party designations in the previous example didn't clarify much; the judge would easily be able to match subsequent references to a party without the duplicative party designation.

Pull Out That Highlighter

Use a highlighter to ensure that your statement of facts is an effective bridge to the argument section. Highlight every fact in yellow. Then use the definitions contained in Chapter 7.1 to determine whether what you've highlighted is truly a fact. Every fact highlighted in yellow should appear in the argument section of the brief with the same degree of specificity.

Check the Story's Sound

Stories were *born* to be read aloud—hence, the universal connection between storytelling and sound. Read the statement of facts aloud to check the sound of your story. Reading the statement of facts out loud will reveal errors in organization, structure, and tone that you might otherwise miss.[35] For example, your eye might glaze over contractions or first- and second-person pronouns, language that is too informal for legal writing.

However, when you read the material aloud, your ear will most likely detect what your eye missed. Similarly, wordiness, an absence of transitions, and grammatical errors can more easily be heard and corrected.[36] What follows are some effective strategies for reading aloud.[37]

---

[34] *See generally* Adam L. Rosman, *Visualizing the Law: Using Charts, Diagrams and Other Images to Improve Legal Briefs*, 63 J. Legal Educ. 70, 78 n.11 (2014) (encouraging practitioners to incorporate visuals into briefs).

[35] *Reading Aloud*, Writing Center, Univ. of N.C. at Chapel Hill, http://writingcenter.unc.edu/handouts/reading-aloud/ (last visited Nov. 3, 2016).

[36] *Id.*

[37] *Id.*

- Read from a printed copy. Working from a printed copy will make it easier for you to flag problem areas in the document.
- Use your finger to keep track of what you're reading. Consider starting at the end of the statement of facts and working back to the beginning. This kind of proofreading strategy will help you focus on each sentence's structure, rather than the story's flow.
- Consider using free or paid speech software applications and Web-based services. A detailed discussion of these resources is outside the scope of this chapter. However, a Google search including terms such as "text to speech," "TTS," or "text reader" will yield valuable information. You can also use the "Read Aloud" function under the Review tab on Microsoft 365.

Chapter 8

Substantiating the Client's Desired Resolution: The Argument Section

"The idea of waiting for something makes it more exciting." —Andy Warhol

If you've successfully used hard- and soft-sell persuasive techniques when crafting the Introduction (or the Summary of the Argument in an appellate brief) and the Statement of Facts, the judge will be like a curious moviegoer eagerly anticipating the clearest, most compelling presentation of your client's best arguments. Because crafting a compelling argument can be intricate, this chapter is divided into four subchapters. Chapter 8.1 teaches you how to draft effective point headings that succinctly announce the client's best arguments, and Chapter 8.2 introduces you to roadmaps, an ethos-generating navigational tool for streamlining the discussion of multiple arguments. The last two subchapters are step-by-step guides for building logos, pathos, and ethos arguments. As discussed in this book's introductory chapters, argument type dictates content and argument structure mimics the plot of a story. Consider the following visual:

Logos	**Step 1: I**dentify any rules or core societal values that support your argument. **Identifying the Status Quo**
Pathos	**Step 2: D**iscuss complex rules or core societal values using legal sources such as cases and non-legal sources such as legislative history, law review articles, statistics, non-legal analogies, etc. **Describing the Status Quo**
Ethos	**Step 3: D**emonstrate how the rules or the core societal values identified and discussed in Steps 1 & 2 substantiate the client's desired conflict resolution. **Articulating the Desired Conflict Resolution**

In the status quo portion of the argument, you'll identify and, if necessary, describe any ambiguous rules or core societal values at the foundation of your argument using soft-sell persuasive techniques that subtly allude to the client's theory and theme. In the desired conflict resolution portion of the argument, you'll use hard-sell persuasive techniques such as rule-based, analogical, and policy-based reasoning to substantiate your proposed solution to the client's legal dilemma. But regardless of their type, all arguments perform three essential functions: **I**dentify a source at the foundation of the argument, **D**iscuss and clarify an ambiguous source, and **D**emonstrate how the source substantiates the client's desired resolution (i.e., the mnemonic device IDD). Remember these principles when reviewing Chapter 8.3 that teaches you how to build logos arguments and Chapter 8.4 that teaches you to build pathos and ethos policy arguments.

Chapter **8.1**

Announcing the Client's Desired Resolution: Drafting Effective Point Headings

"The art of being wise is the art of knowing what to overlook." —William James

Robin-Worrall-sdGcAhK7-02-Q-unsplash (arrow)

Knowing what to overlook—what part of the argument to emphasize and what part to omit—is the key to drafting persuasive point headings. Point headings announce the client's argument via concise sentences that scream: *Hey, pay attention! This is one of my best arguments.* Capturing the judge's attention means condensing the argument so that it could metaphorically fit on the tip of a ballpoint pen. Previous chapters alluded to the importance of point headings. But now we'll fully explore their attention-grabbing power. This chapter begins with a discussion of point headings as ethos-generating navigational tools, guides you through the drafting process, and ends with a drafting checklist.

POINT HEADINGS AS ETHOS-GENERATING NAVIGATIONAL TOOLS

Point headings are the most common ethos-generating navigational tools. And in a storytelling brief, point headings are in two strategic places: the table of contents and the argument section. Including point headings in these two prominent locations facilitates judicial autonomy. With just a quick glance at the point headings, the judge can tally the number of arguments, evaluate each argument's persuasive power, and decide which argument to read first. Without point headings, the judge is forced to hack through the *entire* argument section just to locate the argument that he or she wants to read first.

Recall Chief Justice Roberts's quote from Chapter 5 analogizing a disorganized brief to "hacking through a jungle with a machete." Some judges won't hesitate to hack through the argument section looking for arguments. Other judges, out of deference to the litigants, will begrudgingly hack through the argument section looking for arguments. But some judges won't waste *any* time looking for hard-to-find arguments. Don't risk the possibility that the judge assigned to your case falls in the last category; draft succinct, attention-grabbing point headings.

POINT HEADING BASICS

To draft effective point headings understand their symbiotic relationship to plot headings and appreciate the different types of point headings. Let's begin by exploring some crucial distinctions between plot and point headings. Think of point headings as the assertive cousins of plot headings. Plot headings appear in the statement of facts and subtly allude to the client's arguments. But point headings are assertive, meaning that they overtly tell the judge why the client is entitled to relief. This distinction is important. Plot headings are soft-sell persuasive techniques and thus must be nonargumentative. But point headings are hard-sell persuasive techniques. They're the antithesis of subtlety; they are argumentative, boldly announcing why the client is entitled to relief.

Despite these differences in tone, plot and point headings are complementary; they work together to convey the client's story. Let's explore this symbiotic relationship using the Table of Contents from the employee's brief in the at-will employment scenario:

TABLE OF CONTENTS

Introduction 1

Statement of Facts 2

An Award-Winning Youth Counselor
A Multisection Progressive Discipline Policy 3
A Disclaimer at Odds with Employment Practices 4

Argument 6

Main Point Heading

A Reasonable Juror Could Conclude That the Employer's Disciplinary Practices Created an Implied Contract 6

Subpoint Headings

A. A Multisection Progressive Discipline Policy with Mandatory Language Such as "Shall" and "Must" Created a Contractual Right to a Pretermination Hearing 8

B. The Defendant's Practice of Granting Employee Requests for Pretermination Hearings Invalidates Its Disclaimer 12

C. An At-Will Employment Disclaimer Buried at the Bottom of the Last Page of an Employee Handbook is Ineffective 16

Sub-subpoint Headings

1. The disclaimer is unclear.
2. The disclaimer is inconspicuous.

Conclusion 20

Certificate of Service 21

The three plot headings: **"An Award-Winning Youth Counselor," "A Multi-section Progressive Discipline Policy,"** and **"A Disclaimer at Odds with Employment Practices"** allude to the advocate's arguments about the creation of an implied employment contract that are explicitly announced in the intricate network of point headings. Now that you have a better understanding of the distinction between plot and point headings, let's explore the different point heading types.

The advocate has one main point heading, three subpoint headings, and two sub-subpoint headings. Main point headings announce the primary reasons why the client is entitled to the desired resolution. Subpoint headings are narrower arguments that further support the main point heading. In complex cases, an advocate might have sub-subpoint headings. Sub-subpoint headings are even narrower arguments that further support the subpoint heading. Notice that the advocate has further subdivided the last subpoint heading to create sub-subpoint headings. But effective legal storytellers rarely subdivide arguments beyond sub-subpoint headings because too many point headings overwhelm the judge, creating choppy and disorganized arguments.

The relationship between the different point heading types is analogous to a set of Russian nesting dolls: the advocate's broadest arguments (i.e., the largest doll) are announced in main point headings, narrower supporting arguments (i.e., the two smaller dolls) are announced in subpoint headings, and the narrowest arguments (i.e., the smallest doll) are announced in sub-subpoint headings. The graphic highlights some key features of each point heading type.

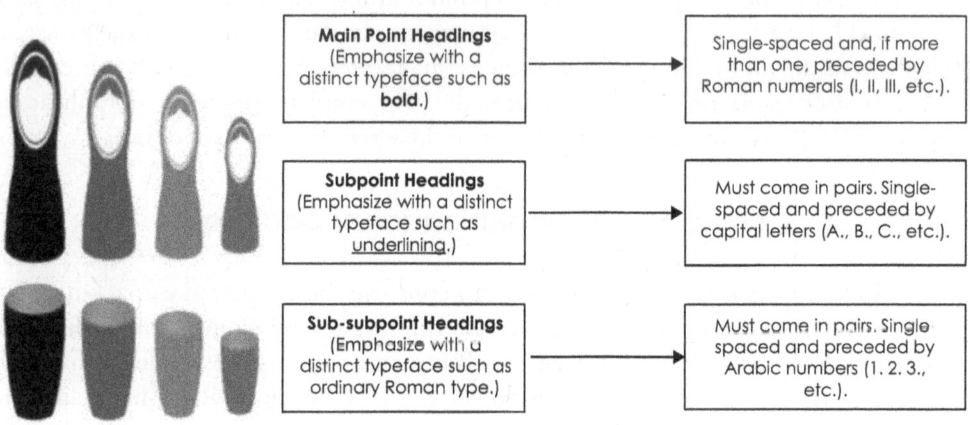

The different typefaces, numerical designations, and alphabetical designations visually represent the relationship between each point heading type. The typeface that you use for each point heading type is stylistic, not substantive.[1] Ask your professor about local customs and preferences. What's important is that you use a *different* typeface for each point heading type.

[1]Traditionally, main point headings were written in all capital letters. However, modern legal storytellers typically avoid all capital letters typeface given cognitive science research that all capital letters are notoriously difficult to read. *See* Ruth Anne Robbins, *Painting with Print: Incorporating Concepts of Typographic and Layout Design into the Text of Legal Writing Documents*, 2 J. Ass'n Legal Writing Directors 108 (Fall 2004).

DRAFTING PERSUASIVE POINT HEADINGS

Now, we'll explore the drafting process.[2] Recall the distinction between arguments and point headings from Chapter 3: all point headings are arguments, but not all arguments become point headings. You'll convert the arguments that survived the processing phase into point headings. Attention-grabbing point headings unite the procedural and substantive argument components in one argumentative, declarative sentence that's no more than *five* single-spaced lines. Brevity is important. Effective point headings are good headlines: They engage judges so that they're eager to read your client's best arguments. Consider the following headlines. Which one is easier to read?

A five-year-old kindergarten student at Eastlake Elementary School kills his sister with a handgun from his father's tool box.

Five-year-old kills sister with father's gun.

Both headlines contain the same content. But the second headline's succinctness encourages you to read it. By eliminating unnecessary words, the writer reduced its length to eight words, making it *much* easier to read than the first headline. The attention-grabbing power of brevity also applies to point headings. Point headings that the judge can quickly read are more persuasive than longer ones. So, let's confront the proverbial elephant in the room: How do you condense an argument into five-single spaced lines? Make smart organizational decisions, use a drafting template, and refine point headings with the PACC (**P**ointed, **A**ssertive, **C**lear, and **C**oncise) mnemonic device.

Make Smart Organizational Decisions

Making smart organizational decisions can conserve space. Instead of packing information into a single point heading, consider drafting several main point headings or a network of main and subpoint headings. But making these kinds of decisions can be daunting. How many point headings do you need? Should you draft only main point headings? A combination of main and subpoint headings?

Sometimes the decision is easy. For example, your client might have only one primary argument and one supporting reason, a 1:1 ratio between the argument and supporting reason. In the following example, the argument is underlined, and the supporting reason is bolded.

---

[2] Many of the techniques and strategies in this chapter have either been inspired by or adapted from the following resources: Mary Beth Beazley, A Practical Guide to Appellate Advocacy (2d ed. 2006); Gerald Lebovitz, *Getting to the Point: Pointers About Point Headings*, 82 N.Y. St. B.J. 64 (Jan. 2010); Robbins, *supra* note 1.

1:1 RATIO BETWEEN THE ARGUMENT AND THE SUPPORTING REASON:

Granting the Motion to Dismiss Is Appropriate **Because the Amount Alleged in the Complaint Does Not Satisfy the $50,000 Jurisdictional Threshold Mandated by the Computer Fraud and Abuse Act.**

When you have a 1:1 ratio, you'll have only one main point heading announcing the client's desired resolution. But in a typical case you'll have several reasons why the client is entitled to relief, a mixed ratio between the argument and supporting reasons. The advocate in the following example has a primary argument about why relocation isn't in the child's best interest and two supporting reasons. The argument is underlined, and the supporting reasons are bolded.

MIXED RATIO BETWEEN THE ARGUMENT AND SUPPORTING REASONS:

Summary Judgment Is Inappropriate, and Relocation Is Not in the Child's Best Interest **Because:**

- **Any Nominal, Material Benefits from Living in a 3000-Square-Foot Home or from Attending a Preschool for Affluent Children Are Outweighed by the Daily Contact That Would Become Financially and Professionally Infeasible for the Non-relocating Parent.**
- **Moving to Boston Would Require the Child to Endure Physically and Mentally Exhausting Cross-Country Travel.**

Mixed-ratio arguments produce multipart arguments, and multipart arguments present organizational challenges. The advocate in the above-referenced example has three organizational options outlined below:

Option 1—One Main Point Heading

I. Summary judgment Is Inappropriate, and Relocation Is Not in the Child's Best Interest Because Any Nominal, Material Benefits from Living in a 3000-Square-Foot Home or from Attending a Preschool for Affluent Children Are Outweighed by the Daily Contact That Would Become

Financially and Professionally Infeasible for the Non-relocating parent and Because Moving to Boston Would Require the Child to Endure Physically and Mentally Exhausting Cross-Country Travel.

The coordinating conjunction "and" connects the supporting reasons.

Option 2—Two Main Point Headings

I. Summary Judgment Is Inappropriate, and Relocation Is Not in the Child's Best Interest Because Any Nominal, Material Benefits from Living in a 3000-Square-Foot Home or from Attending a Preschool for Affluent Children Are Outweighed by the Daily Contact That Would Become Financially and Professionally Infeasible for the Non-relocating Parent.

Roman numerals connect the supporting reasons.

II. Summary Judgment Is Inappropriate, and Relocation Is Not in the Child's Best Interest Because Moving to Boston Would Require the Child to Endure Physically and Mentally Exhausting Cross-Country Travel.

Option 3—Main Point Heading and Two Subpoint Headings

Summary Judgment Is Inappropriate, and Relocation Is Not in the Child's Best Interest.

A network of point headings connect the supporting reasons.

A. Any Nominal, Material Benefits from Living in a 3,000-Square-Foot Home or from Attending a Preschool for Affluent Children Are Outweighed by the Daily Contact That Would Become Financially and Professionally Infeasible for the Non-relocating Parent.

B. Moving to Boston Would Require the Child to Endure Physically and Mentally Exhausting Cross-Country Travel.

These options are substantively identical. The differences are only structural. Choosing the appropriate organizational structure depends on the facts, the relationship between supporting reasons, and your instincts about visual impact. If the supporting reasons are analytically indistinct, the advocate might choose the first option because separating the supporting reasons weakens the argument. An advocate might also choose option one because it avoids overwhelming the judge with disjointed, choppy arguments. Perhaps the biggest drawback of option one is its length. But even if the advocate eliminated excess words, option one is potentially overwhelming because it packs so much information into a small visual plane.

Option two, presenting the supporting reasons in two main point headings, is a more streamlined approach that avoids visual clutter. Furthermore, by separating each supporting reason into a main point heading, the advocate can visually emphasize each argument's importance. Visual separation might be a particularly effective choice if each supporting reason is analytically distinct. But option two has some disadvantages. This option requires the existence of enough relevant primary authority to support two distinct arguments. Another drawback is that creating two separate point headings might appear unduly duplicative to the judge.

Option three, a combination of main and subpoint headings, is the most streamlined; it eliminates the duplicative procedural and substantive components of each supporting reason. But option three shares the same disadvantages of option two: It requires the existence of enough relevant primary authority to support two distinct arguments and risks appearing unduly duplicative. These options demonstrate the extremely flexible nature of point headings. With your professor or managing partner's guidance, select an organizational scheme that maximizes drafting space while visually showcasing the client's arguments.

Use a Drafting Template and the PACC Mnemonic Device

Once you've settled on an organizational scheme, use a drafting template to prioritize the most important aspects of the client's argument. Then, use the PACC mnemonic device, referenced at the beginning of the previous section, to further refine your point headings. The drafting template has three major components: (1) the client's requested relief, (2) the legal buzzwords triggering the requested relief, and (3) the legally relevant facts.

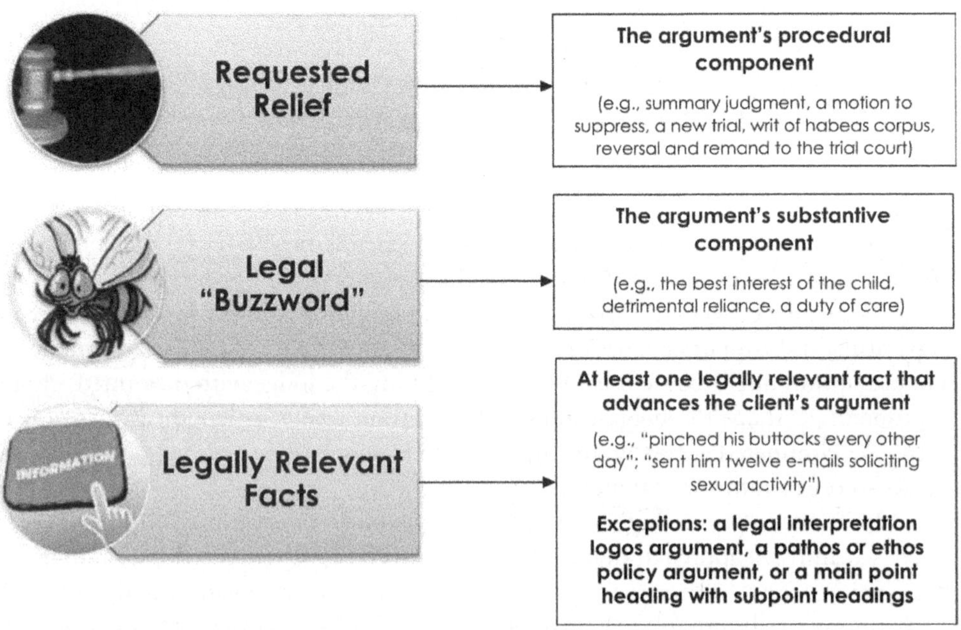

Consider the next graphic; it matches each point heading component with its corresponding location in the drafting template.

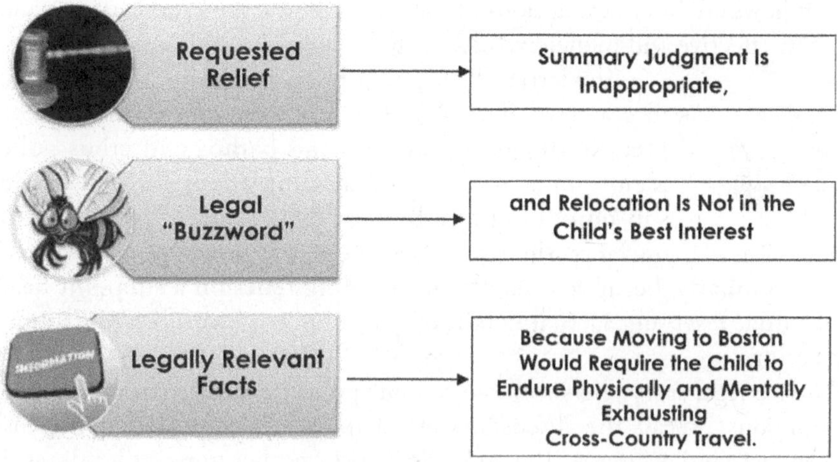

II. Summary Judgment Is Inappropriate, and Relocation Is Not in the Child's Best Interest Because Moving to Boston Would Require the Child to Endure Physically and Mentally Exhausting Cross-Country Travel.

The template prompts you to incorporate procedural, substantive, and factual components. But robotically plugging information into the drafting template won't ensure judge-friendly point headings. For example, the phrase "is not in the child's best interest" is too negative to create a favorable impression of the client's argument, and the phrase "physically and mentally exhausting cross-country travel" is too vague for the judge to understand its meaning. Use the PACC mnemonic device to refine your point headings. The letters of the mnemonic correspond to four attributes of extremely effective point headings. Point headings should

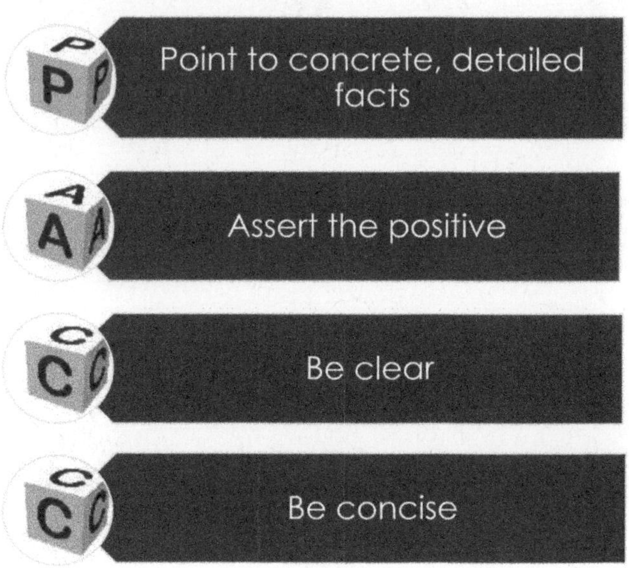

What follows are brief descriptions of each letter in the mnemonic device and examples of its effective and ineffective use.

The letter "P" is a reminder that point headings must point to concrete, detailed facts. The only exceptions are legal interpretation logos arguments, and pathos and ethos policy arguments, or a main point heading that's further developed by sub-point headings. Because these kinds of arguments don't rely on facts, their persuasiveness isn't undermined by the absence of facts. Similarly, because a main point heading relies on a subpoint heading for its meaning, reserving factual detail for the subpoint heading avoids unnecessary duplication.

Novice legal storytellers sometimes draft point headings that are all conclusions and opinions. Recall the discussion in Chapter 7.1 emphasizing the distinction between facts and opinions. The same distinction applies to point headings: Facts are statements that are indisputably true, meaning that they're contained in the pleadings, depositions, or record on appeal. In stark contrast, opinions are statements that can't be indisputably proven because they reflect an advocate's beliefs, feelings, or judgments about the facts.

Furthermore, the soft-sell techniques for drafting a persuasive fact statement discussed in Chapter 7.2 such as accentuation (i.e., detail and repetition) and the use of story words also apply to point headings. Consider the importance of detail. Vague references to material facts dramatically decrease a point heading's persuasiveness. Vagueness is boring. But concrete, detailed facts—ones that evoke images that tell stories—are intensely interesting.[3] Figures are excellent; they demonstrate a familiarity with the record and generate ethos.[4] Story words create images that show the judge, not tell the judge, that the client is entitled to relief. Space is a valuable commodity in a point heading. The mental pictures created by story words conserve valuable space. Consider the following examples of the ineffective and effective use of facts; pay particular attention to the highlighted language.

[3] *See Can You Write a Better Headline Than This? Not Using Old Headline Formulas You Can't*, Kissmetrics Blog, https://blog.kissmetrics.com/how-to-write-headlines/ (last visited Nov. 5, 2016).
[4] *Id.*

Not Pointed	Pointed
II. Summary Judgment Is Inappropriate, and Relocation Is Not in the Child's Best Interest Because Moving to Boston Would Require the Child to Endure Physically and Mentally Exhausting Cross-County Travel.	**II. Summary Judgment Is Inappropriate, and Relocation Is Not in the Child's Best Interest Because Moving to Boston Would Require a Two-and-One-Half-Year-Old Child to Endure Four 3-Hour Airline Flights Per Year.**
Points to opinions and conclusions, not facts	Points to detailed, concrete facts.
The Trial Court Abused Its Discretion by Overlooking Undisputed Evidence That Remaining in Florida Was in the Child's Best Interest.	**The Trial Court Abused Its Discretion by Overlooking Undisputed Evidence That Remaining in Florida Was in the Child's Best Interest.**
A. The Court Overlooked the Financial Infeasibility of Cross-Country Travel for the Non-relocating Parent.	A. The Cost of Cross-Country Travel Would Exceed the Non-relocating Parent's Net Monthly Income by $500.
B. The Court Overlooked the Physical and Emotional Costs of Cross-Country Travel for the Child.	B. Relocation to Boston Would Require a Two-and-One-Half-Year-Old Child to Endure Four 3-Hour Flights Per Year.
The subpoint headings point to opinions and conclusions, not facts.	Detailed, concrete facts help the appellate judges visualize the client's story.

The letter "A" is a reminder that persuasive point headings assert the positive aspects of the client's case. This reminder to draft assertive point headings is consistent with accentuation, a soft-sell persuasive technique for drafting persuasive statement of facts discussed in Chapter 7.2. For example, when you have multiple point headings or subpoint headings, present your strongest point headings in positions of emphasis—either first or last—and "sandwich" weaker point headings in the middle. Using affirmative and noncombative language is another aspect of assertiveness. Your goal is to state information in a way that encourages agreement. Consider the following examples, paying particular attention to the highlighted language.

Not Assertive	Assertive
II. Summary Judgment Is Inappropriate, and Relocation Is Not in the Child's Best Interest Because Moving to Boston Would Require a Two-and-One-Half-Year-Old Child to Endure Four 3-Hour Airline Flights Per Year.	**II. Summary Judgment Is Inappropriate, and Remaining in Florida Preserves the Child's Best Interest by Not Subjecting a Two-and-One-Half-Year-Old Child to Four 3-Hour Airline Flights Per Year.**
↓ Negative statements don't prime the judge for a favorable response.	↓ Positive statements prime the judge for a favorable response.
The District Court Did Not Err in Holding That Prosecuting an Officer for Communicating Publicly Available Information to a Subordinate Did Not Violate the First Amendment.	**The District Court Correctly Held That Prosecuting an Officer for Communicating Publicly Available Information to a Subordinate Was Protected First Amendment Speech.**
↓ Negative statements are confusing, difficult to read, and unpersuasive.	↓ Affirmatively stating the court's holding is less confusing, easier to read, and more persuasive.

Too Assertive or Not Assertive	Assertive
Because Defense Counsel Sat Motionless with His Eyes Closed During Jury Selection, the Trial Court Ignored the Law When It Denied the Plaintiff's Motion to Represent Himself.	**Because Defense Counsel Sat Motionless with His Eyes Closed During Jury Selection, the Trial Court Erred When It Denied the Plaintiff's Motion to Represent Himself.**
↓ Too assertive. The language is combative and insulting.	↓ The language is assertive but not combative or insulting.
Even If a Statement Contains Words Such as "Always" and "Forever," Ohio Law Only Permits Recovery under Promissory Estoppel for Words with Measurable Durations.	**Ohio Law Only Permits Recovery for Promissory Estoppel, Even If a Statement Contains Words Such as "Always" and Forever," for Words with Measurable Durations.**
↓ Not assertive. Because of its placement, the language highlights negative facts.	↓ "Sandwiching" negative facts in the middle of the point heading minimizes the impact of negative facts.

The letter "C" is a reminder that persuasive point headings are clear. Problems with clarity stem from three major sources: (1) vague references to the requested relief, to the reviewing court, or to primary authorities; (2) nonparallel sentence structure; and (3) missing connections between analytically related arguments. Consider the highlighted language in the following examples.

Unclear	Clear
Because Defense Counsel Sat Motionless with His Eyes Closed During Jury Selection, the Lower Court Erred When It Denied the Plaintiff's Motion to Represent Himself.	**Because Defense Counsel Sat Motionless with His Eyes Closed During Jury Selection, the Trial Court Erred When it Denied the Plaintiff's Motion to Represent Himself.**
Vague reference to the reviewing court.	A clearer reference to the reviewing court.
A Reasonable Juror Could Reach Only One Conclusion: § 61.1300(7)(e) outweighs § 61.1300(7)(c).	**A Reasonable Juror Could Reach Only One Conclusion: The Child's Admission to a Nationally Ranked School Outweighs Any Inconvenience to the Non-relocating Parent.**
A vague reference assumes the judge's familiarity with the statute.	A clearer reference to the statutory balancing test improves clarity.

Another common clarity problem is nonparallel sentence structure. A point heading is parallel when it uses an identical pattern of words to clarify connections between analytically related arguments. The nonparallel construction occurs when the advocate breaks the pattern of connection. Problems with nonparallel construction typically occur when mixed-ratio arguments are connected by coordinating conjunctions (e.g., "and," "or," "but") or with subordinating conjunctions such as "because." Consider the following examples.

Unclear	Clear
This Court Should Deny the Motion to Suppress Because the Witness's Testimony That She Saw the Gun Was Credible, and the Physical Evidence Corroborates Her Testimony.	**This Court Should Deny the Motion to Suppress Because the Witness's Testimony That She Saw the Gun Was Credible and Because the Physical Evidence Corroborates Her Testimony.**
Not parallel. The second reason supporting the requested relief does not begin with the word "because."	Parallel. Both reasons supporting the requested relief begin with the word "because."

In complex cases with intricate networks of main point headings, subpoint headings, and sub-subpoint headings, drafting clear point headings can be challenging. Main point headings should be broad enough to "equal" the narrower arguments contained in subpoint headings. Similarly, subpoint headings should provide more details about the broader arguments contained in main point headings. When a point heading doesn't equal the narrower arguments contained in subpoint or sub-subpoint headings, they are mismatched. Mismatched point headings are unclear.

Consider the following example of a mismatched network of point headings. The mismatched portions are highlighted.

Mismatch Between Main and Subpoint Headings:

Issues of Fact About Whether Mr. Simms's Gender Made Him a Target for Sexual Harassment Preclude Summary Judgment.

A. Had He Been Female, Mr. Simms Would Not Have Been Victimized by His Supervisor Who Pinched His Buttocks Every Other Day and Who Sent Twelve E-mails Soliciting Sexual Activity.

B. The Brown Test for Imputing Liability to Bisexual Harassers Is Most Consistent with Congressional Intent to Eliminate All Types of Sexual Harassment.

The first subpoint heading matches the main point heading. They both explicitly relate to gender. But the connection between the second subpoint heading and main point heading is missing. The second subpoint heading is a logos legal interpretation argument, and the main point heading isn't broad enough to encompass it. In the following example, the advocate revises the main point heading so that it's broad enough to encompass both logos arguments identified in the subpoint headings. The matching portions are highlighted.

Appropriately Matched Main and Subpoint Headings:

Summary Judgment Is Improper Because Genuine Issues of Material Fact Exist About Whether Mr. Simms's Gender Made Him a Target for Sexual Harassment and Because a Liberal Interpretation of Causation Is Most Consistent with Congress's Intent.

The "because" clauses connect the two types of logos arguments, eliminating the missing connection.

A. Had He Been Female, Mr. Simms Would Not Have Been Victimized by a Supervisor Who Pinched His Buttocks Every Other Day and Who Sent Twelve E-mails Soliciting Sexual Activity.

B. The Brown Test for Imputing Liability to Bisexual Harassers Is Most Consistent with Congressional Intent to Eliminate All Types of Sexual Harassment.

In the next example, the advocate uses a semicolon in the main point heading to correct the mismatch. Using a semicolon is a clever device for eliminating the missing connection and improving clarity.

Appropriately Matched Main and Subpoint Headings:

Issues of Fact About Whether Mr. Simms's Gender Made Him a Target for Sexual Harassment Preclude Summary Judgment; Furthermore, a Liberal Interpretation of Causation Is Most Consistent with Congress's Intent.

A semicolon connects the two types of logos arguments, eliminating the missing connection.

A. Had He Been Female, Mr. Simms Would Not Have Been Victimized by His Supervisor Who Pinched His Buttocks Every Other Day and Who Sent Twelve E-mails Soliciting Sexual Activity.

B. The Brown Test for Imputing Liability to Bisexual Harassers Is Most Consistent with Congressional Intent to Eliminate All Types of Sexual Harassment.

The second "C" is a reminder that persuasive point headings are concise. Recall the discussion from the first part of the chapter touting the virtues of brevity. But conciseness goes beyond brevity. A concise point heading conveys the crux of the argument in the smallest number of words. Cutting essential information will produce a point heading that's brief but not concise.

Novice legal storytellers struggle with conciseness. They want to include *every* legally relevant fact. But point headings are headlines. They contain only the most riveting, provocative, and interesting factual aspects of the story—they aren't the entire story. When selecting legally relevant facts, identify the ones that are so riveting, provocative, and interesting that they virtually jump off the page and slap the judge in the face with their significance. Those are the essential legally relevant facts that you shouldn't eliminate from a point heading. After identifying the essential legally relevant facts, eliminate any nonessential information. To eliminate nonessential information, eliminate redundancies and excessive detail.

Eliminate Redundancies

Eliminating redundant information that doesn't contribute to the argument yields concise point headings. Consider the following examples. The redundancies are highlighted, and the revised portions are underlined.

Redundant	Concise
II. Summary Judgment Is Inappropriate, and Remaining in Florida Preserves the Child's Best Interest by Not Subjecting a Two-and-One-Half-Year-Old Child to Four 3-Hour Airline Flights Per Year.	**II. Summary Judgment Is Inappropriate, and Remaining in Florida Preserves the Child's Best Interest by Not Subjecting a Two-and-One-Half-Year-Old to Four 3-Hour Flights Per Year.**
A two-and-one-half-year-old is a child. Given the context, the judge will know that the word "flight" means an airline flight.	Two words eliminated. This point heading conveys only essential information.

Redundant	Concise
II. Summary Judgment Is Inappropriate, and Remaining in Florida Preserves the Child's Best Interest by Not Subjecting a Two-and-One-Half-Year-Old to Four 3-Hour Flights Per Year.	II. Summary Judgment Is Inappropriate, and Remaining in Florida Preserves the Child's Best Interest by <u>Protecting</u> a Two-and-One-Half-Year-Old from Four 3-Hour Flights Per Year.
Two words eliminated.	One word conveys the argument more concisely.

Eliminate Excessive Detail

Detail is a popular soft-sell persuasive technique. But excessive detail creates long overwhelming point headings. Point headings only foreshadow the detailed presentation of supporting facts in the argument. Save the details for the argument. To eliminate excessive detail, replace several words with one or two story words. Consider the following point heading from the first part of this chapter. The excessive detail is crossed out, and the revised point headings appear on the right.

Too Detailed	Concise
I. Summary Judgment is Inappropriate, and Remaining in Florida Preserves the Child's Best Interest Because ~~Any Nominal, Material Benefits from Living in a 3000-Square-Foot Home or from Attending a Preschool for Affluent Children~~ Are Outweighed by the Daily Contact ~~That Would Become Financially and Professionally Infeasible for the~~ Non-relocating Parent.	**I. Summary Judgment Is Inappropriate, and Remaining in Florida Preserves the Child's Best Interest Because Daily Contact with the Mother Outweighs Any Material Benefits.**
A forty-nine-word point heading is overwhelming.	Two story words eliminate twenty-six words.

The phrases "Nominal, Material Benefits," "Living in a 3000-Square-Foot Home," and "Attending a Preschool for Affluent Children" are replaced with two story words—Material Benefits—that efficiently present the advocate's theory about a proposed relocation that's in the relocating parent's best interest, not the child's. The advocate saves the complete factual development of the client's desired resolution for the argument section.

A word of caution: Recall the distinction between brevity and conciseness. Don't eliminate the procedural or substantive components of the drafting template. Consider the following examples. The essential information that's been inappropriately eliminated is crossed out. The brief, concise version is on the right.

Brief but Not Concise	Brief and Concise
II. Summary Judgment Is Inappropriate, and Remaining in Florida Preserves the Child's Best Interest by Not Subjecting a Two-and-One-Half-Year-Old to Four 3-Hour Flights ~~Per Year.~~ ↓ The phrase "Per Year" is essential to the client's story about the unduly burdensome nature of the relocation.	**II. Summary Judgment Is Inappropriate, and Remaining in Florida Preserves the Child's Best Interest by Not Subjecting a Two-and-One-Half-Year-Old to Four 3-Hour Flights Per Year.**

Brief but Not Concise	Brief and Concise
II. ~~Summary Judgment is Inappropriate, and~~ Remaining in Florida Preserves the Child's Best Interest by Not Subjecting a Two-and-One-Half-Year-Old to Four 3-Hour Flights Per Year. ↓ Eliminating the requested relief creates an unclear point heading.	**II. Summary Judgment Is Inappropriate, and Remaining in Florida Preserves the Child's Best Interest by Not Subjecting a Two-and-One-Half-Year-Old to Four 3-Hour Flights Per Year.**

One last drafting tip: Don't eliminate excess words by replacing them with contractions; contractions are too informal for legal writing. And don't omit articles such as "the," "a," or "an." Omitting articles make point headings sound robotic, not concise. Packaging so much content into such a small space can be challenging, even for experienced legal storytellers. But with a little effort and practice, even a novice can draft headline-worthy point headings. Review the drafting checklist on the next page, and use it to evaluate your point headings.

POINT HEADING DRAFTING CHECKLIST

General Characteristics

- ☑ Is each argument introduced by a point heading?
- ☑ Is each point heading no more than five single-spaced lines?
- ☑ Can the judge immediately understand your point headings?
- ☑ Do your point headings appropriately use editorial enhancements such as bolded typeface for main point headings and underlining for subpoint headings?
- ☑ Do your point headings appropriately use Roman numerals and/or alphabetical or numerical designations?
- ☑ When read comprehensively, do the point headings completely and persuasively outline your arguments?
- ☑ When read comprehensively, do the point headings allude to the client's theory and theme?

Specific Considerations

- ☑ Does each point heading comply with the drafting principles memorialized in the PACC mnemonic device?
- ☑ Does each main point heading make a positive assertion about the conclusion or action that you want the judge to take?
- ☑ Does each main point heading allude to the case's procedural posture?
- ☑ Does each point heading contain at least one legally relevant fact from the case (with the exceptions of pure questions of law, point headings introducing a policy CREAC, or main point headings with subpoint headings)?

Chapter **8.2**

Using Roadmaps to Streamline Multiple Arguments

"Nature is pleased with simplicity. And nature is no dummy." —Isaac Newton

Streamlining the complex sounds impossible. But multipart arguments demand streamlining. Most judges are burdened by enormous time constraints and dislike the suspense created by having little inkling about how a multipart argument will unfold.[1] Roadmaps are the advocate's best antidote to detrimental suspense. Also known as umbrellas, **roadmaps** aren't arguments but ethos-generating navigational paragraphs that streamline arguments by announcing the route through their intricate organization of main and subpoint headings. Without a roadmap, the judge might be distracted by questions about the relationship between arguments, the order that the advocate will present those arguments, and whether any common legal rules, public policies, traditions, or customs govern distinct parts of the argument. And a distracted judge will have difficulty processing the client's arguments. This chapter begins with a brief discussion of roadmap placement and function and ends with tips for tackling arguments requiring multiple roadmaps.

ROADMAP PLACEMENT AND FUNCTION

Roadmaps aren't labeled or identified in the table of contents. But judges can quickly spot them because of their placement and function. Roadmaps appear in the argument section immediately before multipart arguments. Multipart arguments are easy to identify because they're divided into multiple point headings. The number

[1] *See* Raoul G. Cantero, *Three Simple Ways to Improve Your Briefs*, 85 Fla. B.J. 31, 33 (Feb. 2011) (encouraging the use of roadmap paragraphs in briefs with multiple subsections).

of subdivisions, *not* the number of point headings, equals the number of roadmaps. Consider the following nonlegal example.

Roadmap 1

I. Nontropical Fruit

Roadmap 2

- A. Apple
- B. Grapes
- C. Peaches

II. Tropical Fruit

Roadmap 3

- A. Passion Fruit
- B. Coconut

Number of Roadmaps = Number of Subdivisions

Subdivision 1: Nontropical vs. Tropical Fruit

Subdivision 2: Specific types of Nontropical Fruit

Subdivision 3: Specific types of Tropical Fruit

Don't be overwhelmed by the number of roadmaps in the example. Novices often assume that roadmaps must be a predetermined length. But effective roadmaps don't have to be long or intricate. Length is based on the complexity of the arguments. Instead of focusing on length, concentrate on function. Roadmaps typically perform the following functions.

Identify "lowest common denominator" substantive and procedural rules, public policies, traditions, or customs

Preview and outline arguments

Explain the omission of extraneous arguments

This list of roadmap functions is nonexclusive. The substance of your arguments and their organizational structure will dictate whether your roadmap performs some or all of these functions. Consider the following example. The roadmap provides context for the arguments announced in the main point headings. Each essential roadmap function is identified in bold type.[2]

Argument

Mr. Bryan is entitled to discover the identity of the deponent's sources, information that is vital to his employment discrimination claim. **[Lowest common denominator procedural rule]** This Court has discretion when ruling on motions to compel discovery, discretion that extends to ruling on the journalist's privilege. **[Lowest common denominator substantive rule]** The Second Circuit limits the applicability of the journalist's privilege, reasoning that "the privilege's viability is dictated by the purposes it serves. The privilege follows where reason leads; where the reason stops, there stops the privilege." **[Preview and outline of arguments]** In this case, reason weighs against the privilege. First, the deponent is not a journalist. Her website—a gossip clearinghouse doubling as a job search tool—is an uncorroborated hodgepodge of cherry-picked information cut and pasted from public sources, not investigatory reporting intended to benefit the public. Second, applying the privilege would extend First Amendment protection beyond its purpose: ensuring public access to investigatory reporting about matters of substantial importance. **[Explain the omission of extraneous arguments]** Because the deponent cannot satisfy her burden of proving intent to engage in investigatory reporting, this brief does not address other elements of the privilege. If the journalist's privilege is to have any reasonable limitation, the motion to compel must be granted.

I. **The Deponent Is Not a Journalist and Should Be Compelled to Identify Her Sources Because Creating a Blogpost to Find a Job and to Gather Evidence for Her Sister's Divorce Is Not Investigatory Reporting Intended for Public Benefit.**

II. **Extending the Privilege to Recycled Gossip Would Undermine the First Amendment's Purpose of Ensuring Public Access to Hard-Hitting Investigatory Reporting About Matters of Substantial Importance.**

---

[2] Citations have been omitted to conserve space.

Without this roadmap, the judge wouldn't understand the relationship between the arguments announced in the point headings or the advocate's reasons for omitting arguments about undisputed elements of the privilege. Furthermore, without the roadmap, the advocate would have to repeat the motion to compel standard and the substantive rules governing the journalist's privilege in each argument. Such unnecessary duplication would impair the judge-friendliness of the argument section and waste valuable space.

ARGUMENTS REQUIRING MULTIPLE ROADMAPS

The previous example was straightforward. But what if the advocate opted for an organizational scheme requiring multiple roadmaps? Novices often struggle with decisions about content when drafting multiple roadmaps. Location governs content. Each roadmap must be broad enough to streamline the arguments that it proceeds. Information that relates to only one argument belongs in the body of the argument, not the roadmap. Assume that the advocate in the previous example opted for a different organizational scheme with slightly different point headings:

Roadmap 1

I. **The Deponent Is Not a Journalist, Has No Standing to Assert the Journalist's Privilege, and Should Be Compelled to Identify Her Sources.**

Roadmap 2

A. <u>Only People Serving the Public's Interest in Investigatory Reporting, Not Those Gathering Information for a Job Search or a Sister's Impending Divorce, Have Standing.</u>

B. <u>Only People Intending to Publicly Disseminate Information, Not Those Gathering Information for a Job Search or a Sister's Impending Divorce, Have Standing.</u>

II. **Extending the Privilege to Recycled Gossip Would Undermine Established Canons of Journalistic Ethics.**

Also assume that the advocate's research yielded a plethora of information. The chart that follows describes what information belongs in a roadmap and what information belongs in the body of the argument.

Information	Placement
"Work experience as a professional journalist can create an inference of an intent to disseminate."	**Body of the Argument** (Narrow legal rule that relates only to the logos argument announced in subpoint heading B)
"The Committee of Concerned Journalists identifies three ethical obligations of professional journalists: (1) to report accurate, truthful information to the public for its benefit; (2) to maintain independence and loyalty to the public; and (3) to avoid 'sensationalism and trivia' to protect privacy interests."	**Body of the Argument** (Narrow quasi-legal custom that relates only to the pathos argument announced in main point heading II)
"In the Second Circuit, entitlement to the privilege is governed by two mandatory elements: (1) investigatory reporting and (2) an intent to disseminate information to the public at the inception of the newsgathering process."	**Roadmap 2** (Broad governing rule for the privilege that governs both logos subpoint headings)
"The First Amendment provides that Congress shall make no law . . . abridging freedom of the press."	**Roadmap 1** (Broad legal rule that relates to both arguments announced in the main point headings)
"Investigatory reporting requires a reliable fact-gathering process and explores topics related to social justice."	**Body of the Argument** (Narrow legal rule that relates only to the logos argument announced in the subpoint heading A)

If you find yourself repeating rules in the roadmap and in the body of the argument, then the information is the kind of lowest dominator information that belongs in a roadmap.

A word of caution: Too many roadmaps make the argument section choppy and disjointed. Only the most complex cases, those with multiple arguments and multiple, interrelated networks of supporting reasons should have multiple roadmaps.

One last drafting tip: The presentation of your arguments should track the order of their presentation in the roadmap. So, in the journalist's privilege example, the argument that the deponent's online activities aren't investigatory reporting should appear first in the argument section. This symmetry between the roadmap and the argument enhances your brief's judge-friendliness. Although a good brief must tell a compelling legal story, save suspense for creative writing. And use roadmaps to help the busy judge seamlessly navigate multiple arguments.

Chapter 8.3

Crafting Persuasive Logos Arguments

"I didn't fail 3,000 times; I documented 3,000 ways not to make a light bulb." —Thomas Edison

Thomas Edison skillfully redefined what some might characterize as failure into success. In much the same way, judges expect advocates to redefine or reconceptualize familiar mnemonic devices such as CREAC or IRAC. Instead of using mnemonic devices as vehicles for substantiating objective predictive analysis, judges expect advocates to reconceptualize these mnemonic devices, using them to reframe objective descriptions of rules, facts, holdings, and rationales—information comprising the status quo of a logos argument—so that they're written from the client's unique point of view.[1] For example, if you're objecting to a summary judgment motion, then you'll define the procedural rule as one protecting your client's right to a jury trial. If you're the party filing the motion for summary judgment, then you'll define the procedural rule as protecting judicial integrity by ensuring that purely legal issues are decided by judges.[2] Similarly, if you're representing an Internet journalist who's asking the judge to extend the protection of the journalist's privilege to nontraditional forms of media, then you'll use soft-sell persuasive techniques to identify rules at the foundation of your argument and describe cases interpreting those rules in ways that advance the emerging story outlined in the theory and summarized in the theme.

[1] See Helen E. Hoens, *Writing Persuasively at the Trial Court Level: Practical Tips on Style and Substance*, N.J. Law., Aug. 2001, at 2.
[2] *Id.*

Novice legal storytellers often struggle to reconceptualize commonly used mnemonic devices to identify, explain, and substantiate their logos arguments. The techniques and strategies outlined in this chapter are designed to minimize that struggle.[3] This subchapter begins with a discussion of key distinctions between objective and persuasive CREAC, a modified version of the traditional mnemonic device that's more appropriate for legal storytelling. The remainder of this subchapter teaches you how to craft compelling logos arguments. First, you'll learn some of the most common soft-sell techniques for persuasively identifying legal rules and then you'll explore a three-step process for persuasively articulating the rules at the foundation of your logos arguments. Then, you'll learn how to persuasively use case law authority to provide the judge with a succinct explanation of how courts have interpreted ambiguous or complex rules. Next, you'll learn how to substantiate the desired conflict resolution by applying the rule that you identified and explained via hard-sell persuasive techniques such as rule-based and analogical reasoning. The last portion of this subchapter teaches you how to combat adverse facts that might undermine the client's requested relief.

UNDERSTANDING PERSUASIVE CREAC

Beginners often need assistance when learning something new. For example, when you first learned to add and subtract, you might have used your fingers. In the law school context, your first introduction to exam writing was in the form of an organizational tool such as IRAC. Similarly, your first introduction to memo writing came in the form of memory-enhancing mnemonic devices such as CREAC, TREAT, or CRUPACC. Mnemonic devices are also useful in persuasive writing. They remind novice advocates about what judges need to understand their arguments. Don't be intimidated by the novelty of persuasive CREAC. Comfort yourself with the knowledge that the rule application section of persuasive CREAC is identical to the rule application section of an objective CREAC—they both highlight the attorney's desired resolution using hard-sell persuasive techniques such as rule-based and analogical reasoning. However, there are differences between the two mnemonic devices. One of the key differences is that persuasive CREAC is organized around arguments, not elements, factors, or other components of a legal rule. And consequently, a persuasive CREAC is a discrete logos argument written from the client's unique perspective that reflects a unifying theory and theme. Persuasive CREAC differs from objective CREAC in four other distinct ways:

Let's explore the first distinguishing feature: persuasive CREACs begin with a point heading. In an objective memo, the analysis begins with a conclusion articulating a prediction about the outcome of a legal issue. The conclusion in an objective CREAC is a neutral, objective statement. Consider the following graphic:

---

[3] Many of the techniques and strategies in this chapter have either been inspired by or adapted from materials in the following textbooks: Beazley, *supra* note 2; Linda H. Edwards, Legal Writing: Process, Analysis, and Organization (1999); Laurel Currie Oates et. al., The Legal Writing Handbook—Analysis, Research, and Writing (2d ed. 1998); Robin Wellford Slocum, Legal Reasoning, Writing, and Other Lawyering Skills (3d ed. 2009).

Attributes of Persuasive CREAC

- Begins with a Point Heading
- Embraces the Client's Perspective
- Uses Strategic Case Placement Strategies
- Ends with the Desired Conflict Resolution

> **Ms. Ramon will not recover under the promissory estoppel exception to at-will employment because her employer's oral assurance that she would "always have a job" was too indefinite to constitute a binding promise.**

But in legal storytelling, the conclusion—the first "C" in the persuasive CREAC mnemonic device—morphs into a point heading that announces the advocate's argument. Review the objective CREAC conclusion heading transformed into a persuasive CREAC point heading:

> **I. The Church is entitled to summary judgment because an offhand, casual remark praising the plaintiff's job performance is too indefinite to trigger the promissory estoppel exception to at-will employment.**

The point heading commands the judge's attention because of its distinctive typography (i.e., bolded text preceded by a Roman numeral) and because of its location (i.e., separated from the body of the argument). Furthermore, in addition to alluding to the substantive legal rule (i.e., the promissory estoppel exception), the point heading identifies the relevant procedural rule (i.e., the summary judgment standard). Point headings are more comprehensive than conclusions; they reference the governing substantive *and* procedural rules. Also notice that the point heading contains words with negative connotations such "offhand" and "casual." Connotations are emotions or feelings that a word triggers in the reader. By identifying the employer's statement as "an offhand, casual remark," the advocate subtly suggests to the judge that the employer's words aren't a legally binding promise. Lastly, notice that the point heading omits the phrases "oral assurance" and "always have a job" referenced in the objective conclusion because they emphasize aspects of the case that the advocate wants to deemphasize. Chapter 8.1 teaches you how to draft persuasive point headings.

The second distinction between persuasive and objective CREAC, embracing the client's unique perspective, relates to persuasive CREAC's reliance on soft-sell techniques to persuasively identify legal rules—the "R" in the persuasive CREAC mnemonic device. Recall that soft-sell persuasive techniques subtly reference the client's theory, theme, and arguments and prime the judge for a favorable response to the client's story. In objective CREAC, the counselor objectively states the rule. Whether written for the plaintiff or the defendant, the rule in an objective memo is the same. Review the following excerpt from a rule section in an objective CREAC.

In Ohio, the promissory estoppel exception requires proof of a specific, definite promise of continued employment. When looking for evidence of specificity, courts carefully evaluate whether the employer's statement contains a concrete duration of continued employment.

But in persuasive CREAC, advocates use soft-sell persuasive techniques such as word choice, detail, and positions of emphasis to persuasively identify legal rules. Your description of the legal rules is persuasive when the judge *immediately* knows the identity of the attorney that drafted it. Review the following excerpt from a rule section in a persuasive CREAC.

Ohio courts construe the specificity element narrowly, rigorously evaluating the employer's comments for language suggesting a concrete duration of continued employment such as six months or three years. Without this level of specificity, Ohio courts are more likely to find that comments made by employers are too indefinite to survive summary judgment.

The drafter is clearly the employer's attorney. The description of the substantive and procedural rules—"narrowly," "rigorously evaluating," "without this level of specificity, Ohio courts are more likely to find," "too indefinite to survive summary judgment"—subtly suggests that the employer's language was too indefinite to create a legally binding promise. To the untrained eye, these distinctions may seem subtle. But effective legal storytellers are experts in subtly, using soft-sell persuasive techniques to prime the judge for a favorable response to the client's argument.

The third distinction between persuasive and objective CREAC, using strategic placement strategies, relates primarily to the rule explanation section or the "E" of the persuasive CREAC mnemonic device. The advocate's tools for explaining case law authority—case illustrations and explanatory parentheticals—are identical in objective and persuasive CREAC. A **case illustration** is an in-depth discussion of a case that contains a description of the legally relevant facts, the court's holding, and the court's rationale. Unlike a case illustration, an **explanatory parenthetical** is a more succinct description of the case (commonly no more than 35 words). But in rule explanation section of a persuasive CREAC, advocates use the memory enhancing power of primacy and recency, the practice of placing information that the advocate wants the judge to remember at the beginning and ending of sentences and paragraphs. Principles of primacy and recency explain why advocates begin the rule explanation section of a persuasive CREAC with an assertion. Rule explanation assertions function like thesis sentences, meaning that they don't merely reiterate rules but succinctly and persuasively articulate clarifying information about ambiguous rules. Rule explanation assertions are supported by case illustrations, explanatory parentheticals, or a combination of both. Without a strategically placed assertion, a judge would be forced to read *all* the advocate's case illustrations and parentheticals and figure out how they advance the client's argument.

The rule explanation assertion is the kind of ethos-generating navigational tool discussed in Chapter 5. A busy judge should be able to read the assertion and immediately understand how the case law authority supports your argument and undermines your opponent's. According to one prominent federal judge, "Putting your main point up front gives your readers the conclusion in case they don't read further. It tempts readers to continue and puts everything in context."[4] For these reasons, effective advocates *always* begin the persuasive rule explanation with an assertion—a location where the judge can't miss it.

Assertions aren't objective. Think of an assertion as a "thesis with an attitude." They embrace the client's point of view by subtly highlighting case law authority that's consistent with the client's theory and theme. Consider the following illustration.

Thesis Sentence	Assertion
To determine if an employer's statement contains a concrete duration of continued employment, courts evaluate whether it promises employment for a measurable time or whether it is based on a clearly discernable event.	Ohio courts routinely hold that, unless they are based on a measurable time or a clearly discernable event, an employer's statements about job performance are indefinite.

[4] Gerald Lebovits, *Do's, Don'ts, and Maybes: Legal Writing Do's—Part I,* N.Y. St. B.J., May 2007, at 64, 56

The assertion's attitude comes from the advocate's strategic use of phrases such as "routinely hold" and "unless they are based," soft-sell persuasive techniques that prime the judge for the advocate's argument that the promissory estoppel exception to at will employment is narrowly construed.

Principles of primacy and recency also explain why effective advocates think strategically about the placement of case illustrations and explanatory parentheticals. And consequently, another distinctive feature of a persuasive rule explanation section is its use of a preemptive case selection strategy. A **preemptive case selection strategy** neutralizes the negative impact of unfavorable case law authority by discussing it in inconspicuous places such as in the middle of sentences and paragraphs and highlights favorable case law authority by discussing it in conspicuous places such as the beginning and ending of sentences and paragraphs. Let's explore the impact of soft-sell persuasive techniques and a preemptive case selection strategy by comparing the rule explanation section of an objective CREAC to the rule explanation section of a persuasive CREAC. Review the following excerpt from the rule explanation section of an objective CREAC.

In <u>Case X</u>, the plaintiffs alleged that various supervisors told them that they could work "until retirement." Based on these statements, the plaintiffs argued that the doctrine of promissory estoppel precluded their termination. The court agreed, reasoning that retirement was a clearly discernable event and thus sufficiently specific to constitute a legally binding promise. However, in <u>Case Y</u>, the employer's casual remarks that he envisioned a "very long" business relationship with the plaintiff lacked the requisite specificity. The court reasoned that the phrase "very long" had no quantifiable duration and was more properly construed as a remark about an undetermined event in the future.

Now review the following excerpt from the rule explanation section of a persuasive CREAC.

In <u>Case Y</u>, the plaintiff alleged that her employer's casual remark that he envisioned a "very long" business relationship triggered the promissory estoppel exception to at-will employment. The court disagreed, reasoning that the phrase "very long" was not premised on a clearly discernable event and thus was too indefinite to be anything more than a random remark instead of a legally binding promise of continued employment. However, in <u>Case X</u>, the plaintiffs, who were 62 when hired, were told that they could work for the company "until retirement." Pursuant to the company's employee handbook, the mandatory retirement age was 65. The court held that the employer's statement was sufficiently definite because it constituted a finite, measurable time period that was clearly outlined in the employee handbook. <u>But see Case A</u> (holding that employer's statement that plaintiff could work "until he wanted to quit" was too vague and indefinite to constitute a promise).

Notice the advocate's use of a preemptive case selection strategy in the second example. The advocate begins with Case Y, a case with similar facts of the client's case, a favorable holding, and ends with an explanatory parenthetical to Case A, another case with similar facts and a favorable holding. Instead of omitting Case X, a case with an unfavorable holding, the advocate downplays it by burying it in the middle of the paragraph. By utilizing principles of primacy and recency, the advocate neutralizes the negative impact of unfavorable case law authority while highlighting favorable case law authority. Also notice the advocate's use of soft-sell persuasive techniques such as the detail used to describe Case X's holding and rationale. The amount of "airtime" that the advocate devotes to describing the mandatory retirement age outlined in the employee handbook is intentional. The detail subtly suggests to the court that Case X is factually distinguishable. So, its unfavorable holding doesn't prevent a favorable outcome in the client's case.

The fourth distinction between persuasive and objective CREAC, ending with desired conflict resolution, relates the final "C" in the persuasive CREAC mnemonic device. In objective CREAC, the final conclusion reasserts the prediction about the outcome of the client's legal problem. By starting and ending at the same point, the legal writer completes the storytelling arc for the judge. Compare these two simple circles:

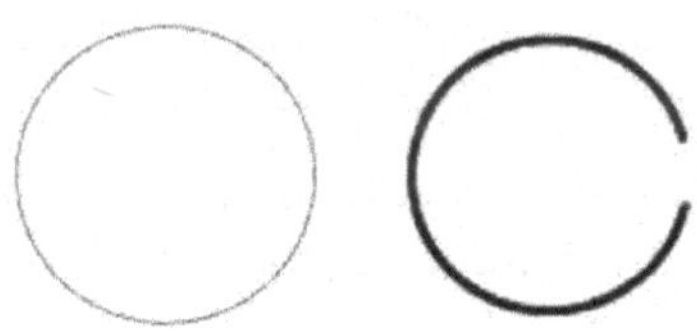

Which one seems more "complete"?

Advocates who don't end their persuasive CREACs with a final conclusion create a conspicuous gap in the client's argument that's unpersuasive because it strips the judge of certainty. So, both objective and persuasive CREACs must have initial and final conclusions. How, then, do these final conclusions differ? Review the following conclusion from an objective CREAC.

Consequently, Ms. Ramon will not recover under the promissory estoppel exception to at-will employment.

In persuasive CREAC, the final conclusion—the last "C" in the persuasive CREAC mnemonic device—reasserts the advocate's desired conflict resolution. Review the following conclusion from a persuasive CREAC.

The facts of this case simply do not substantiate the existence of a binding promise of continued employment. Consequently, the motion for summary judgment should be granted.

The rest of this chapter explores the process of drafting each component of a persuasive CREAC in greater detail.

PERSUASIVELY IDENTIFYING RULES

This section explores strategies and tips for drafting the rule section of a persuasive CREAC. Your goal is to use soft-sell persuasive techniques to highlight rules that are consistent with the client's theory and theme and to downplay unfavorable rules that are inconsistent with the theory and theme or that must be disclosed to avoid losing credibility with the judge. Soft-sell techniques aren't tricks but useful strategies. Judges expect advocates to employ these techniques, but demand that they use them responsibly. Effective advocates *never* misled the court or inaccurately describe authority under the guise of legal storytelling. When advocates lose credibility, they lose their ability to persuade via ethos. The following soft-sell techniques are particularly helpful tools for persuasively identifying legal rules:

Now that you're familiar with the most widely used soft-sell persuasive techniques for persuasively identifying rules, let's begin drafting. Rules are like puzzle pieces. Your persuasive version of the rule doesn't have to use the same words as

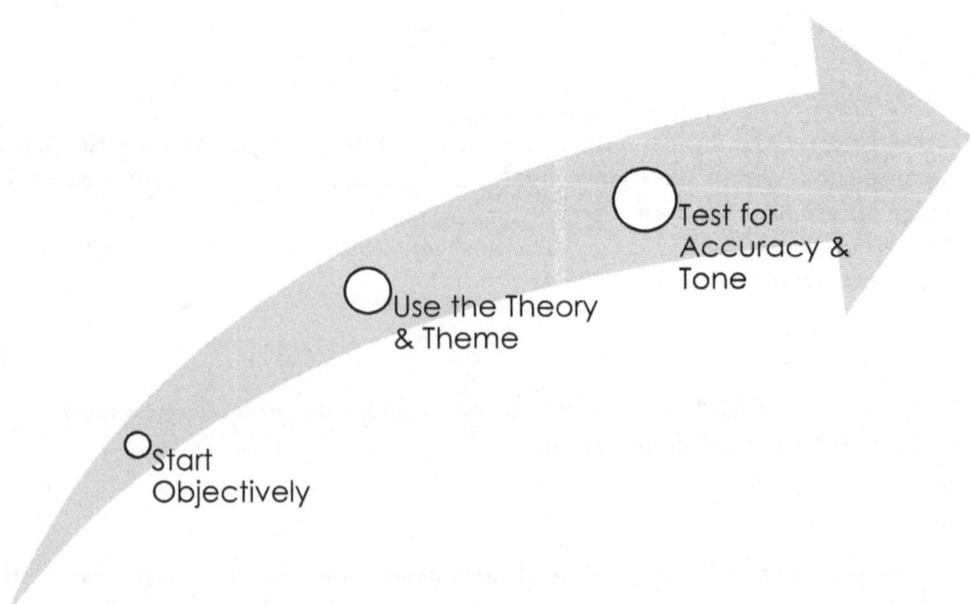

Highlight Favorable Rules with:	Downplay Unfavorable Rules with:
Word Choice	**Word Choice**
Use words with favorable connotations (e.g., **"released from employment"** rather than **"fired"**).	Describe unfavorable rules with unfavorable connotations (e.g., **"Courts only recognize promissory estoppel as an exception to the at-will employment doctrine when . . ."**).
Detail	**Lack of Detail**
Use detail to describe favorable rules (e.g., **"multidistrict, area-wide remedy"** instead of **"remedy"**).	Describe unfavorable rules broadly (e.g., **"remedy"** instead of **"multidistrict, area-wide remedy"**).
Context	**The Absence of Context**
Highlight historical context and purpose to emphasize the rule's legitimacy (e.g., **"The promissory estoppel doctrine has been the established law of Ohio since 1913 . . ."**).	Avoid mentioning the rule's historical context, purpose, or similar background information (e.g., **"In Ohio, the promissory estoppel doctrine requires . . ."**)
Repetition	**The Absence of Repetition**
Use a distinct word pattern to highlight key information about the rule (e.g., **"absent any X, absent any Y, or absent any Z"**).	Broadly describe unfavorable information about the rule.
Positions of Emphasis	**Positions of Emphasis**
Place favorable language in conspicuous places (e.g., at the beginning or end of sentences and paragraphs).	Place unfavorable language in inconspicuous places (e.g., in the middle of sentences and paragraphs).
Strategic Use of Punctuation and Typeface	**Strategic Use of Punctuation and Typeface**
Use editorial enhancements to highlight relevant language such as quotes, italics, underlining, numbering, bullets, numbered lists, colons, and dashes.	Avoid editorial enhancements such as quotes, italics, underlining, numbering, bullets, numbered lists, colons, and dashes.
Burdens of Proof/Procedural Rules	**Burden of Proof/Procedural Rules**
Emphasize the burden of proof if your opponent has the burden. Emphasize favorable procedural rules.	Deemphasize the burden of proof if you have the burden. Deemphasize unfavorable procedural rules.

the objective version. Condense, combine, synthesize, and re-arrange the rules to highlight favorable rules, downplay unfavorable ones, and foreshadow the client's arguments, theory, theme. Your rule is persuasive when it's written in a way that makes a favorable seem inevitable. Consider the following three step process for drafting rules persuasively.

Start Objectively and Use the Theory and Theme

Highlighting favorable information about the rules at the foundation of your logos argument doesn't mean distorting their substance. Ensure that you don't cross the line from persuasion to distortion by drafting the rule objectively, in much the same way that you would in a predictive memo. Then, use the theory and theme to identify aspects of the rule that you should highlight and information about the rule that you should downplay. We'll explore these first two drafting steps with an example. Let's revisit the promissory estoppel exception to at-will employment discussed at the beginning of this chapter. During the processing phase, the employee's advocate brainstormed a logos argument and crafted a compelling theory. The employee's advocate also brainstormed a logos argument and crafted a compelling theory. The objective statement of the governing rule appears below.

Objective Rule Statement:

Ohio courts require the following elements to establish the promissory estoppel exception to at-will employment: a clear, unambiguous promise, reasonable reliance on that promise, and an injury based on that reliance. The plaintiff has the burden of proof by a preponderance of the evidence.

Because your theory and theme emphasize employer autonomy, your description of the legal rule must subtly highlight that an employer's autonomy would be jeopardized if the promissory estoppel exception were permitted to swallow the general rule of at-will employment. In stark contrast, the employee's attorney will use soft-sell persuasive techniques to downplay the at-will employment rule and to suggest the suitability of the promissory estoppel exception. In the examples that follow, notice how the advocates use soft-sell persuasive techniques (highlighted in bold type) to describe the legal status quo from their clients' point of view.

Pro Employer Rule Statement:

Ohio courts **only** recognize promissory estoppel as an exception to at-will employment when **all three** of the following **mandatory elements** are satisfied: (1) a clear, unambiguous promise; (2) reliance on that promise; and (3) an injury based on that reliance. The plaintiff **must** prove **all three** elements by a preponderance of the evidence.

Pro Employee Rule Statement:

The promissory estoppel doctrine has been the **established law of Ohio since 1913**. Since that time, **more than 100 years ago**, Ohio courts have **routinely** found employers liable for wrongful termination under the promissory exception to at-will employment.

The distinctive use of language telegraphs the identity of the advocate that drafted each rule statement. Notice that the employee's persuasive rule statement doesn't mimic or use the same pattern of words as the objective version of the rule. That's the beauty of persuasion; as long as the rule is accurate and comprehensive (i.e., not omitting important rules), advocates can arrange the rules to subtly highlight the client's arguments, theory, and theme. Let's evaluate your understanding of soft-sell persuasive techniques. Can identify the soft-sell persuasive techniques used by each advocate?

Pro Employer Rule Statement	Pro Employee Rule Statement
Highlights Favorable Aspects of the Rule Using: ?	**Downplays Negative Aspects of the Rule Using:** ?

Test for Accuracy and Tone

Evaluating your persuasive rule statements for accuracy and tone is the last and most important drafting step. Your identification of the rule is accurate when it doesn't distort the objective version of the rule. And your persuasive rule section has the appropriate tone when it's not overtly or subtly argumentative. Consider the following rule statements that either distort the objective rule or are argumentative. The inaccurate and argumentative language is bolded.

Inaccurate Pro Employer Rule Statement:

Ohio courts almost never recognize promissory estoppel as an exception to at-will employment because the exception requires that all three of the following mandatory elements are satisfied: (1) a clear, unambiguous promise; (2) reliance on that promise; and (3) an injury based on that reliance. The plaintiff must prove all three elements by a preponderance of the evidence.

Overtly Argumentative Pro Employee Rule Statement:

The promissory estoppel doctrine has been the established law of Ohio since 1913. Since that time, more than 100 years ago, Ohio courts have routinely found employers civilly liable when employees are victimized by the illegal termination practices of unscrupulous employers.

Subtly Argumentative Pro Employer Rule Statement:

The at will employment doctrine protects employers like the defendant. Requiring the defendant, a small business owner, to retain an employee because of the casual use of the word "always" jeopardizes the enterprising spirit embodied in the at will employment doctrine. Under Ohio law, an employer's decision to release an employee does not subject him to civil liability when an employee handbook clearly and unambiguously proclaims the employer's intent to bypass any judicially created exceptions to the at will employment doctrine.

The first example is inaccurate because it makes the rule appear more rigorous than it is. The second example is argumentative because it's an ad hominem attack against all Ohio employers, including the employer in this case. The last example avoids ad hominem attacks. Nevertheless, it's still argumentative because alluding to the client destroys the subtly of the persuasive rule section, crossing the line from soft-sell to hard-sell. The following graphic outlines some common persuasive rule section drafting culprits. Use it as a guide when drafting your persuasive rules for your client.

Persuasive Rule Section Drafting Culprits

Argumentative Tone

- Could offend the judge or opposing counsel by crossing the line from subtle to overt persuasion

Too Neutral

- Can't immediately tell which party drafted the rule

Not Comprehensive

- Omits important rules that form foundation of the argument

PERSUASIVELY EXPLAINING LEGAL RULES

This section explores the process of drafting persuasive rule explanation sections—the "E" in the persuasive CREAC mnemonic device. Sometimes the rules will be so straightforward that they don't need an in-depth explanation. Consider the following rule: "A person is closely related to the victim if the person is the parent, sibling, child, or grandparent of the victim."[5] But consider the following rule: "Prison officials' deliberate indifference to a prisoner's serious medical need violates the Eighth Amendment's prohibition against cruel and unusual punishment." Unlike the previous rule that unambiguously defines the phrase "closely related to the victim," the deliberate indifference standard is ambiguous. When the legal rules supporting the client's argument are ambiguous, the brief must contain a rule explanation section that clarifies the ambiguity while subtly suggesting how the case law authority supports the client's argument. In addition to clarifying ambiguous rules in a way that subtly advances the client's argument, effective persuasive rule explanation sections have the following attributes: they (1) begin with a powerful assertion, (2) skillfully use case illustrations and explanatory parentheticals, (3) strategically implement a preemptive case selection strategy, and (4) strategically use soft-sell persuasive techniques.

Begin with a Powerful Assertion

Recall the discussion from the previous section: A persuasive rule explanation section without an assertion shifts the burden to the judge to decipher how the case law authority supports the argument. The attributes of effective assertions are summarized in the following graphic:

[5] Christine Coughlin et al., A Lawyer Writes Ch. 7.2 (3d Ed. 2018).

Attributes of Effective Assertions	❑ Has an "attitude" (i.e., written from the client's point of view) ❑ Signal the beginning of a persuasive rule explanation ❑ Is an ethos-generating navigational tool

Each rule explanation assertion is a distinct unit of explanation. So, the number of assertions depends on the rule's complexity. Let's return to the deliberate indifference standard. To prove deliberate indifference, an inmate must prove that a requested treatment is medically necessary and that prison officials' refusal to provide that treatment consciously disregarded an excessive risk to the inmate's health. Given the rule's ambiguity, your brief must address how courts have interpreted the phrases "medically necessary" and "conscious disregard to an excessive risk to the inmate's health." So, you'll need *two* rule explanation assertions chock-full of language that makes the client's desired relief seem inevitable.

Drafting effective assertions is more art than science; they're no clear-cut standards. Instead the goal is abstract: making the client's requested relief seem inevitable, leaving the judge to wonder how the opposing party could possibly prevail. Effective assertions typically come in two varieties: assertions that synthesize how courts have interpreted ambiguous rules and assertions that identify patterns in the case law that have led to favorable rulings in cases similar to the client's case. To maximize effectiveness, avoid cluttering persuasive rule explanation sections with too many assertions. Limit your explanation to no more than three assertions. If you're struggling to follow this guideline, consider combining similar assertions. Consider the following assertions.

Pro Prison Synthesis Rule Explanation Assertion:

The Eleventh Circuit adopts the reasoning of Fourth and Fifth Circuit Courts of Appeal and several district courts within the Eleventh Circuit that sex reassignment surgery is not medically necessary without evidence of unanimity in the medical community about the appropriateness of sex reassignment surgery for treating inmates with severe gender dysphoria.

Pro Inmate Pattern-Identifying Rule Explanation Assertion:

When doctors who earn their living treating incarcerated persons with severe gender dysphoria unanimously agree that gender affirming surgery is medically necessary, the majority of circuit courts considering this issue of first impression hold that a prison's refusal to provide incarcerated persons with access to life sustaining gender affirming surgery creates an excessive risk that satisfies the deliberate indifference standard.

These assertions are effective. They both clarify how courts have interpreted the meaning of medical necessity and conscious disregard. And the advocates' effective use of soft-sell persuasive techniques such as using words with favorable connotation (e.g. sex-reassignment surgery versus gender affirming surgery; inmate versus incarcerated person) subtly convey the message that a ruling in the client's favor seems inevitable. Let's return to the at will employment scenario. The at will employment doctrine permits employers to avoid civil liability for terminating an employee when a disclaimer in an employee handbook clearly and unambiguously proclaims the employer's intent to bypass the exceptions to the doctrine. The phrases clearly and unambiguously require a clarifying assertion. Now, consider the following assertions.

Pro Employer Synthesis Rule Explanation Assertion:

Colorado appellate courts shield employers from wrongful discharge claims when the employer has a clearly worded, prominently displayed at will employment disclaimer.

Pro Employee Pattern-Identifying Rule Explanation Assertion:

If an at will employment disclaimer in an employee handbook contradicts the employer's employment practices, then Colorado appellate courts typically deny the employer's motion for summary judgment, reasoning that its inconsistent employment practices create a genuine issue of material fact about the validity of the disclaimer that precludes summary judgment.

Both assertions are effective. The first assertion highlights the employer's theory: any exception to the at will employment doctrine must be construed in ways that protect employer autonomy. Similarly, the second assertion highlights the employee's theory: the exceptions to at will employment are consistent with free principles because they enhance employers' ability to recruit and retain highly qualified job candidates. Paradoxically, the criteria for evaluating dysfunctional assertions are more clear-cut than the criteria for drafting effective assertions. An assertion is dysfunctional when it (1) restates governing rules without clarifying them, (2) is too neutral, or (3) is too long or confusing. Consider the following assertions drafted by the advocates in the parental relocation scenario. The governing rule requires that relocation be in the child's best interest, an ambiguous standard that requires a clarifying assertion. Use the criteria discussed in this section to identify the *best* rule explanation assertion from the following options.

Option 1: Relocation must be in the child's best interest.

Option 2: Florida's Third and Fourth District Courts of Appeal have reasoned that relocation is in the child's best interest if the child will benefit from life-changing educational opportunities, even when access to those opportunities will disrupt the non-relocating parent's work schedule or career ambitions.

Option 3: When considering whether relocation is in the child's best interest, Florida courts evaluate factors such as (1) whether the non-relocating parent or the non-relocating parent's family members are actively involved in the child's life, (2) whether the relocation will have a negative impact on the child's ability to physically and mentally engage with the non-relocating parent, and (3) whether the relocating parent has a history of obstructing visitation.

Option 4: Florida courts typically give very little weight to even dramatic improvements in the relocating parent's quality of life—even when the proposed move is born of a legitimate economic necessity such as a new job or employment opportunities—when the non-relocating parent would be unable to maintain a parental bond because of unduly burdensome travel that negatively affects the child's interest in extracurricular activities or because of a proposed visitation plan that substantively alters the current custodial arrangements.

The second option is the best assertion. It has an attitude that comes from the following language: ". . . life-changing educational opportunities . . . even when access to those opportunities will disrupt the non-relocating parent's work schedule or career ambitions." Because of its language, the judge can immediately tell that it was written by the non-relocating parent. The first option simply restates the governing rule without clarifying it. The third option clarifies the best interest of the child standard and strategically uses a numbered list. But despite these positive attributes, its language (e.g., "Florida courts evaluate factors such as . . .") is too neutral; it's akin to a thesis sentence in an objective rule explanation section. The fourth option skillfully uses soft-sell persuasive techniques such as favorable word choice (e.g., . . . "typically give very little weight to even dramatic improvements in the relocating parent's quality of life") and strategic use of punctuation (i.e., the en dash that highlights favorable language). However, it's too long. Because of its length, it could overwhelm the reader.

Use the following scenario to test your ability to distinguish a functional assertion from a dysfunctional one. Your client is a recent journalism school graduate who created a blog that divulges sensational information about celebrities. A famous actor featured on the blog alleges that the post caused her employer to terminate her. The actor filed suit against her employer. To substantiate her allegations of wrongful termination, she filed a motion compelling the client to divulge the names of his confidential sources. The client refused, arguing that he's a reporter with standing to assert the reporter's privilege. If the judge rules that the client has standing, the actor cannot compel the client to identify confidential sources. Standing depends on whether the person claiming the privilege engaged in activities traditionally associated with investigatory reporting and published information with the intent to publicly disseminate it. Given the ambiguity of this standard, a portion of your brief must explain how courts have defined "activities traditionally associated with investigatory reporting." Evaluate the following options.

Option 1: The Second Circuit has not identified the kind of activities traditionally associated with investigatory reporting. But several federal circuit courts of appeal have limited the protection of the privilege to persons engaged in active fact gathering and rigorous verification procedures about matters of substantial public importance—not purely private matt. Ers.

Option 2: Mr. Cantwell is entitled to the protection of the reporter's privilege because he engages in activities traditionally associated with investigatory reporting.

Option 3: In the Second Circuit, persons asserting the protection of the privilege have the burden of proving that they are engaged in activities traditionally associated with investigatory reporting.

Option 4: The United States Supreme Court endorses a limited interpretation of evidentiary privileges because they impede a litigant's search for truth.

Can you identify the *best* rule explanation assertion using the criteria and examples discussed in this section?

Skillfully Use Case Illustrations and Explanatory Parentheticals

Assertions are the stars of persuasive rule explanation sections. And case illustrations and explanatory parentheticals are the back-up singers. Like any good back-up singer they hang back and handle the grunt work: substantiating the assertions' bold proclamations about how courts have interpreted ambiguous rules.[6] The following chart

[6] Eric P. Voigt, *Explanatory Parentheticals Can Pack a Persuasive Punch*, 45 McGeorge L. Rev. 269, 273 (2013) (internal quotations omitted).

illustrates some key distinctions between case illustrations and explanatory parentheticals discussed at the beginning of this chapter.

Type of Support	Definition	Example
Case Illustrations	An in-depth discussion of a case containing a description of the legally relevant facts, holding, and rationale that supports an assertion.	**[Assertion]** Ohio courts routinely hold that an employer's statements about job performance are indefinite unless they are premised on a measurable time or a clearly discernable event. **[Case Illustration]** In Case Y, the plaintiff alleged that her employer's casual remark that he envisioned a "very long" business relationship triggered the promissory estoppel exception to at-will employment. The court disagreed, reasoning that the phrase "very long" was not premised on a clearly discernable event and thus was too indefinite to be anything more than a random remark instead of a legally binding promise of continued employment.
Signals, Explanatory Parentheticals, and String Citations	A signal appears at the beginning of the citation and sends a message about the relationship between the assertion and one cited case or several cited cases (i.e., a string citation).[7] Each case in a string cite is separated by a semicolon. An explanatory parenthetical is an abbreviated case discussion that typically begins with a present participle (a verb ending in "ing") and explains how a court's action supports an assertion.	**[Assertion]** Utilizing a multi-tiered procedure for identifying privileged documents is a reasonable precaution against inadvertent disclosures of confidential information. **[Signal & Parenthetical]** Compare Case A (upholding privilege when attorney implemented a tripartite system of checks and balances that required secretarial staff, paralegals, and junior associates to review documents) with Case B (waiving privilege when plaintiff's counsel produced documents without reviewing them for privilege); Case C (waiving privilege when plaintiff's counsel had only one member of the firm's clerical staff reviewing documents for privilege).

[7] *See* The Bluebook: A Uniform System of Citation R. B3, 1.2 (Columbia Law Review Ass'n et al. eds, 20th ed. 2015).

Because case illustrations are in-depth discussions, advocates have space to transcend superficial explanations that one seasoned appellate lawyer characterized as "skitter[ing] along the surface . . . as if reaching an incontestable result were simply a matter of mechanically entering data into a formula."[8] Case illustrations are the perfect vehicle for deeper, transcendent explanations that can withstand scrutiny from judges and opposing counsel.[9] Their expansive format enables advocates to subtly advance the client's story—the theory, theme, and arguments—with soft-sell persuasive techniques while subtly undermining the opponent's theory, theme, and arguments.

But transcendent rule explanations come at a price. Judges dislike rule explanation sections riddled with redundant, lengthy case descriptions. As one legal writing expert observed, "[j]udges do not want a book report . . . few things [are] more boring than . . . page after page of case discussion[s]."[10] Because they present relevant information in a condensed, concise manner, some judges prefer explanatory parentheticals.[11] For example, Justice Ruth Bader Ginsburg championed explanatory parentheticals, proclaiming "a first-rate brief contains citations with parenthetical explanations."[12] But some judges aren't fans. Persuasive explanation sections with assertions supported by pages of signals, string cites, and explanatory parentheticals are cumbersome to read.[13] As one prominent judge explained, "A sentence . . . followed by a lengthy string cite, then another sentence . . . and another long citation, invites the reader's mind to wander."[14]

Poor writing can also make explanatory parentheticals cumbersome. As one legal writing expert observed "explaining the holding and reasoning of a case in just a few lines . . . requires strong analytical skills.[15] Given this lack of consensus, you're probably wondering which side has the winning approach. The good news is that you don't have to choose a side. Much like drafting effective assertions, supporting an assertion with case illustrations, explanatory parentheticals, or a combination of both isn't governed by clear-cut standards. The decision is stylistic. The following scenarios and corresponding examples will help you make reasoned, considered choices about which cases merit an in-depth discussion and those that should be explained in a more cursory fashion.

Scenario #1: Use case illustrations to support assertions when the case law consists primarily of "Ferrari cases."

As the name suggests, Ferrari cases are the crème de la crème of your research results. Like their namesake, they're flashy, supporting the assertion with panache. Ferrari

[8] David J. Pearlman, *The Legal Brief: The New Paradigm, Writing Manuals, Volumes of Appeals, Electronic Shorthand All Have Influenced Legal Writing*, PHILADELPHIA LAWYER, 11 Fall 2011).
[9] *Id.*
[10] Voigt, *supra* note 6, at 271 (internal quotations omitted).
[11] Mary Matthews, *Explanatory Parentheticals Are Your Friends*, 88 J. KAN. B.A. 10 (May 2019).
[12] Voigt, *Supra* note 6, at 271 (internal quotations omitted).
[13] Matthews, *supra,* note 13, at 10 (noting the disagreement among judges about their effectiveness).
[14] Margaret Oertling Cupples, *Appellate Briefing: Some Thoughts on Writing Briefs That Can Clear a Path through the Jungle*, 30 MISS. C. L. REV. 1, 10 (2011).
[15] Voigt, *supra* note 6, at 276 (internal quotations omitted).

cases are binding or persuasive cases with facts, holdings, or rationales that advance the client's argument or that undermine the opponent's argument. For example, a binding case that contains a thorough analysis of the relevant legal issues would definitely be a Ferrari. Now, suppose that the assertion relates to an issue of first impression. A case from another jurisdiction that thoroughly analyzes the relevant issues would also be a Ferrari, although it's not binding case law authority. A word of caution. Recall the discussion at the beginning of this section: Judges dislike rule explanation sections riddled with redundant, lengthy case descriptions. Maximize the persuasiveness of your case illustrations and avoid the common drafting errors outlined in the graphic below:

Persuasive Rule Explanation Drafting Culprits

Structural Errors

- Missing or imprecisely stated components

Unfocused

- Case description doesn't support the assertion

Blurred

- Material facts not described with specificity

Compare the strong assertion with the weak one, paying particular attention to the shaded portions of each example.

Weak Case Illustration: [Assertion] All the federal circuit courts of appeal agree that a new work is a transformative fair use of copyrighted materials when its primary purpose is different from the original one. **[Case Illustration]** For example, In Campbell, the new work was a rap group's lyrical modification of a popular song, "Oh, Pretty Woman." The rap group did not present any evidence that its song, marketed to a different market and demographic, harmed the copyright holder's current or future market. Despite this lack of evidence, the Supreme Court nevertheless denied the copyright holder's motion for summary judgment.

Strong Case Illustration: [Assertion] All the federal circuit courts of appeal agree that a new work is a transformative fair use of copyrighted materials when its primary purpose is different from the original one. **[Case Illustration]** For example, In Campbell, the new work was a rap group's

> lyrical modification of the popular song, "Oh, Pretty Woman." While the copyrighted work was a romantic and sentimental rock ballad, the new song was a scathing commentary about the idealized, romantic love at the heart of the original work. The Supreme Court held that the rap group's use was transformative, reasoning that the new song conveyed an overarching meaning markedly distinct from that of the copyrighted work.

The weak example demonstrates all three drafting culprits. It's blurry, unfocused, and improperly structured. The key term in both assertions is the word "transformative." However, the advocate's comparison of the new work and the copyrighted one in the weak example is too blurry to support the assertion. For example, although the advocate's language about the nature of the two works is sufficiently detailed, the description of the relative purpose of the two works is vague. Compare this vague language with the detailed language of the strong example. The strong example adeptly identifies the purpose of both works (e.g., "a romantic and sentimental rock ballad" versus "a scathing commentary about the idealized, romantic love at the heart of the original work"). Without a detailed comparison of the distinct purposes of both songs, the judge can't determine whether the new work was transformative. The weak example is also unfocused because the case description doesn't prove the assertion. The advocate's discussion veers off course, discussing markets and demographics, concepts that aren't related to a transformative use.

But in the strong example, the advocate's description of the relative purpose of the new work and the copyrighted one supports the assertion by connecting these distinct purposes to the definition of a transformative fair use of copyrighted material. The last drafting culprit in the weak example is a structural error. Notice how the advocate abruptly ends the discussion without including a discussion of the court's rationale. In stark contrast, the advocate in the strong example connects the dots, explaining how the material facts support the court's holding about the nature of the transformative use. Use these examples of ineffective and effective case illustrations as an interpretive guide when drafting your case illustrations.

Scenario #2: Use explanatory parentheticals to support assertions when the case law consists primarily of "Camry cases."

The headline in a popular automotive blog described the Toyota Camry as *The Long Running Reliable Staple Built with Precision,* a testament to its reputation as a dependable, fuel-efficient car.[16] In the same way, Camry cases are dependable, no-frills cases that conclusively support the assertion but whose facts are only marginally similar to the facts of the client's case. Let's return to your client, the recent journalism school graduate, who created a blog that divulges sensational information about celebrities. To prevent the compelled disclosure of the client's confidential sources, you allege that even non-traditional members of the media such as a bloggers have standing to assert

---

[16] Quinn Osha, *The Long Running Reliable Staple Built with Precision,* TOPMARQ, available at https://tinyurl.com/muc48uz6 (last visited June 13, 2023).

the privilege. If your research results yielded only marginally similar cases involving non-traditional members of the media claiming the protection of the privilege—a commercial publisher for a bond rating agency, a documentary film maker, or a press secretary for a prominent politician—you'd discuss these cases in an explanatory parenthetical. Or a case might be a Camry because you want to highlight only a portion of it such as an insightful quote or eloquent language that succinctly highlights a comparison or consensus in the case law. A case might also be a Camry because of its potential to undermine the assertion such as an adverse case that, even with the use of soft-sell persuasive techniques, you can't distinguish in a case illustration. However, you must discuss the case because of an ethical obligation (a topic discussed in the next section) or because it's the pièce de résistance of your opponent's case. In these kinds of scenarios, consider discussing the case in an explanatory parenthetical. Highlighting it in a case illustration would emphasize the deficiencies of the client's case. So, the abbreviated format of an explanatory parenthetical minimizes its impact.

But remember the warning at the beginning of this section: condensing the facts, holding, and reasoning in just a few words can challenge the ability of even the most skilled legal writers. The same drafting culprits that apply to case illustrations—lack of focus, blurriness, or structural errors—also apply to explanatory parentheticals. To ensure clarity and concision, ruthlessly edit your explanatory parentheticals so, as one legal writing expert explained, they "provide only the information that is necessary so that the judge will understand—and accept—the rule or the argument without having to read the citied authority itself."[17] Also, pay attention to the number of citations supporting an assertion. Consider supporting the assertion with more than one citation and accompanying explanatory parenthetical when the issue is one of first impression or when supporting an assertion that highlights a comparison or consensus in the case law. But don't overdo it. A good rule of thumb is no more than two or three citations and explanatory parentheticals per assertion. Keeping these general principles in mind, consider the following examples of weak and strong parentheticals, paying particular attention to the shaded portions.

Weak Explanatory Parenthetical: [Assertion] Courts have routinely held, in a variety of contexts, that prison officials act with deliberate indifference if they adopt an easier and less efficacious treatment plan that does not adequately address a prisoner's serious medical needs. **[Signal, Citation & Explanatory Parenthetical]** See e.g., De'lonta v. Johnson, 708 F.3d 520, 522_(granting prisoner's request for gender affirming surgery because hormone therapy was insufficient to address the prisoner's severe gender dysphoria as demonstrated by four suicide attempts in four months); Greeno v. Daly, 414 F.3d 645, 653-54 (7th Cir. 2005) (denying motion for summary judgment and granting the prisoner's request for referral to specialist because of insufficient treatment); Langford v. Norris, 614 F.3d 445, 460 (8th Cir. 2010) (explaining that "a doctor's decision to take an easier and less efficacious course of treatment" constitutes

[17] Voigt, *supra* note 6, at 280.

deliberate indifference); Jones v. Muskegon County, 625 F.3d 935, 944 (6th Cir. 2010) (explaining that prison officials may not entirely insulate themselves from liability under §1983 simply by persistently providing ineffective treatment); Roe v. Elyea, 631 F.3d 843, 861 (7th Cir. 2011) (summarizing cases explaining that prison officials cannot abandon medical judgment and avoid deliberate indifference by persisting in a course or treatment known to be ineffective).

Strong Explanatory Parenthetical: [Assertion] Courts have routinely held, in a variety of contexts, that prisoner officials act with deliberate indifference if they adopt an easier and less efficacious treatment plan that does not adequately address a prisoner's serious medical needs. **[Signal, Citation & Explanatory Parenthetical]** See e.g., De'lonta v. Johnson, 708 F.3d 520, 522_ (denying motion to dismiss and granting prisoner's request for gender affirming surgery because hormone therapy insufficient to address severe gender dysphoria as demonstrated by four suicide attempts in four months); Greeno v. Daly, 414 F.3d 645, 653-54 (7th Cir. 2005) (denying motion for summary judgment and granting inmate's request for referral to a gastroenterologist because a panoply of over-the-counter medications insufficient to address severe heartburn as demonstrated by numerous requests spanning two years).

The shaded portions in the weak explanatory parenthetical illustrate the drafting culprits. The most obvious culprit is a structural error—the number of supporting citations in the weak explanatory parenthetical (five) versus the number of supporting citations (two) in the strong explanatory parenthetical. An avalanche of citations and corresponding explanatory parentheticals is visually distracting and invites the judge's mind to wander. The next drafting culprit is the lack of focus in the explanatory parentheticals corresponding to the Langford, Jones, and Roe cases in the weak example. Instead of supporting the assertion with examples of each inmate's requested treatment, severe medical need, and the prior less efficacious treatment offered by prison officials, the advocate simply parrots the assertion. By parroting the assertion, the advocate forces the judge to read the cited authority. And consequently, the assertion loses its gravitas as an ethos-generating navigational tool.

The explanatory parentheticals corresponding to the De'lonta and Greeno cases in the weak example illustrate two distinct types of blurriness. Although the language in the second portion of the explanatory parenthetical is vivid and detailed (e.g., "request for gender affirming surgery," "hormone therapy," and "severe gender dysphoria as demonstrated by four suicide attempts in four months"), the first portion is an example of procedural blurriness. It omits the procedural posture (i.e., a motion to dismiss). Because the motion to dismiss standard is easier to satisfy than other dispositive pre-trial motions such as a motion for summary judgment, omitting weakens the advocate's credibility, especially since the explanatory parenthetical to the Greeno case mentions the more favorable summary judgment procedural posture.

The culprit in the Greeno explanatory parenthetical is its substantive blurriness. The advocate's description of the prison officials' action (e.g., "because of insufficient treatment") is too vague to support the assertion. It doesn't identify the specific nature of the inmate's requested treatment, the severe medical need, or the prior less efficacious treatment offered by prison officials. Compare this vague language to the vivid, detailed language in the Greeno explanatory parenthetical of the strong example. After reading it, the judge immediately understands the inmate's requested treatment (e.g., a referral to a gastroenterologist), the serious medical need (e.g., severe heartburn), and the prior less efficacious treatment offered by prison officials (e.g., "a panoply of over-the-counter medications"). Use these examples as interpretive guides when drafting your explanatory parentheticals.

Scenario #3: Use a combination of case illustrations and explanatory parentheticals to support assertions when the combination enhances your argument.

The disclaimer in the heading bears repeating. When used effectively, assertions supported by case illustrations and explanatory parentheticals (also known as a hybrid) capitalize on the persuasive power of both. If you elect to use a hybrid explanatory scheme, the explanatory parenthetical should always come after the case illustration. But if overused the combination mires the rule explanation section with unnecessary detail and risks becoming the kind of repetitive explanation that judges don't enjoy reading. To avoid overwhelming the reader, use a combination of introductory signals, explanatory parentheticals, and case illustrations *only* when their combination is absolutely necessary to advance the assertion and when their use isn't unduly duplicative. One scenario where a hybrid approach might be effective is demonstrating the depth of your research. In the example below, the signal "see also" and explanatory parentheticals are used to complement a case illustration:

Strong Hybrid Example: **[Assertion]** All of Florida's District Courts of Appeal broadly define the severe emotional distress element, conditioning it on the plaintiff's ability to demonstrate an ongoing pattern of life-altering behavioral changes—not whether a doctor prescribed medication—defined as observable evidence of continuing, noticeable symptoms that disrupt the plaintiff's lifestyle, demeanor, and relationships. **[Case Illustration]** In Smith, the plaintiff's husband testified that the plaintiff was a "nervous person" and experienced sleep problems. Smith, 415 So. 2d at 1100. There was little testimony as to the nature or duration of the sleep problems and anxiety, and there was no evidence presented to compare the plaintiff's behavior before and after the defendant's outrageous conduct. Id. at 1101. Therefore, in Smith, the trial court reasoned that the plaintiff's sleep problems and nervousness were not so severe that no reasonable person could be expected to endure them. Her vague testimony failed to adequately prove that her symptoms were life-altering and of a continuing nature. Id. As a result, the court held that the plaintiff's emotional distress was not severe enough to support an intentional infliction of emotional distress cause of action. Id. **[Signal, Citation & Explanatory Parenthetical]** See also Ziegler v. Elmore

Cnty. Health Ctr., 56 F. Supp. 2d 1324, 1329 (M.D. Fla. 1999) (reasoning that there was no severe emotional distress when plaintiffs failed to prove any behavioral changes or evidence of long-lasting complications); Grantham, 802 So. 2d at 1081 (reasoning that the plaintiff's generalized fear, without a basis in fact, was not proof that emotional distress was ongoing or life-altering).

Notice that *Smith* is the Ferrari case because it is discussed in a case illustration. The *Ziegler* and *Grantham* cases play supporting roles in the form of explanatory parentheticals. Although *Ziegler* and *Grantham* are only Camry cases, they provide additional examples of the kind of continuing, noticeable symptoms that constitute severe emotional distress, and their inclusion alerts the reader about the depth of the writer's research without using too much space.

Strategically Implement a Preemptive Case Selection Strategy

After deciding which cases merit an in-depth discussion in the rule explanation section and which ones should be explained in a more cursory fashion, you must decide the order of their presentation. A successful case preemption strategy harnesses the power of primacy and recency. Whenever possible, begin or end your explanations with the discussion of favorable cases. For example, you might choose to highlight a Ferrari case in a case illustration located at the beginning or end of a paragraph and to downplay a case with unfavorable facts, holdings, or rationales by burying it in the middle of a sentence or paragraph. Beginning and ending explanations with highly favorable case law is an effective use of positions of emphasis, a popular soft-sell persuasive technique.

A preemption case selection strategy is extremely important for another reason. It ensures that you don't violate ethical rules requiring advocates to disclose unfavorable case law that is binding, even if that case law isn't referenced in opposing counsel's brief.[18] Furthermore, a preemptive case selection strategy that voluntarily discloses unfavorable information facilitates ethos. According to one trial judge, a strategy of voluntary disclosure facilitates ethos because "[i]t appears you are less concerned about [the negative authority] when you admit its existence—and it is even more devastating for the other side when you cite [adverse] cases . . . that they have not found."[19]

Strategically Use Soft-Sell Persuasive Techniques

If assertions are the stars of the persuasive rule explanation section, and case illustrations and explanatory parentheticals are the back-up singers, soft-sell persuasive techniques

---

[18] *See* MODEL R. PROF'L CONDUCT R. 3.3 (AM BAR ASS'N 2016).

[19] *See* Michael J. Higdon, *When the Case Gives You Lemons: Using Negative Authority in Persuasive Legal Writing*, TENN. BAR ASS'N J., Mar. 2010, http://www.tba.org/journal/archive/2010-03 (citing Illinois Judge Mark Drummond).

are the stagehands. They are the engines that fuel the persuasive power of assertions, case illustrations, and explanatory parentheticals. Many of the soft-sell persuasive techniques discussed in Chapter 7 in conjunction with the statement of facts and those discussed in conjunction with drafting persuasive rule statements also apply to persuasive rule explanation. But the following soft-sell techniques are particularly helpful.

Highlight Favorable Case Law with:	Downplay Unfavorable Case Law with:
Detail Describe favorable facts, holdings, and rationales in case illustrations that emphasize their relationship to the status quo assertion.	**Lack of Detail** Describe unfavorable facts, holdings, and rationales using introductory signals and explanatory parentheticals.
Positions of Emphasis Use case illustrations in the beginning or at the end of paragraphs.	**Positions of Emphasis** Use case illustrations, introductory signals, and explanatory parentheticals in the middle of sentences and paragraphs.
Breadth Describe favorable facts, holdings, and rationales broadly to emphasize their significance.	**Narrowness** Describe unfavorable facts, holdings, and rationales narrowly to downplay their significance.
Emphasize Weight of Authority Emphasize favorable holdings and rationales from binding authorities by identifying the issuing court in the text and in citations.	**Deemphasize Weight of Authority** Downplay unfavorable holdings and rationales from binding authorities by identifying the issuing court only in citations.

When read in its totality, the rule explanation section of a persuasive CREAC should generate a spark of insight that enables the judge to predict the desired conflict resolution articulated in the rule application section.

PERSUASIVELY APPLYING LEGAL RULES

This section explores the process of drafting persuasive rule application sections—the "A" in the persuasive CREAC mnemonic device, the portion of the argument where you substantiate the client's desired resolution. This section is the most important part of a logos argument. It's the main event, the place where you'll wrap up the client's argument in a tidy little package. Nothing about this section is subtle. You'll use hard-sell persuasive techniques such as rule-based and analogical reasoning to present the most explicit, comprehensive analysis of why the conflict should be resolved in the client's favor. And if you've used soft-sell persuasive techniques to identify and explain the legal status quo, then the judge will be primed for a favorable response to your argument. In this section, you'll learn how to (1) make smart decisions about structure, (2) select the most appropriate combination of reasoning tools to substantiate your argument, and (3) combat adverse facts that could potentially undermine your argument.

Make Smart Structural Decisions

Just as rule explanation assertions succinctly and persuasively clarify ambiguous rules, rule application assertions succinctly articulate the reasons why the client is entitled to the requested relief. Typically, the number of rule explanation assertions mirrors the number of rule application assertions, especially if the rule is complex. As an illustration, let's return to the deliberate indifference standard. To satisfy this standard, an inmate must prove that the requested treatment is medically necessary and that prison officials' refusal to provide that treatment consciously disregarded an excessive risk to the inmate's health. The rule's complexity requires two rule explanation assertions: one clarifying the meaning of medical necessity and another clarifying the meaning of conscious disregard. So, to substantiate the client's desired conflict resolution, you'll need two rule application assertions, one articulating why the requested treatment is or isn't medically necessary and another articulating why prison officials' refusal to provide that treatment did or didn't consciously disregard an excessive risk to the inmate's health. Structure is particularly important when your argument requires multiple rule explanation and rule application assertions. When you have multiple assertions, you have two organizational options. Consider the following chart.

The first option mimics the structure of an objective CREAC. Select option one if your argument is straightforward or if separating the explanation of the

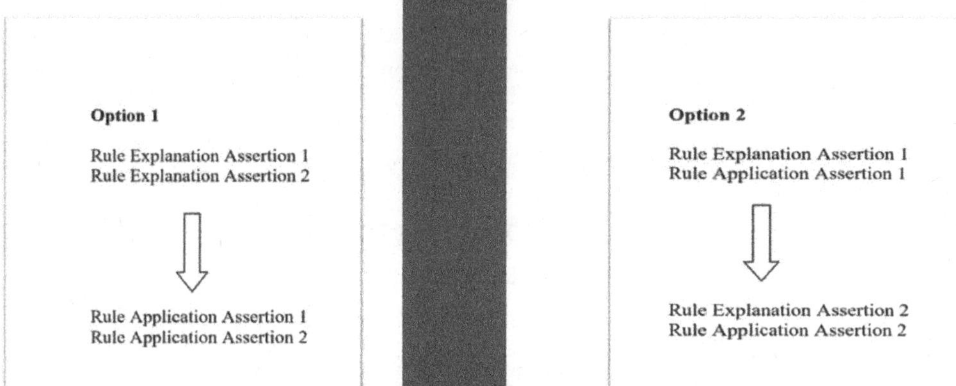

rule from its application enhances overall narrative flow. But if the rule application section is complex (e.g., contains copious amounts of supporting facts or involves a multi-part rule structure), then consider option two. When evaluating complex rule application sections, some judges prefer that the rule application section immediately follow the identification or explanation of the rule. But the organizational scheme you select is stylistic instead of substantive. With your professor or managing partner's guidance, critically evaluate the options and select the one that clearly and concisely articulates why the client is entitled to relief.

Substantiate the Desired Resolution

Now you're ready to begin the all-important process of substantiating the client's desired conflict resolution. To substantiate your argument, select the most appropriate reasoning tools and decide how to confront adverse facts that could potentially undermine your argument.

Use rule-based reasoning (RBR), analogical reasoning (AR), or a combination of both to support each rule application assertion. The legally relevant facts—not your subjective feelings—will dictate the tool that you use to substantiate your assertions. The graphic below discusses some guidelines about when to use rule-based, analogical reasoning, or both to support an assertion.

RBR

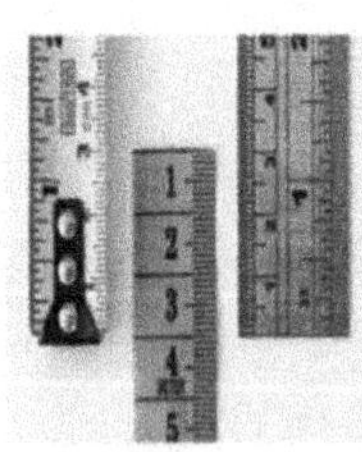

Use when the material facts supporting your assertion **aren't analogous** to the facts of a prior case (i.e., one previously identified or explained).

AR

Use when the material facts supporting your assertion **are analogous** to the facts of a prior case (i.e., one previously identified or explained).

Let's explore these guidelines with an example. Your client is a legal writing professor who's won numerous awards for innovative teaching. To introduce first-year legal writing students to fundamental brief writing principles, he created "*How to Write a Brief*," a song that mimicked the lyrics and rhyming pattern of a popular song, *"How to Save a Life,"* written and performed by an internationally acclaimed rock band. The band sued the professor for violating its copyright. The professor countersued, arguing that "*How to Write a Brief*" is a permissible use protected by the fair use doctrine. Fair use depends upon several factors such as whether the new work is transformative. A new work is transformative when its primary purpose is different from the original one. Furthermore, a new work may produce some monetary gain and still constitute a good faith, transformative fair use. Given these legal principles, you've drafted two rule application assertions, one related to the primary purpose facet of the rule and another related to the monetary or professional gain facet. Consider the following example, paying particular attention to how the facts dictate which reasoning tool the advocate uses to support the assertions.

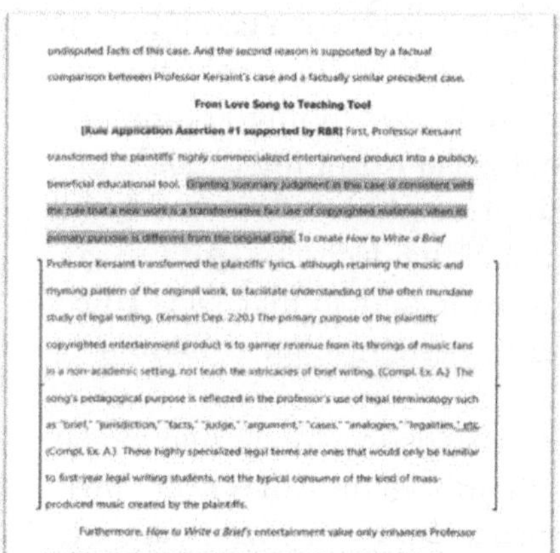
undisputed facts of this case. And the second reason is supported by a factual comparison between Professor Kersaint's case and a factually similar precedent case.

From Love Song to Teaching Tool

[Rule Application Assertion #1 supported by RBR] First, Professor Kersaint transformed the plaintiffs' highly commercialized entertainment product into a publicly beneficial educational tool. Granting summary judgment in this case is consistent with the rule that a new work is a transformative fair use of copyrighted materials when its primary purpose is different from the original one. To create *How to Write a Brief* [Professor Kersaint transformed the plaintiffs' lyrics, although retaining the music and rhyming pattern of the original work, to facilitate understanding of the often mundane study of legal writing. (Kersaint Dep. 2:20.) The primary purpose of the plaintiffs' copyrighted entertainment product is to garner revenue from its throngs of music fans in a non-academic setting, not teach the intricacies of brief writing. (Compl. Ex. A.) The song's pedagogical purpose is reflected in the professor's use of legal terminology such as "brief," "jurisdiction," "facts," "judge," "argument," "cases," "analogies," "legalities," etc. (Compl. Ex. A.) These highly specialized legal terms are ones that would only be familiar to first-year legal writing students, not the typical consumer of the kind of mass-produced music created by the plaintiffs.]

Furthermore, *How to Write a Brief's* entertainment value only enhances Professor Kersaint's argument about the transformative nature of its use. Professor Kersaint

13

Material facts **not analogous** to any prior case but relevant to black-letter rules.

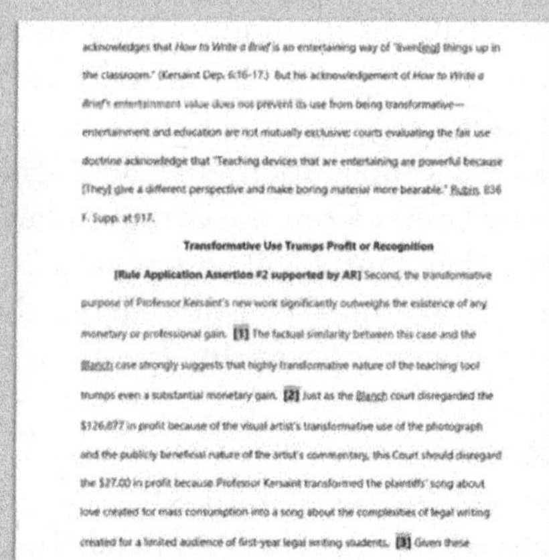
acknowledges that *How to Write a Brief* is an entertaining way of "liven[ing] things up in the classroom." (Kersaint Dep. 6:16-17.) But his acknowledgement of *How to Write a Brief's* entertainment value does not prevent its use from being transformative—entertainment and education are not mutually exclusive: courts evaluating the fair use doctrine acknowledge that "Teaching devices that are entertaining are powerful because [they] give a different perspective and make boring material more bearable." Rubin, 836 F. Supp. at 917.

Transformative Use Trumps Profit or Recognition

[Rule Application Assertion #2 supported by AR] Second, the transformative purpose of Professor Kersaint's new work significantly outweighs the existence of any monetary or professional gain. **[1]** The factual similarity between this case and the Blanch case strongly suggests that highly transformative nature of the teaching tool trumps even a substantial monetary gain. **[2]** Just as the Blanch court disregarded the $126,877 in profit because of the visual artist's transformative use of the photograph and the publicly beneficial nature of the artist's commentary, this Court should disregard the $27.00 in profit because Professor Kersaint transformed the plaintiffs' song about love created for mass consumption into a song about the complexities of legal writing created for a limited audience of first-year legal writing students. **[3]** Given these similarities, this Court should hold that the substantially transformative purpose of Professor Kersaint's engaging teaching tool outweighs any nominal return of $27.00.

14

Material facts **are analogous** to material facts from any prior case.

Scenario #1: Two assertions supported exclusively with rule-based reasoning or analogical reasoning

Notice that the advocate doesn't apply analogical and rule-based reasoning to the same set of material facts. This kind of duplication is confusing and undermines the persuasiveness of the advocate's reasoning. Instead, the advocate allocates the materials facts according to the assertion that they're designed to prove. The advocate supports the first assertion with rule-based reasoning. The material facts related to the new work's purpose are enclosed in brackets. They aren't analogous to any of the cases identified in the rule section or explained in the rule-explanation sections. So, the advocate applies the material facts to the black-letter rule shaded in gray about the new work's transformative purpose. Since it's straightforward, rule-based reasoning is the simplest reasoning tool. In a logos argument, rule-based reasoning is the default reasoning tool. Advocates can always default to rule-based reasoning. Because even if the material facts of the client's case aren't analogous to a prior case, the rule is always available to substantiate an assertion.

However, the facts supporting the second assertion dictate a different reasoning tool. Because the material facts related to the monetary or professional gain facet of the rule *are* analogous to the *Blanch* case, the advocate supports the second assertion with analogical reasoning. The bracketed numbers represent the three parts of an analogy: [1] the proposition that the analogy will prove, [2] the comparison between the client's facts and the facts of a prior case, and [3] the significance of the comparison. Without *all* three steps, the judge would have to either flip back to the rule explanation section or even worse, read the *Blanch* case in its entirety. Commenting on the angst of reading briefs with undeveloped and unsupported arguments, one judge lamented that "A skeletal argument, really nothing more than an assertion, does not preserve a claim . . . [j] udges are not like pigs, hunting for truffles buried in briefs."[20] This colorful and memorable language highlights the importance of fully developing arguments, especially complex, multi-step analogical ones. Analogical reasoning is powerful. Its power comes from the common law system and principles of *stare decisis*, the doctrine that courts will adhere to precedent when making decisions. And so, an argument that another court facing the same legal issue and similar facts ruled in a way that supports the assertion and the client's desired relief is extremely persuasive.

Consider another client's dilemma. The client sued his stepfather for the intentional infliction of emotional distress based on the stepfather's revocation of the client's invitation to attend his mother's funeral. The stepfather filed a motion to dismiss, arguing that the client cannot prove that he experienced severe emotional distress. Under the applicable law, a plaintiff's emotional distress is sufficiently severe when it results in an ongoing pattern of life-altering behavioral changes. And consequently, you've drafted one rule application assertion related to the life-altering behavioral change facet of the rule.

---

[20] *United States v. Dunkel*, 927 F.2d 955, 956 (7th Cir. 1991) (internal quotation marks and citations omitted).

Consider the following example, paying particular attention to how the advocate supports the assertion.

This Court should deny the motion to dismiss. Mr. Calhoun's distress was severe because he has experienced continuing, haunting nightmares, leading to the disruption of his lifestyle and demeanor. **[Foreshadowing Reasoning Tools]** This request for relief is supported by rule based reasoning applying the definition of severe emotional distress adopted by Florida courts and an analogy between Mr. Calhoun's case and precedent case.

[Rule Application Assertion] Mr. Calhoun's disruptive, recurring nightmares have resulted in an ongoing pattern of life-altering changes. **[RBR]** In Florida, a plaintiff's emotional distress is sufficiently severe when it results in an ongoing pattern of life-altering behavioral changes. Mr. Calhoun has endured anxiety-inducing recurring nightmares for nine consecutive nights where he hears the defendant saying, "Your relationship may be recognized by the State of Florida, but God's law is the only law that matters in this church" and sees those words flashing on and off like a strobe light, an experience that he equates to a physical assault. Because of these nightmares, Mr. Calhoun averages only three hours of sleep per night instead of the ten hours of sleep per night that he enjoyed before the defendant excluded him from his mother's funeral.

[Transitioning to AR] Furthermore, Mr. Calhoun has experienced demeanor changes that have tainted cherished memories of his life with his mother. **[AR]** **[1]** His inability to mourn a loved one make this case like Gray Brown. **[2]** Like the plaintiff in Gray Brown whose good memories of his wife were tainted by anger because of the disinterment of his wife's remains that resulted in handfuls of odor-reducing chemicals being thrown in her face, Mr. Calhoun's cherished memories of his mother's pride in and acceptance of his sexual orientation that prompted her to make a homemade signs with the words "I gave birth to a Grand Marshal" were tainted by the defendant's characterization of his mother's acceptance as an "abomination." **[3]** Given the similarities between the tainted memories and resulting changes in demeanor experienced by Mr. Calhoun and the Gray Brown plaintiff, the Court should deny the motion to dismiss.

Scenario #2: One assertion supported with a combination of rule-based and analogical reasoning

Because of the restrictive nature of analogical reasoning and the default nature of rule-based reasoning, the second scenario is the one that most advocates encounter. Support an assertion with a combination of rule-based and analogical reasoning when some of the material facts of the client's case are analogous to a prior case but others aren't. Notice how the advocate prepares the reader for the combination with foreshadowing language and signals the shift to analogical reasoning with a transition sentence. Similar to the first scenario, the advocate's analysis isn't duplicative.

However, because the advocate has only one assertion, the allocation process is different than the one in the previous scenario. The advocate allocates the material facts based on whether they're analogous to prior cases previously identified in the rule section or explained in the rule explanation section. The non-analogous material facts enclosed in brackets substantiate the assertion via rule-based reasoning while the analogous material facts following the second bracket substantiate the assertion with analogical reasoning. Both scenarios constitute the advocate's primary argument. A primary argument consists of the rule application assertions, the corresponding material facts, any supporting rule-based or analogical reasoning that substantiates the client's desired relief. After selecting the most appropriate reasoning tools for your primary argument, you must decide how to confront adverse facts that could potentially undermine that argument.

Decide How to Confront Adverse Facts

Your opponent will fight back, seeking to dismantle your primary argument. As one legal writing expert observed, "When faced with a strong opposing argument, persuasive legal writers are sometimes tempted to shrink away from the argument, combat it with a barrage of unfounded responses, or as a last resort, simply lodge ad hominem attacks."[21] The quote underscores the challenge of confronting adverse facts. Should you concede them? Address them immediately after your primary argument in counterargument or preempt them in your primary argument? **Preemption** subtly alludes to adverse facts in the advocate's primary argument instead of highlighting them in a separate counterargument. Advocates typically preempt adverse facts in one of two ways: by redefining or "flipping" them to support the client's argument or by deemphasizing them and burying them in the middle of sentences or paragraphs. Consider the following examples of these different approaches. The adverse facts are shaded.

Preempting by Flipping Adverse Facts:

Mr. Cantwell collects a fifty-dollar fee from subscribers—an amount equal to a dinner in a typical Manhattan restaurant—to nominate a media gatekeeper as the person of the week.

Preempting by Burying Adverse Facts:

Consequently, even if the client's screams that his stepfather was "a sanctimonious, homophobic asshole," drew attention to their conversation, the stepfather put the client in a position to be subjected to abuse by publicly revoking the invitation in view of 100 mourners and within earshot of 30 people.

The first example relates to the client who created a blog that divulges sensational information about celebrities. Recall that the client refused to divulge the identity of his confidential sources, arguing that he's a reporter with standing to assert the reporter's privilege. One aspect of standing relates to whether the person claiming the privilege disseminated information with the intent to disseminate it to the public. The advocate flips the argument by attacking the assumption at the heart of these adverse facts: specifically, that the nomination fee and his solicitation of private subscribers demonstrate that the client's motive was purely personal. Adverse facts aren't

[21] Stacey Rogers Sharp, *Crafting Responses to Counterarguments: Learning from the Swing-Vote Cases*, 10 J. Legal Comm. & Rhetoric 201, 201 (Fall 2013).

simply buried in the middle of the sentence. Instead, punctuation is used strategically (i.e., the en-dash). So, instead of undermining the argument, they highlight the gratis amount of the subscription fee, undermining opposing counsel's argument that the client's motive was purely personal.

The second example relates to the client who sued his stepfather based on the stepfather's revocation of the client's invitation to attend his mother's funeral. Assume that the stepfather amended his motion to dismiss, arguing that the revocation wasn't extreme and outrageous conduct, another element of an intentional infliction of emotional distress cause of action. Under the applicable law, conduct becomes extreme and outrageous when the defendant abuses a relationship of authority. The shaded facts are adverse. They undermine the argument that the revocation was abusive because it occurred in a public place within view of approximately 100 people. Burying adverse facts in the middle of the sentence deemphasizes them because they're surrounded by a sea of favorable facts.

But sometimes you aren't able to completely preempt the opponent's argument without shifting the focus from the client's desired resolution. For example, if preemption requires you to discuss information that's inconsistent with the client's desired resolution or that interrupts its narrative flow, then affirmatively disclosing and neutralizing that unfavorable information in a counterargument is appropriate. Counterarguments should appear *after* your primary argument—the rule application assertions and any supporting rule-based or analogical reasoning that substantiates the client's desired relief.

Think of a **counterargument** as a "fallback"[22] argument that supplements a primary argument. But don't get carried away. Resist the urge to over-anticipate your opponent's argument. An explicit counterargument should never be longer than your primary argument and should addresses only those considerations that merit rebuttal. Give the counterargument only the amount of consideration needed to briefly explain why the information doesn't undermine the client's desired resolution. As an illustration, let's revisit the relocation scenario. Assume that you're cloistered in your office working on the brief when you receive the following e-mail from opposing counsel:

> By withdrawing her objection to the motion, your client would avoid the embarrassment that would undoubtedly occur if the judge learned about last weekend's incident where your client showed up unannounced at my client's home yelling profanities and declaring her intent to vigorously oppose relocation.

Incorporating this added information into the brief would interrupt the flow of the rule-based and analogical reasoning supporting your logos argument. But you're concerned that ignoring the incident might undermine your argument. Given these facts, including a brief counterargument after your rule-based and analogical reasoning would better substantiate the client's desired conflict resolution. Building an effective counterargument is a three-step process.

[22] Thanks to our colleague, Professor Roma Perez, for this creative terminology to describe the relationship between primary arguments and counterarguments.

Step 1: Briefly explain the opposing argument (e.g., "The opposing side may argue that . . ."). Avoid defensive language (e.g., "Although my opponent may attempt to rely on Case X, this case is not applicable because . . .).

Step 2: Use rule-based or analogical reasoning to explain why the judge should reject the argument (e.g., "The court will likely reject this argument because . . .").

Step 3: Explain why the client's desired resolution invalidates the counterargument (e.g., "However, desired resolution X is more appropriate because . . .").

Test your understanding of the drafting principles discussed in this chapter and carefully scrutinize the sample counterargument. Pay particular attention to the highlighted information.

Sample Counterargument:

Nothing in the handbook logically conditions the right to progressive discipline on an employee's personal sexual practices.

> Persuasive, not defensive, transition to the counterargument

The immorality clause is a four-line paragraph in a subsection relating to work rules while the progressive discipline policy contains its own heading and spans two handbook pages. Nothing connects the immorality clause to the promissory and mandatory language contained in the progressive discipline policy.

> Brief reference to the opponent's argument

At best, a reasonable juror could conclude only that the relationship between the immorality clause and the progressive discipline clause is ambiguous. Under general contract principles, ambiguous contract language must be construed against the drafter. See, e.g., Kuta v. Delta, 799 P.2d 379, 390 (Colo. 1990). As the handbook's drafter, the defendant had the flexibility to design its handbook to unambiguously convey its intent to condition the availability of progressive discipline on an employee's personal sexual practices. In short, the very existence of an interpretive ambiguity makes summary judgment inappropriate.

> Rule-based reasoning substantiating the client's desired resolution

---

Chapter 8.4

Crafting Persuasive Pathos and Ethos Policy Arguments

"A lawyer is either a social engineer or . . . a parasite on society . . . ." —Charles Hamilton Houston

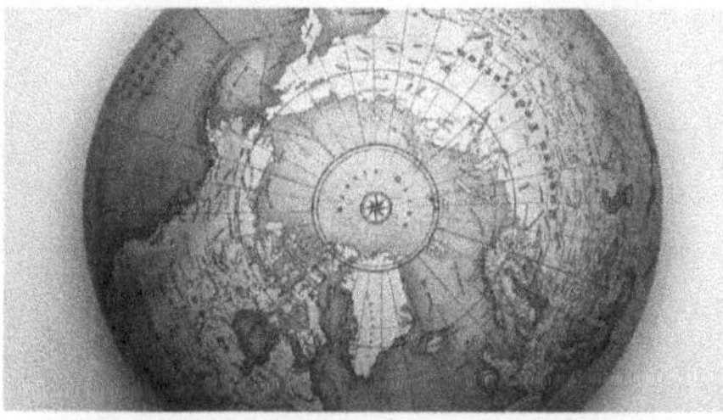

Charles Hamilton Houston was the legendary teacher, lawyer, and activist who designed the litigation strategy that resulted in *Brown v. Board of Education*, one of the most influential Supreme Court cases of the twentieth century.[1] Houston described a social engineer as "a highly skilled, perceptive, sensitive lawyer who [understands] the Constitution of the United States and [knows] how to explore its uses in the solving of problems of local communities and in bettering conditions of the [*sic*] underprivileged citizens."[2] Houston's words are a call to action, challenging lawyers to embrace the social justice aspects of their professional identity. The American Bar Association echoes Houston's call to action in its Model Rules of Professional Conduct. The preamble describes the lawyer as "a public citizen having special responsibility for the quality of justice" who "should cultivate knowledge of the law beyond its use for clients, [and] employ that knowledge in the reform of law . . . ."[3] Consequently, lawyers are not only counselors predicting the outcome of a legal dilemma or advocates urging judges to resolve a dispute in a way that benefits a client, but social engineers—activists who use the law to affect real-world change.

---

[1] *See* Leland Ware, *The Story of Brown v. Board of Education: The Long Road to Racial Equality*, *in* Education Law Stories 19, 20, 22, 24, 36–40 (Michael A. Olivas & Ronna Greff Schneider, eds., 2008).

[2] H. Timothy Lovelace, Jr., Revisiting "*The Need for Negro Lawyers*": *Are Today's Black Corporate Lawyers Houstonian Social Engineers*? 9 J. GENDER RACE & JUST. 637, 642 (2006).

[3] ABA Model Rules of Professional Conduct, Preamble, available at https://tinyurl.com/54t3f7fs (last visited on July 10, 2023)

Policy arguments are one way that advocates affect real-world change. Unlike logos arguments, policy arguments aren't premised on legal rules but on core societal values undergirding those rules and the real-world concerns. A typical policy argument might address how the resolution of a legal conflict might affect the court system, broad concepts such as justice, liberty, and equality (pathos), or specific concerns related to tradition, custom, or precedent (ethos). Sometimes novice legal writers assume that policy arguments are only for appellate courts. Nothing could be further from the truth. Trial court judges are often persuaded by policy-based reasoning in a case of first impression or when the relevant authorities are ambiguous, inconsistent, or conflicting. Furthermore, trial judges want to be aware of and make decisions that are consistent with the core societal values embedded in the existing law because their decisions are subjected to appellate review.[4]

As this discussion indicates, the shift to legal storytelling requires that you expand your horizons beyond rule-based logos arguments and embrace the persuasive power of policy arguments. This chapter will teach you how to expand your horizons. It begins with a discussion of the different types of policy arguments and then moves to a discussion of various techniques and strategies for crafting each component of a persuasive policy argument. This chapter ends with a chart summarizing all the soft- and hard-sell techniques at your disposal for crafting persuasive logos, ethos, and pathos arguments.

TYPES OF POLICY ARGUMENTS

All policy arguments emanate from core societal values. But advocates employ those values to support policy arguments in a variety of ways. Experts divide policy arguments into four basic types: (1) judicial administration arguments, (2) normative arguments, (3) institutional competence arguments, and (4) economic arguments.[5] The following graphic briefly defines each type of policy argument.

[4] *See* Ken Swift, *The Writer's Corner: Making Policy Arguments*, 61 Bench & B. Minn. 30, 30 (Oct. 2004).

[5] Many of the concepts and techniques discussed in this chapter have either been inspired by or adapted from the following noted legal writing scholars and teachers. *See generally*, Michael R. Smith, *The Sociological and Cognitive Dimensions of Policy-Based Persuasion*, 22 J.L. & Pol'y 35 (2013); Ken Swift, *The Writer's Corner: Making Policy Arguments*, 61 Bench & B. Minn., 30 (October 2004); Ellie Margolis, *Closing the Floodgates: Making Persuasive Policy Arguments in Appellate Briefs*, 62 Mont. L. Rev. 59 (Winter 2001); Ellie Margolis, *Beyond Brandeis: Exploring the Uses of Non-Legal Materials in Appellate Briefs*, 34 U.S.F. L. Rev. 197 (Winter 2000).

Types of Policy Arguments:

- ❑ **Judicial Administration Arguments:** Arguments about core societal values that focus on the role of the courts or on the difficulty of judicial enforcement.
- ❑ **Normative Arguments:** Arguments about core societal values that focus on broad concepts such as morality, social utility, and corrective justice.
- ❑ **Institutional Competence Arguments:** Arguments about core societal values that focus on which branch of the government should address a particular issue.
- ❑ **Economic Arguments:** Arguments about core societal values that place economics at the center of judicial decision-making.

Consider the shaded language in the following examples illustrating each type of policy argument.

Judicial Administration Argument: At a time when professional journalists are worried about the integrity of the press—a core societal value enshrined in the First Amendment—amid the unregulated nature of the Internet, courts should revisit Section 230 of the Communications Decency Act of 1996 that shields online services from civil liability. Revisiting the issue of liability in an increasingly digital age would provide uniformity in federal case law and drastically reduce the volume of appeals.

Normative Argument: The core societal values enshrined in the First Amendment promoting the unfettered communication of information from journalists to the public would be undermined if courts could exclude "bad journalism" from the protection of the reporter's privilege. Such arbitrary distinctions between inherently ambiguous concepts such as "good" and "bad" journalism have no social utility and create artificial barriers to entry, especially among novices or those with non-traditional experiences and credentials.

Institutional Competence Argument: A new standard for child relocation cases focused on empirical evidence about what is in a child's best interest should come from the courts, not state legislatures. Courts are better positioned to craft this kind of empirically based standard that would promote the kind of familial stability at the root of parental relocation statutes.

Economic Argument: The judicially created exceptions to the at-will employment doctrine should be abolished because they unduly burden traditional notions of employer autonomy that facilitate free markets and entrepreneurship.

Let's return to the parental relocation scenario to revisit the distinction between logos and policy arguments discussed at length in Chapter 3 and test your understanding of the different types of policy arguments. Recall that your client is a litigation associate at a large national law firm who objects to her ex-husband's petition to relocate their child to another state. The governing rule requires the court to weigh several statutory factors to determine if relocation is in the child's best interest. One factor relates to whether relocation will "foster a continuing meaningful relationship" between the child and the non-relocating parent and another factor evaluates whether relocation will enhance quality of life of the child and the relocating parent. Now, evaluate the point headings from the petitioner and the respondent's briefs.

TABLE OF CONTENTS
(Respondent's Brief)

Introduction 2

Statement of Facts 3

A Shared Love of Soccer 4
The Petitioner's Dissatisfaction in Florida 5
Fighting a Loss of Continuous Weekly Interaction 7

Argument 8

Genuine Issues of Material Fact Exist Regarding Whether Relocation Is the Child's Best Interest 8

A. The Post-Relocation Visitation Schedule's Inability to Foster a Continuing, Meaningful Relationship through a Combination of In-Person Weekly and Bi-Weekly Visitation Outweighs Any Quality of Life Benefits of a 6,477 Square Foot Home or a Pre-School for Affluent Children 9

B. Remaining in Florida Avoids Jeopardizing a 2 ½ Year-Old Child's Access to Individualized Instruction and the Non-Relocating Parent's Right to Actively Participate in the Child's Educational Life 12

Conclusion 13

Certificate of Service 13

TABLE OF CONTENTS
(Petitioner's Brief)

Introduction 2

Statement of Facts 3

The Consistent Primary Caregiver 4
Unemployment Threatens Family Stability 5
A Desire to Embrace New Opportunities 5

Argument 8

I. The Petitioner is Entitled to Judgment as a Matter of Law Because Florida's Parental Relocation Statute Violates Custodial Parents' Constitutional Right to Travel 9

II. A Reasonable Juror Could Only Conclude That Relocation is in the Child's Best Interest because Weekly, Biweekly, and Summer Visitation Foster the Non-Relocating Parent's Bond, Preserves Family Stability, and Ensures the Child's Free Access to a Highly Ranked Preschool Reading Program 13

Conclusion 13

Certificate of Service 13

Does either advocate make a policy argument? If so, can you identify the specific *type* of policy argument that the advocate makes? Now that you know the specific types of policy arguments at your disposal, you're ready to begin the drafting process. The remainder of this chapter explores the process of crafting persuasive policy arguments.

CRAFTING PERSUASIVE POLICY ARGUMENTS

Don't let the novelty of policy arguments intimidate you. All persuasive arguments, regardless of their type, perform three essential functions: identify a source at the foundation of the argument, discuss and clarify an ambiguous source, and demonstrate how the source substantiates the client's desired resolution (i.e., the mnemonic device IDD). Consider the following graphic.

Logos

Pathos

Ethos

Step 1: **I**dentify any rules or core societal values that support your argument.

Identifying the Status Quo

Step 2: **D**iscuss complex rules or core societal values using legal sources such as cases and non-legal sources such as legislative history, law review articles, statistics, non-legal analogies, etc.

Describing the Status Quo

Step 3: **D**emonstrate how the rules or the core societal values identified and discussed in Steps 1 & 2 substantiate the client's desired conflict resolution.

Articulating the Desired Conflict Resolution

The good news is that all the strategies and techniques for crafting effective logos arguments discussed in Chapter 8.3 apply to crafting effective policy arguments such as:

- ☑ Beginning with a powerful assertion.
- ☑ Skillfully using case illustrations and explanatory parentheticals.
- ☑ Strategically implementing a preemptive case selection strategy.
- ☑ Strategically using soft-sell persuasive techniques

To avoid unnecessary repetition, the remainder of this chapter explores drafting strategies and techniques that relate specifically to persuasive pathos and ethos policy arguments.

Persuasively Identifying and Explaining the Status Quo

This section explores strategies and tips for drafting the status quo component of a pathos or ethos policy argument. You'll use the same soft-sell persuasive techniques that you used to persuasively identify legal rules to persuasively identifying the core societal values at the foundation of your policy argument. Because of the "root" and "branch" relationship between logos and policy arguments, core societal values are often reflected in the case law. Recall the root and branch analogy discussed in Chapter 3. Logos arguments are "branch" arguments; pathos and ethos policy arguments are "root" arguments. Use the process discussed in Chapter 3 to extract those core societal values. And don't forget to avoid those drafting culprits outlined in Chapter 8.3.

But sometimes the core societal values undergirding your policy argument aren't reflected in a pre-existing rule. For example, when grappling with issues of first impression or a significant expansion or restriction of an existing rule, there isn't any pre-existing "branch" from which to extract a core societal value. In these scenarios, advocates work backwards, making an inverse policy argument. In an **inverse policy argument**, the advocate seeks to "institutionalize a [core societal] value by encouraging a court to establish a new rule that would protect or advance that value."[6] In an inverse policy argument, you don't have the kind of safety net that you have when building a traditional policy argument based upon core societal values reflected in rules. Recall the discussion in Chapter 3. Core societal values identified in a traditional policy argument are credible because a court, regulatory, or legislative body determined that they were so important that they created civil or criminal sanctions for those who undermine those values. In this scenario, select core societal values that appeal to the judge's value system. To identify those values, one noted legal writing scholar advised, "Pay close attention to long decisions or often-cited ones. Dissents are also a big giveaway. These samples are more likely to reflect the judge's deeply-held feelings."[7] Also consider geopolitical influences. Geopolitical influences are beliefs, assumptions, or values that are shared by persons of a particular region, city, state, or country. For example, the conventional wisdom is that judges on the West and East Coasts of the United States are more liberal while judges in the South and the Midwest are more conservative. Judges within the same state can also be influenced by geopolitical pressures. But regardless of the approach you select, you'll use the strategies for persuasively identifying legal rules discussed in Chapter 8.3. to identify the core societal value at the foundation of your inverse policy argument.

As an illustration of these concepts, consider the following scenario. Your client is a transgender inmate who alleges that prison officials' refusal to evaluate him for gender-affirming surgery violates the Eighth Amendment. Your logos argument reflects the deliberate indifference standard. However, your research reveals that the deliberate indifference standard emanates from the tension between core societal values related to evolving standards of decency and penological concerns about health and safety. Consequently, the status quo component of your logos argument (i.e., the branch argument) will be premised on the deliberate indifference standard. The status quo component of your policy argument (i.e., the root argument) will thus be premised on the core societal values undergirding the deliberate indifference standard. Consider the shaded portions in following examples.

---

[6] Smith, *supra*, note 5, at 46-47.

[7] Joe Regalia, *How to Use Policy Arguments to Boost Your Legal Arguments*, available at https://write.law/blog/policing-policy (last visited July 19, 2023).

Pro Prison Identification of the Status Quo: An inmate's Eighth Amendment rights are not absolute, and courts defer to the judgment of correctional officials, even if those judgments offend evolving standards of decency, when the denial of care is based on legitimate penological concerns regarding prisoner safety and institutional security. Turner v. Safely, 482 U.S. 78, 89 (1987).

Pro Inmate Identification of the Status Quo: Prison administrators must balance the conflicting demands related to the safety and security of incarcerated persons with evolving standards of care reflected in the Eighth Amendment. Turner v. Safely, 482 U.S. 78, 89 (1987).

The shaded language properly reflects the emphasis on the core societal values at the root of the deliberate indifference standard. Although neither example explicitly uses the phrase "core societal value," the judge reviewing the brief immediately knows that the advocate is making a policy argument because of the reference to real-world concerns such as evolving standards of care and the impact of competing concerns related to cost and safety. Also notice that each example incorporates soft-sell persuasive techniques such as word choice (e.g., "inmate" versus "incarcerated person") and positions of emphasis (e.g., burying the phrase "even if those judgments offend evolving standards of decency" in a dependent clause in the middle of the sentence). Sometimes the identification of the status quo will be more complex. Consider the shaded portions from the respondent's brief in the parental relocation scenario.

Identification of the Status Quo: The current version of Florida's child relocation statute is premised on the fundamental principle that the best interest of the child is inextricably linked to the non-custodial parents' right to actively participate and make decisions about their child's education. This foundational premise is based on the overwhelming body of psychological research establishing that separating young children from non-custodial parents who are actively involved in their children's educational lives impairs developing attachment relationships. J. Wallerstein & T. Tanke, *To Move or Not to Move: Psychological Considerations in the Relocation of Children Following Divorce*, FAMILY LAW QUARTERLY, Vol. 30, No. 2, summer 2016. Based on the conclusiveness of these findings, the Florida legislature made a policy-based decision to abandon presumptions, opting for a standard embracing holistic considerations such as the quality of the child's educational opportunities and the degree of parental participation in the child's educational life. See Naime v. Corzo, 208 So. 3d 296, 302-03 (Fla. 3d DCA 2016).

The shaded language properly highlights the core societal values (i.e., non-relocating parents' inalienable right to actively participate in their child's educational life) at the foundation of the advocate's policy argument. Although the identification of the core societal values in this example is more detailed than the previous example, notice that the advocate doesn't lose focus, saving the detail for the explanation of the status quo.

You'll also use the strategies and techniques discussed in Chapter 8.3 to draft the explanation of the status quo component of a policy argument. However, in a policy argument, you can support an assertion with non-legal materials such as law review articles, legislative history, statistics, and information from reputable sources. As an illustration, let's revisit the scenario involving the transgender inmate who alleges that prison officials' refusal to provide him with gender affirming surgery violates the Eighth Amendment. Evaluate the following options and select any option that an advocate could include in the explanation of the status quo in a policy argument.

Option 1: Prison officials cannot abandon medical judgment and avoid deliberate indifference by persisting in a known course of treatment known to be ineffective.

Option 2: According to recent statistics from California Department of Corrections, the annual cost to incarcerate an inmate is $106,131 per year per inmate. About three-quarters of these costs are for security and inmate health care.

Option 3: To establish deliberate indifference to an inmate's serious medical needs based on a prisoner's current course of treatment, the inmate must prove that the course of treatment was (1) medically unacceptable under the circumstances and (2) prison officials chose the course of treatment in conscious disregard of an excessive risk to the inmate's health.

Option 4: The average cost of gender affirming surgery ranges between $20,000 and $50,000.

Option 5: Deliberate indifference cases are by their nature fact-specific and fact intensive, and consequently, inmate medical care decisions must be fact-based with respect to the inmate, the severity and stage of the condition, and the efficacy of available treatments.

Option 6: Several courts have recognized that empirical assumptions related to cost at the root of many early cases categorically denying treatment for gender dysphoria such as hormone therapy and gender affirming surgery are no longer valid.

Any of the even numbered options could be included in the explanation of the status quo in a policy argument. An advocate could use the statistics about the annual cost of incarceration and the approximate cost of gender affirming surgery identified in options two and four to discuss the real-world impact of the tension between evolving standards of medical care and cost and safety. Option six would also be a good choice because information about how courts have grappled with striking the balance between competing core societal values would substantiate the inmate's assertion that evolving standards of decency outweigh prison officials' concerns about cost and safety. However, because the odd numbered options relate to the deliberate indifference standard, they belong in the rule or rule explanation section of a logos argument, not the explanation of the status quo in a policy argument.

Lastly, consider the complete status quo section (i.e., identification and explanation) from the respondent's brief in the parental relocation scenario as an illustration of the concepts discussed in this section.

Identification of the Status Quo: The current version of Florida's child relocation statute is premised on the fundamental principle that the best interest of the child is inextricably linked to the non-custodial parents' right to actively participate and make decisions about their child's education. This foundational premise is based on the overwhelming body of psychological research establishing that separating young children from non-custodial parents who are actively involved in their children's educational lives impairs developing attachment relationships. J. Wallerstein & T. Tanke, *To Move or Not to Move: Psychological Considerations in the Relocation of Children Following Divorce*, FAMILY LAW QUARTERLY, Vol. 30, No. 2, summer 2016. Based on the conclusiveness of these findings, the Florida legislature made a policy-based decision to abandon presumptions, opting for a standard embracing holistic considerations such as the quality of the child's educational opportunities and the degree of parental participation in the child's educational life. <u>See Naime v. Corzo</u>, 208 So. 3d 296, 302-03 (Fla. 3d DCA 2016).

Explanation of the Status Quo: Educational psychologists have long recognized that parental participation in a young child's life resulting in access to an individualized pre-school education can be superior to highly structured learning environments, especially when that education is delivered by active, involved parents via a homeschooling curriculum. A recent article by Harvard child development specialists, titled "*Is Kindergarten the New First Grade?*" criticized the current trend of highly structured educational experiences for pre-school-aged children. Poniewozik, James. 20 Nov. 2020, pp. 70-71. According to that study, preschool classrooms have become increasingly fraught spaces, with teachers cajoling their charges to finish their "work" before they can go play, resulting in less inquisitive and less engaged kids than those of earlier generations. <u>Id.</u>

But most alarmingly, researchers found that although children who had attended preschool initially exhibited more "school readiness" skills when they entered kindergarten than did their non-preschool-attending peers, by the time they were in first grade their attitudes toward school were deteriorating. <u>Id.</u> And by second grade they performed worse on tests measuring literacy, language, and math skills. <u>Id.</u> Another study from psychologists at the University of Colorado and the University of Denver studied the schedules of 70 six-year-olds found that the kids who spent more time in less-structured activities had more advanced self-directed executive function. Liu, Alaknanda. University of Denver Sociological Studies, vol. 15, no. 1, 2022, pp. 329-30. The researchers opined that when children are in control of how they spend their time, they learn how to work toward achieving goals and solving problems proactively. Id. Lastly, the study concluded that young children who were homeschooled had a more stable, empathetic relationships with their parents than children who were educated in more formal settings. Id.

Use the examples and illustrations discussed in this section when drafting the status quo component of your policy argument. For additional guidance, review the policy argument drafting checklist at the end of the next sub-section.

Persuasively Substantiating the Client's Desired Conflict Resolution

When substantiating the client's desired resolution in a policy argument, you'll use policy-based reasoning instead of rule-based or analogical reasoning. And consequently, your focus will shift from the application of legal rules and fact-to-fact analogical comparisons. Instead, your task will be to demonstrate why the core societal values previously identified and explained in the status quo entitle your client and similarly situated persons to the requested relief. To formulate this aspect of your policy argument, ask yourself the following types of questions:[8]

- How will people other than your client (i.e., stakeholders) be impacted?
- Is the client's requested relief in tension with those of other stakeholders? If so, how might you resolve those tensions in a way that doesn't undermine the client's requested relief?
- Will the client's desired relief result in any unintended societal consequences?
- Will the client's desired relief result in any tangible costs such as money or any intangible costs such as time or impairment of reputational interests?

Once you've answered these questions and revised your requested relief accordingly, you must consider where to place your policy-based reasoning. Because of the symbiotic relationship between logos and policy arguments, some advocates include policy-based reasoning in the conflict desired resolution section (i.e., the rule application section) of their logos argument. Consider this placement option when your policy-based reasoning is relatively straightforward or when it complements your rule-based and analogical reasoning. Other advocates include their policy-based reasoning in the desired conflict resolution section of a freestanding policy argument. Consider this placement option when your policy-based reasoning is complex or lengthy. Additionally, some advocates prefer the freestanding placement option because it makes their policy arguments more memorable.[9] The placement option you ultimately

[8] *See* Doretta McGinnis, *How to Construct a Policy Argument*, Law School Toolbox, https://lawschooltoolbox.com/11074-2amp/(lasts visited February 20, 2023).
[9] Smith, *supra,* note 5, at 46-47.

select is stylistic. But with your professor or managing partner's guidance, critically evaluate the options and select the one that most clearly substantiates the client's desired resolution. Consider the following examples of each organizational option.

Policy-Based Reasoning Incorporated into a Logos Argument:

[Rule Application Assertion] The Church's motion to dismiss should be granted because Father Van Helsing's casual use of the word "always" did not contain a specific duration of continued employment and did not reference a clearly discernable event. Instead, Father Van Helsing's casual remark that Father Greg would "always" have a job was an indefinite reference to the existence of future job opportunities with the Church. **[Analogical reasoning]** The indefinite, congratulatory remarks in this case are distinctly different from the concrete employment promise made by the employer in the Patrick case. Unlike the employer's representation in Patrick that contained a definite term of employment for ten years, Father Van Helsing's remark did not create any specific, measurable term of employment upon which Father Greg could have reasonably relied. Because the challenged remarks in this case are so different from those alleged by the plaintiff in Patrick, this Court should deny the motion. Instead, Father Van Helsing's congratulatory remarks are the kind of indefinite statement that the Daup court rejected. Like the indefinite statements made by the employer in Daup referencing a "very long" business relationship, Father Van Helsing's statements that Father Greg would "always" have a job were similarly indefinite because they were gratuitous statements about the potential for career advancement, not promises of a term of employment measurable by a discernable time. Based on the foregoing comparison of binding case law authorities, Father Van Helsing did not make a definite promise of continued employment and thus, the Court should grant the motion to dismiss.

[Policy-Based Reasoning] Furthermore, denying the Church's motion to dismiss would extend the protection of the promissory estoppel exception to vague, indefinite employer statements and would circumvent the underlying policy of the at-will employment doctrine. The at-will employment doctrine is premised on the principle that religious employers have a right "to decide for themselves free from interference, matters of church government as well as those of faith and doctrine." Kedroff v. St. Nicholas Cathedral of the Russian Orthodox Church, 344 U.S. 94, 116 (1952). Requiring the Church to permanently retain an employee like the plaintiff based solely on the casual use of the word "always" would seriously infringe upon the autonomy of religious employers like the Church and thus, circumvent the public policy of the employment at will doctrine. For example, if the Father Van Helsing's casual remark that the plaintiff would "always" have a job as a youth pastor was interpreted as a promise of lifetime employment, then the Church and similarly-situated religious employers would face (1) civil liability for wrongful discharge if it subsequently fired the plaintiff and (2) potential civil liability in excess of ten million dollars based on the inappropriate and unprofessional behavior of employees like the plaintiff that falls short of criminal behavior.

Policy-Based Reasoning Incorporated into a Freestanding Policy Argument:[10]

[Desired Conflict Resolution Assertion] The foregoing shows that the beliefs about lesbians and gay men relied on by Congress in enacting DOMA—about their capacity for committed, long-lasting relationships, and their ability to raise healthy well-adjusted children—are contradicted by the scientific evidence and instead reflect an unreasoned antipathy towards an identifiable minority. **[Policy-Based Reasoning]** In institutionalizing greater access by heterosexuals than gay men and lesbians to the many federal resources and benefits accorded married couples and their children, the Act conveys the federal government's judgment that committed intimate relationships between people of the same sex—even when recognized as legal marriages by the couple's state—are inferior to heterosexual relationships. This is the essence of stigma.

A stigmatized condition or status is negatively valued by society, defines a person's social identity, and thus disadvantages that person. A classic work in this area characterized stigma as "an undesired differentness." It can be manifested both in social institutions, such as the law, and in individual behaviors. Laws that accord majority and minority groups differing status highlight the perceived "differentness" of the minority and thereby tend to legitimize prejudicial attitudes and individual acts against the disfavored group, including ostracism, harassment, discrimination, and violence. Large numbers of lesbian, gay, and bisexual people experience such acts of prejudice because of their sexual orientation.

DOMA is an instance of institutional stigma. It conveys the government's judgment that, in the realm of intimate relationships, a legally married same-sex couple is inherently less deserving of society's full recognition through the provision of federal marriage-linked benefits than are heterosexual couples. By devaluing and delegitimizing the relationships that constitute the very

[10] Excerpt from the Amicus Brief of the American Psychological Ass'n, *et. al.*, p. 34, *United States v. Windsor*, 570 U.S. 744 (2013). In this landmark case, the United States Supreme Court held that Section 3 of the Defense of Marriage Act, which denied federal recognition of same-sex marriages, was a violation of the Due Process Clause of the Fifth Amendment.

core of a homosexual orientation, the Act compounds and perpetuates the stigma historically attached to homosexuality. Indeed, this effect of the statute condemns it quite apart from its denial of tangible financial benefits to married same-sex couples, for the Supreme Court has repeatedly recognized the unconstitutional nature of stigmatizing legislation based on stereotypic classifications. See Heckler v. Mathews, 465 U.S.728, 739-40 (1984) ("[A] s we have repeatedly emphasized, discrimination itself, by perpetuating 'archaic and stereotypic notions' or by stigmatizing members of the disfavored group as 'innately inferior' and therefore as less worthy participants in the political community * * * can cause serious noneconomic injuries to those persons who are personally denied equal treatment solely because of their membership in a disfavored group.") (footnote and citations omitted).

Once you've scrutinized all the examples in this chapter, use the following checklist to evaluate your policy argument. Consider modifying it to include any additional considerations suggested by your professor.

POLICY ARGUMENT DRAFTING CHECKLIST

- ☑ Does your identification of the status quo clearly articulate the core societal values (CSV) upon which your argument depends?
- ☑ Does your explanation of the status quo begin with an assertion that persuasively articulates interpretive information about ambiguous core societal values?
- ☑ Is the assertion followed by detailed explanation of any legal or non-legal sources that will clarify or help the reader understand the CSVs supporting your argument?
- ☑ Have you clearly demonstrated how the CSV identified and discussed in the status quo would or wouldn't be advanced in the client's case?
- ☑ Have you clearly demonstrated how the client and others similarly situated will benefit from the requested relief?

PERSUASIVE TECHNIQUES COMPARISON CHART

The following chart summarizes the soft- and hard-sell persuasive techniques discussed in this chapter and in Chapter 8.3 and identifies the section of the argument where each technique is particularly effective. Use it as a guide when drafting your client's logos and policy arguments.

Persuasive Argument Component	Soft-Sell Persuasive Technique
Generally Applicable	• **Favorable Context** • **Positions of Emphasis** (beginnings of sentences and paragraphs to highlight; middle of sentences and paragraphs to downplay) • **Sentence Length** (short to highlight; long to downplay) • **Word Choice** (words with favorable connotations to highlight; neutral words to downplay) • **Level of Detail** (detailed descriptions to highlight; general descriptions to downplay) • **Repetition**
Identifying the Status Quo	• **Level of Detail** (broad for favorable information; narrow for unfavorable) • **Context** (highlight historical context and purpose; omit context to downplay context and purpose) • **Burden of Proof** (emphasize if you have burden; deemphasize if you don't) • **Strategic Use of Punctuation and Typeface** (quotes, italics, underlining, numbering, bullets, numbered lists, colons, dashes, etc.)
Explaining the Status Quo	• **Preemptive Selection Strategies** • **Weight of Authority** (in favorable cases, emphasize the court issuing the decision in text and citations; in unfavorable cases, deemphasize by identifying the issuing court only in case citations) • **Breadth/Narrowness** (describe favorable facts, holdings, and rationales broadly; describe unfavorable facts, holding, and rationales narrowly)
Substantiating the Desired Conflict Resolution	• **Strategic Use of Reasoning Tools** (rule-based reasoning, analogical reasoning, and policy-reasoning)

Chapter 9

Storytelling at the Appellate Level: Understanding the Difference Between Trial and Appellate Briefs

"It's got to be a good story. I mean every lawsuit is a story. I don't care if it's about a dry contract interpretation; you've got two people who want to accomplish something and they're coming together. That's a story. And you've got to tell a good story." —Chief Justice John Roberts

Even among the Supremes—the highest court in the country—storytelling is key. As the Chief Justice of the United States suggests, even the most dry, mundane case can be examined through a more interesting storytelling lens. As we address appellate briefs in this chapter, it is important to remember everything you've already learned about narrative techniques and brief writing at the trial level. Much of what you've learned will translate nicely into the arena of appellate arguments. You are not reinventing the wheel. Rather, you are moving it to another car.

There are a few important distinctions between trial and appellate briefs, however. This chapter begins by highlighting the common narrative techniques used in each type of brief. We introduce you to the different levels of standards of review that are the hallmarks of the appellate process. Next, this chapter highlights the stylistic differences between trial and appellate briefs, using the Rules of Appellate Procedure as an outline.

THE COMMONALITIES

Hopefully, through the course of this text, you have become more comfortable with the principles of storytelling, and you understand how important these techniques are at boosting the persuasive power of your briefs. Those same principles—everything from the development of theory and theme, the appeal to core societal values, and presentation of a narrative thread—should inform your approach to your appellate brief.

In fact, because of the long reach of appellate cases, you may want to work even harder to highlight the core societal values raised by your appellate brief. As you develop the theme—the fundamental message that tells the court who your client is and why the court should care about the legal issue—remember that you are casting a very wide net. The court ruling on your appeal will have the ability to impact other courts within its jurisdiction, so appellate judges are even more sensitive to the policy implications of their rulings. The higher the court, the wider the scope of the brief's potential impact. The Supreme Court of the United States, for instance, has to consider the public policy implications for the entire nation. These overarching concerns should compel you to fully address both direct and collateral policy implications. You also need to work harder to counter any negative policy implications.

In addition to developing a compelling theme that will emerge from your question presented, summary of the argument, facts and argument, you should apply the persuasive writing techniques you learned about the presentation of the brief. The details—ranging from document design, word choice, and sentence construction—also translate to the appellate brief.

> ***A well-written brief should argue a point of law in a manner that appeals to the reader's natural sense of right and wrong.***
>
> —Warren Kwavnick, appellate attorney

UNDERSTANDING THE APPELLATE PROCESS: STANDARDS OF REVIEW

One of the defining distinctions between the trial and appellate court concerns the standards of review. The standard of review for a particular issue—often contested between parties because of the benefits and burdens each confers—has to be addressed and supported at the start.

The **standard of review** dictates the level of deference that the appellate court will give to the decision below. The more deference the appellate court gives to the lower court, the tighter the

> ***The applicable standard of review forms the lens through which the appellate court views a case. Cases are often won or lost on which standard of review is applied.***
>
> —Duane A. Daiker, in The Florida Bar[1]

arenas for consideration. Conversely, when the appellate court is given less deference, the area of consideration is expanded significantly. Here are the most common standards of review at the appellate level:

- **Clear Error**
  The clear error standard shows the highest deference to the lower court. It is used to review a court's findings of fact. Because the trial court is in a much better position to review the facts, the appellate court will usually accept the trial court's findings of fact.
- **De Novo**
  This standard recognizes the appellate court's important role in resolving legal disputes. It is used to resolve questions of law. Under this standard, the appellate court takes a fresh or "new" look at the legal issue. It does not give any deference to the trial court's decision on the law.
- **Abuse of Discretion**
  This standard applies to discretionary decisions from the trial court. Judges make several judgement calls in the course of a trial, and this standard does not call into question every minor or major discretionary ruling. It is limited to an examination of whether the trial court *abused its discretion* in exercising its judgment.
- **Mixed Questions**
  Some questions present both factual and legal issues that need resolution. These mixed questions of law and fact may require the court to apply two or more standards of review. Essentially, the issues are addressed independently, and the court gives deference to the trial court on the factual issue but examines the legal issue freely.

The standard of review is an important part of the litigation strategy. When trying to decide which standard of review applies, research case law. Precedent will often make clear the governing standard of review. When it isn't so clear, however, you have an opportunity to persuade the court to adopt the standard of review most beneficial to your client.

> ***The standard of review must be interwoven throughout the argument and come full circle at the end to show why the appellate court should or should not reverse the trial court.***
>
> —Richard Kraus and Bridget Brown Powers, attorneys[2]

---

[1] *See* Duane A. Daiker, *Avoiding Appellate Mistakes: A Primer for the General Practitioner*, Fla. B. J., July/Aug. 2008, at 51. Duane A. Daiker has served as Chair of the Appellate Practice Section of The Florida Bar.

[2] Richard Kraus & Bridget Brown Powers, *Appellate Practice: Brief-Writing Tips for the Infrequent Appellate Attorney*, Mi. B. J., Sept. 2019, at 22, 24.

Experienced attorneys will work to redefine the issue to support a more favorable standard of review. But this is a difficult process, one still confined by a realistic assessment of the lower court's actions and precedent. In addition to consideration of these matters at the start of the process, many jurisdictions are now requiring a discussion of relevant standards of review. Do the necessary research, strategize, and consider whether you have any options. If you are locked into a standard, build your argument within the appropriate framework. An informed discussion with your professor may also be helpful. Finally, this is merely a snapshot of some of the most common standards of review used. If you are writing an appellate brief for class, it will likely be helpful to better familiarize yourself with this material by consulting specialized material.[1]

UNDERSTANDING THE KEY DIFFERENCES BETWEEN TRIAL AND APPELLATE BRIEFS

While there are numerous similarities between the trial and appellate brief, there are some key differences worth noting. Essentially, however, the changes are stylistic. While much of what you have learned about trial briefs will transfer to the appellate arena, you must research and follow the rules governing appellate briefs in your jurisdiction.

Rules of Appellate Procedure dictate certain requirements that are unique to the appellate brief. There are multiple layers of rules that control appellate briefs. If you are in federal court, you will start with Rule 28 of the Federal Rule of Appellate Procedure. (But note that if you are in the U.S. Supreme Court, the briefs are governed by a special rule tailored for U.S. Supreme Court briefs.) It is imperative that you follow the governing court rules regarding the brief requirements.

If you are in federal court, the guidelines of Rule 28 offer a great deal of specificity regarding the brief requirements. The rule also breaks down the requirements for the appellant's brief versus the respondent's brief. Take a look at an excerpt of the rule itself:

Rule 28. Briefs.

(a) Appellant's Brief. The appellant's brief must contain, under appropriate headings and in the order indicated:

(1) a corporate disclosure statement if required by Rule 26.1;

(2) a table of contents, with page references;

(3) a table of authorities—cases (alphabetically arranged), statutes, and other authorities—with references to the pages of the brief where they are cited;

[3]One frequently cited, comprehensive book on the subject is Harry T. Edwards & Linda A. Elliott, Federal Courts Standard of Review: Appellate Court Review of District Court Decisions and Agency Actions (2007).

(4) a jurisdictional statement, including:

(A) the basis for the district court's or agency's subject-matter jurisdiction, with citations to applicable statutory provisions and stating relevant facts establishing jurisdiction;

(B) the basis for the court of appeals' jurisdiction, with citations to applicable statutory provisions and stating relevant facts establishing jurisdiction;

(C) the filing dates establishing the timeliness of the appeal or petition for review; and

(D) an assertion that the appeal is from a final order or judgment that disposes of all parties' claims, or information establishing the court of appeals' jurisdiction on some other basis;

(5) a statement of the issues presented for review;

(6) a concise statement of the case setting out the facts relevant to the issues submitted for review, describing the relevant procedural history, and identifying the rulings presented for review, with appropriate references to the record (see Rule 28(e));

(7) a summary of the argument, which must contain a succinct, clear, and accurate statement of the arguments made in the body of the brief, and which must not merely repeat the argument headings;

(8) the argument, which must contain:

(A) appellant's contentions and the reasons for them, with citations to the authorities and parts of the record on which the appellant relies; and

(B) for each issue, a concise statement of the applicable standard of review (which may appear in the discussion of the issue or under a separate heading placed before the discussion of the issues);

(9) a short conclusion stating the precise relief sought; and

(10) the certificate of compliance, if required by Rule 32(a)(7).[2]

As you can see, the rules are detailed and link to other rules for clarification on certain issues. In fact, as addressed below, the rules are so detailed that they even specify the typeface and margins, among other things, for the brief submission. It is your responsibility to review and adhere to all of the appellate court rules for the brief.

Most of the substantive appellate brief components would already appear in some form in a trial brief. The new requirements include subparagraphs (1)–(5), (7), and (10). Even some of these—such as the table of authorities—are included in trial briefs by attorneys who believe these additions make their brief more compelling and complete. To focus on the key distinctions, a simple breakdown of the requirements might be helpful.

[4] Fed. R. App. P. 28.

Subparagraph (1)—Corporate Disclosure Statement

This statement is needed only when there is a nongovernmental corporate party to a proceeding. Any party corporation or corporation that owns at least 10 percent of its stock must be identified. This is governed by Federal Rule of Appellate Procedure 26.1.

Subparagraph (2)—Table of Contents

The table of contents is just what it sounds like, though it must link to the actual page numbers that start the identified section. But in the brief, the table of contents takes on a very important purpose. It is the very start of the story. Through the table of contents, readers will get their first introduction to your argument.

The heart of your argument and the structure of your argument are revealed through concise, persuasive, and credible headings and subheadings. An important formatting tip for beginners: Go back and add the page numbers once you are done with the final brief edits. Page numbers will no doubt change with subsequent revisions.

Subparagraph (3)—Table of Authorities

This includes all the sources cited in your brief. It includes specific page references where the sources can be found. Though not required, it is most helpful to break down sources by type. Cases are grouped together, constitutions are grouped together, statutes are grouped together, and regulations are grouped together. These groupings give the reader a quick look at the breadth of your research. It therefore is an early opportunity to be persuasive; the more thorough your research, the more likely you will protect your credibility with the judge.

There are several word-processing programs available that can make this time-consuming process more manageable. Of course, you are building ethos or credibility here, so take the time to ensure that your citations are accurate. The rules require that the cases are alphabetically arranged to ease the burden on readers, but you have flexibility. Your goal is not to make substantive arguments here; rather, you build credibility by presenting a thorough table of authorities that is easy for busy readers to understand. If you move beyond cases and statutes, you can use the term "Other Authorities" for the catch-all to include law review articles, treaties, and other sources. Again, it is more efficient to actually wait until all revisions are concluded before you add the page numbers. And though you should start with a computer program to expedite the process, use your own two eyes to double-check the page references.

Subparagraph (4)—Jurisdictional Statement

This statement explains the court's basis for jurisdiction over the appeal. Beyond the scope of this book is the threshold question for any appeal; specifically, should you file an appeal? Once that decision is made, the jurisdictional statement helps the court clearly resolve the issue of jurisdiction. It should include some statute or other authority that cements the court's jurisdiction over the case. Essential content here includes the basis for the appellate court's jurisdiction and demonstration that the appeal is timely through the announcement of filing dates.

Subparagraph (5)—Statement of the Issue Presented for Review

This section of the brief presents another important opportunity to persuade. The very act of framing the question before the court is key to guiding the decision-maker to the correct outcome. (Depending on your jurisdiction, this section of the appellate brief is called the "question presented" or "issue presented." Use the term that is used in your jurisdiction or preferred by your instructor.)

Take time to draft a persuasive question presented that primes readers for your client's narrative. Do not merely write a dry statement of the issue that can be used for either side; instead, commit to your theory and theme. Now use that knowledge to inform your presentation of the issue. A well-crafted question presented will set the stage for the main event.

The format most commonly employed for the question presented is broken down into three parts:

1. Under [identify the applicable law]
2. Does [identify the legal issue]
3. When [identify the legally significant facts][5]

Unlike the question presented drafted for your objective memo—you may recall a question presented section in your predictive interoffice brief, if you wrote one—this question presented is not neutral. An effective question presented for the persuasive appellate brief attempts to create a foundation for the narrative. At the same time, however, it must maintain a professional tone that is rooted in ethical lawyering. Do not use hyperbole, exaggeration, or condescension when drafting the question presented.[6]

That's the easy part. The hard part is getting the key facts into the question presented in a fluid and readable manner. Begin by stating the applicable law and work from there to clarify the legal issue before the court. Then walk through outcome-determinative facts.

But how can you identify the key facts? Just as you did in predictive writing, allow the law to guide you. It is best to make a chart that tracks the legal elements you need

[5] This format has been credited to Laurel Currie Oates, Anne Enquist & Kelly Kunsch, The Legal Writing Handbook: Analysis, Research, and Writing (1st ed. 1993); *see also* Joan Rocklin, Robert Rocklin, Christine Coughlin & Sandy Patrick, An Advocate Persuades (2016).

[6] At times, you may have more than one legal question before the court that needs resolution. At that point, use the plural form, "Questions Presented" or "Issues Presented."

to prove under your applicable law to resolve the legal issue. Then match it with compelling facts that support your client's case.

For false imprisonment in Georgia, for instance, a deprivation for any length of time can support a claim.[7] The plaintiff must be held against his will and detained through the use of force or fear. Rather than make a legal conclusion in the question presented, ask the question through the incorporation of the key facts. Eliminate all irrelevant facts. And choose strong words and details that support your client's point of view.

Here is a quick sketch of how to best identify the legally significant facts in a false imprisonment claim involving a store security guard and a customer:

Element	Significant Facts
Against plaintiff's will	The plaintiff cried
Use of force	Security guard grabbed the plaintiff's arm
Use of fear	Store threatened to call the police
	~~Detention lasted 20 minutes~~

Based on the description of the facts, who do you think the brief writer represents? And what kind of theory and theme could such a presentation of facts support?

Why is the 20-minute detention eliminated from the list of included language in the question presented? If you are stuck, recall that the law in this jurisdiction does not consider the length of the detention when examining a claim for false imprisonment. Given that limitation, does the length of the detention really matter? If not, it should not be included in the question presented.

This particular presentation is sufficient to support a brief for the customer. But what if you were charged with writing a brief to support the store-defendant where the security guard worked? If the brief were written in support of the store facing a false imprisonment claim, it would be helpful to include some additional facts for context. Specifically, it would be central to theme of "mistakes happen" to include the fact that the customer was a suspected shoplifter. Though the outcome-determinative facts would still need to be included, adding the facts about suspected shoplifting helps paint a more favorable picture of the store.

Just as you learned to search for credible but emotionally charged words when crafting the statement of facts, take your time as you draft the question presented to choose the best words to support your narrative. Give extra consideration to the identifiers used for the parties. For example: Is your client "unemployed" or an "entrepreneur"? Is the Rottweiler a "family pet" or a "vicious animal"? The limits of the flexibility here should be governed by common sense and an ethical duty to relay a persuasive but accurate account of the events.

---

[7] *See* GA. CODE ANN. §51-7-20 (2015).

Subparagraph (7)—Summary of the Argument

Imagine there is a continuum of arguments captured within one brief. The shortest presentation of the argument is in the table of contents. Next on the continuum is the summary of the argument. It is much less detailed than the full argument but has more "meat on the bones" than the table of contents.

While the summary of the argument tracks the same arguments captured in the argument section, it doesn't get into deep analysis or details. It does not usually include citations. Nor does it generally raise counterarguments. Envision a movie description or book jacket summary of the text. The summary of the argument serves the vital function of alerting the judge to the core arguments that will be addressed in greater detail elsewhere in the brief. Most important, it provides context for the rest of the story. As for organization, it most closely tracks the format for the roadmap. Above all, it is succinct. You will have an entire argument section to address your points in great detail; there is no need to do so twice. This is the preview, not a first run of the entire show.

Experienced appellate attorneys will warn you, however, that even though you want to be persuasive, always remain professional. You may feel extra pressure to escalate your language in the short but sweet summary of the argument, but such tactics are unprofessional and undermine your credibility.

Subparagraph (10)—Certificate of Compliance

This section certifies that the attorney submitting the appellate brief has complied with page limits. Research the applicable rules to determine how many words or how many lines you can submit. Attorneys face sanctions for noncompliance.

Remember that the above guidelines are the requirements for the federal appellate brief. If you are writing an appeal in state court, you must research the brief requirements for that jurisdiction. They are readily available online. And, of course, don't forget to sign your brief. But think hard about your license before you "sign off" on anything—including an appellate brief. That signature and hard-earned bar card means that you stand by the accuracy of the brief contents.

ONE MORE THING

Don't forget the format. In addition to the substantive differences outlined above, remember that there are some formatting requirements that govern the submission of appellate briefs. Just as you did with your trial brief, check for governing rules to make sure you are in compliance. Everything from the margins, to the fonts, to fastening requirements, to the length of the brief is governed by formatting guidelines. Even small things such as whether the text is justified may be subject to the rules.

As you map out your time for completing the brief, remember to build in additional time to dig through the multiple layers of rules that govern the same court. For instance, in addition to the Federal Rules of Appellate Procedure, you need to review the Circuit Court rules and, of course, any local rules that apply to your court. Even individual judges sometimes have rules that may apply.

COGNITIVE CORNER

Appellate Briefs

Consider the following questions about appellate brief writing:

1. Which storytelling techniques can be imported from trial briefs to appellate briefs?
2. What are the key differences between trial-level briefs and appellate briefs?
3. How can you ensure that your appellate briefs are significantly different from the trial briefs you will be writing?

Intermission #1: Moving from Packaging to Revising

Victory!

If you have stayed the course and held on tight with both hands, you may be looking at a very good draft of a completed brief right now. You deserve high praise for getting this far. The work required to craft a strong brief featuring hallmark storytelling techniques throughout probably wasn't easy. You've come a long way from those first days of objective writing. Kudos on that.

But hold off on the celebratory dance for a little while. This important milestone marks the end of the packaging stage. But the fireworks and parade should be reserved for the conclusion of the entire process, which does not wrap until you are done with your revisions. For now, however, take a little time out for some self-care to walk, stretch, or listen to your favorite podcast as you clear your head momentarily of your client's theory and theme. You are about to move into the last stage of process, and you will function best if you are (1) kind to yourself and (2) recharged to tackle the work ahead.

> ***Law school can be demanding, so it's crucial to prioritize self-care. Whether it's going for a walk, practicing meditation, indulging in a hobby, or spending quality time with loved ones, prioritize these activities to recharge and rejuvenate.***
>
> —Eric Rosen, attorney[8]

The final section of this book will give you the tools you need to put the finishing touches on the story you have worked so hard to package. After working meticulously to craft a cohesive narrative throughout your brief, don't be tempted to take shortcuts now. The editing process is intense. And you may not be as practiced in critical self-evaluation of your writing as you should be. But as we've stressed throughout the book, lawyers are lifelong learners who should develop both the cognitive and metacognitive skills needed to succeed. That means that you should focus both on the task and *process* of revision to make your brief stand out. What's more, now that you may believe you have what looks like a finished product, it might be even harder to develop the drive and fortitude to complete the revision process. Even professional writers acknowledge how difficult it can be to push on through the editing stage.

[8] Eric Rosen is the founder of Rosen Injury Law, P.A., in South Florida. He is former President of the Broward County Trial Lawyers Association.

Despite the difficulty you may feel when moving from the hard and important work of packaging to the hard and important work of revising, you need to be equally committed to this step. The story is not complete until it is ready for public screening. So before you go "live" with your work, give it a serious review. Chapter 10 walks you through both the large- and the small-scale steps you should take to make your brief your best work.

> ***Writing is like riding a bike. Once you gain momentum, the hills are easier. Editing, however, requires a motor and some horsepower.***
>
> —Gina McKnight, author

This editing material in Chapter 10 is truly only the beginning of the end, however. You will be most successful in the editing process if you build in time to craft and complete a personalized editing checklist. More than any professor or supervisor, you are most qualified to assess your personal writing strengths and weaknesses. Use that expert knowledge to make the editing process meaningful.

Part III

Bonus Materials: A Little Something Extra

Chapter 10

Delivering a Cohesive Story Through Strong Editing: Hands-on Tips for Large- and Small-Scale Revisions

"I didn't have time to write a short letter, so I wrote a long one instead." —Mark Twain

It feels good to finally wrap up a writing project after the long, stressful period of writing. Once that final sentence is put on the paper, the last thing that anyone wants to do is read it again and look for more work to do. But editing is one of the most important components of the writing process. There is no point to toiling over a draft only to lose all credibility with readers through sloppy mistakes, narrative holes, or basic grammatical errors that undermine your arguments.

This chapter examines the importance of editing in the writing process. It focuses on editing as another strategy to generate ethos in a storytelling brief. It first makes explicit the connection between effective editing and strong storytelling. It then addresses the emotional challenges of editing and the professional repercussions of skimming on editing. Next, it offers several tips and techniques that can be used to make editing as simple and effective as possible. The strategies section especially focuses on editing techniques designed to strengthen persuasive writing. While many editing tips are universal, some are specifically designed at improving persuasive writing.

EDITING IS ESSENTIAL TO ANY GOOD STORY

A good story must be free of "plot holes." If your story is engaging, readers will follow the plot line with anticipation. If your story is persuasive, readers will also look forward to a positive resolution in favor of your client—this is the result you want.

On the other hand, a plot with holes will disorient readers. Without a complete plot line, the story falls apart. Before the proofreading and technical editing can occur, the first editing task involves reading for plot development. No matter how stellar the grammar and syntax of a novel, it is unfulfilling if the plot is incomplete.

A good storyteller is willing to draft the initial document, revise for story development, proofread for technical glitches, and redraft where needed. Without the editing process, the story you hope to produce is reduced to a draft. The client deserves more.

> *Writing without revising is like the literary equivalent of waltzing gaily out of the house in your underwear.*
>
> —Patricia Fuller, author

THE EMOTIONAL SIDE OF EDITING

People may resist editing their own work for any of several reasons. They are rushed for time or tired of the brief. Sometimes they are too emotionally invested in their work product to make any changes. Try your best to view your work objectively. Now try harder. The fact is that editing is hard because it is emotional. Unlike some other disciplines that test your knowledge of a particular subject, writing anything always feels personal. It reveals something about the sophistication of your arguments, your judgment, your personal style, and your ability to manage your workload.

It is usually easier to edit someone else's work because you do not bring the same emotional baggage to the editing table with you. But since you need to be self-sufficient in law school—and your school likely bans you from receiving assistance from anyone else—you must commit to overcoming your emotional resistance to editing. At the same time, you must learn how to use your "emotional brain" in the editing process. You will soon learn that an effective edit will help you feel more "zen" about the writing process.

How does this happen? Expert legal writers are able to evaluate their work because they are more practiced in the art of metacognition. They are more aware of thinking about how they think. Professor JoAnne Sweeny describes "emotional editing" as an important tool in evaluating effective writing.[1] She suggests that when you wear your editing hat, you think about how you feel after reading something. Ask yourself what emotional reaction you are having to what you are reading. Such an exercise may give you the focus to process your emotional investment in your writing. Getting in touch with your feelings connected to your writing will help you guide your reaction to your draft and make you a better editor.

Too touchy-feely? Remember that you are seeking to create in your readers both an intellectual and an emotional response to your product, so you must first measure your own emotional response to your work. Try an initial reading without looking for any mistakes, narrative holes, typos, or grammatical errors. Write down and consider your emotional response to your document and allow the emotional response to inform your assessment of whether you think the writing accomplishes its purpose. Then continue your edits from there.

THE PROFESSIONAL COSTS OF NOT EDITING

Making the decision to skimp on editing and revisions carries heavy professional costs for the legal writer. A weak brief can undermine your credibility with the judge and expose you to sanctions—both will impair your ability to effectively represent your client. Whenever you build in time to complete a new assignment, build in plenty of time to edit and revise. The best editing occurs when the writer is able to review the draft with care and attention. A "rush job" will probably fail to pick up all the errors in a draft. A rush edit also prevents the writer from crafting the best revision. If you rush in the writing process, you will make more mistakes. If you rush in the editing process, you will not catch your mistakes. Take your time when editing.

> *Poor editing is usually a problem of pace, and it is usually that the pace is too fast. Go slow.*
>
> —Johnathan K. Van Patten[2]

Careful, effective editing requires a thoughtful approach to time management (as discussed in Chapter 12) and a commitment to honoring those "soft" deadlines. The professional costs of not making time to edit are too high.

One risk you run by not editing is hurting your goodwill with judges. Judges are very busy human readers who will not respond favorably to additional, needless work created by a lawyer too busy to submit a clean, well-reasoned memo. Judges have issued bench-slaps to lawyers who have filed briefs too deficient to be helpful. One

[1] JoAnne Sweeny, *Emotional Editing*, 20 Perspectives: Teaching Legal Res. & Writing 109 (2012).
[2] Jonathan K. Van Patten, *On Editing*, 60 S.D. L. Rev. 1, 25 (2015).

court called a brief "wretched" and "almost unintelligible."[3] The court then ordered the attorney to show cause as to why she was not subject to sanctions.[4]

Another risk created by shortchanging the editing process is the threat of hurting your own credibility. Even something as simple as a citation error or typo can make readers question your expertise in the substantive law. Making sure that your brief does not show track changes or that formatting guidelines are honored demonstrates to the court that you are serious about your work product. Failing to make even these small commitments sends the wrong signal.

Finally, the cost of weak edits frustrates the fair administration of justice. Numerous courts have challenged attorneys for incomplete or inadequate briefs. Not including cites to records or not making accurate pinpoint citations creates several handicaps for the advocate. From a practical point of view, such failures force the court to do the work of the attorney and make it difficult for the judge to access key information. The extra layer of work makes it more difficult for the court to rule in a party's favor. If the court is not willing to function as a litigation support team to help you complete your record or citations, the court may decline to consider the underlying arguments. One court, for instance, declined to review the party's arguments to the extent that it would have to review a 4,712 page record to do so.[5] A rush job restricted the court's review of the argument. This was not effective or persuasive advocacy. Making time to fully edit, proof, and revise bolsters your credibility and honors professional obligations to the client.

> *An attorney's written work product is a reflection of the individual's professionalism and competence; every word matters. Spelling, grammatical, and typographical errors cause the reader to question the care with which the attorney prepared the document.*
> —Heidi K. Brown, *Converting Benchslaps to Backslaps*

BEST PRACTICES FOR EDITING

Depending on your writing skill and learning style, there are several options to improve your editing. Pick and choose and be creative. Learn from your mistakes. And be flexible. If one method does not work for you, make adjustments on the next assignments and go from there. Also, reflect on your best writing projects and your writing failures. What were you doing then? Are there any steps that you can import into upcoming projects?

[3] Sambrano v. Mabus, 663 F.3d 879, 880-81 (7th Cir. 2011).
[4] Heidi K. Brown, *Converting Benchslaps to Backslaps: Instilling Professional Accountability in New Legal Writers by Teaching and Reinforcing Context,* 11 JALWD 109, 118 (2014).
[5] Murken v. Solv-Ex Corp., 124 P.3d 1192, 1196 (N.M. Ct. App. 2005).

> *Whenever you feel an impulse to perpetrate a piece of exceptionally fine writing, obey it—whole-heartedly—and delete it before sending your manuscript to press. Murder your darlings.*
>
> —Arthur Quiller-Couch, author and literary critic

Don't forget to use technology to improve your editing. If you learn better by listening, have your computer "read" your draft to you so you can detect errors or gaps. Use the spell check or grammar check on your computer. But recognize the limits of technology. One student learned the hard way, for instance, that spell check is often set to ignore all caps. That meant the memo she submitted featured glaring spelling errors in the point headings. The computer does not account for the unique—and sometimes frustrating—hallmarks of English grammar. Consider the homophone. These words sound the same but have different meanings and ofter different spelling. Think: council and counsel. Another unlucky student did a spell checker on her computer, and the system did not catch the mistake. Imagine how much credibility she lost when she argued numerous times that "[t]he Court should deny Opposing Council's Motion for Summary Judgment." (Do you see why this is incorrect? Hint: Spell check will not pick up the difference between "council" and "counsel.") While you should not be shy about using technology to assist in your editing, remember that there is no substitute for a dedicated edit by a human being.

A Word about Artificial Intelligence

While technology such as spell check has been around for decades to help humans improve their writing, the explosion of more sophisticated artificial intelligence (AI) programs in recent years has changed the landscape of tech-assisted writing support in significant ways. Chat GPT, an AI language model produced by Open AI that is free for users,[6] has had a transformative impact on writing and other forms of creative expression. The Chat GPT program, also known as Generative Pre-Trained Transformer 3, has been hailed at "the best artificial intelligence chatbot ever released to the general public."[7] Since its release, Chat GPT has produced essays, song lyrics, press releases, research papers and a host of other content. Other similar emerging sophisticated AI programs include Google's Bard and Microsoft's Bing Chat.

But the use of generative AI in the legal profession is the topic of great debate. Some experts promote the use of Chat GPT and similar programs as a miracle of efficiency that can save time and money, therefore making legal services more affordable for clients. A small survey found that lawyers were already using Chat GPT for an expansive array of legal services. This work included prediction of case outcomes, e-discovery, brief composition, contract review, legal research, brief analysis, writing

[6] *See* Judge Mark W. Klingensmith, *Let's Talk ChatGPT: What Will the Judiciary's Future Look Like?* 97 FLA. BAR J. 26 (May 2023).

[7] Nico Grant & Cade Metz, *A New Chat Bot Is a 'Code Red' for Google's Search Business*, N.Y. TIMES, Dec. 21, 2022, *available at* https://www.nytimes.com/2022/12/21/technology/ai-chatgpt-google-search.html # comments.

briefs, predictive analytics, deposition questions, document review, billing and litigation support, due diligence, jury screening, online dispute resolution, and composition of emails.[8]

Other experts, however, warn of the dangers of AI and its limitations. "This is because the legal system involves complex ethical, moral, and societal issues that computers may not be able to fully understand and make decisions on."[9] The reliance on Chat GPT and other forms of generative AI tools could therefore trigger ethics violations and lead to bad lawyering. Just a few of the problems caused by lawyers using generative AI included inaccurate results, misleading results, plagiarism, bias, and lack of supervision.[10] There is also concern fueled by the lack of human judgment and empathy—essential components of effective client counseling and decision-making.

So what does this mean for today's law student? The experience with AI in the practice of law reveals that Chat GPT and other generative AI tools can be invaluable at improving efficiency but may expose the human writer to errors or ethical violations. It is your responsibility to speak to your professor and review the class and law school rules about the use of Chat GPT and other AI tools in the preparation of your briefs. Just as lawyers are split on the ethics of AI, law professors are split about the appropriate use of Chat GPT and generative AI in the classroom. Get clear guidance from your professor about the extent to which you can use generative AI in your assignments. Don't risk an honor code violation in an effort to cut a few corners. There may be pedagogical reasons your professor wants you to do something on your own. When in doubt, ask.

CHECKLISTS AND SELF-ASSESSMENT

As you already know, this text is committed to helping you take control of the writing process through self-reflection, self-assessment, and self-regulation. In a perfect world, you could rely on an editor to carefully proof and evaluate your writing. In practice, you may be able to rely on colleagues in your office to proof important documents with you. Time limitations, however, may limit the amount of feedback colleagues or supervisors can give you on your drafts. You must learn to be accountable for your own work product. The ethical rules regarding confidentiality and client communications may also restrict how much outside assistance is available to you.

More important, most law schools and law professors have strict honor code policies that prohibit sharing work product with others. Unless your professor has given you explicit instructions to do so, you should not attempt to get editing assistance from anyone. Receiving or giving unauthorized assistance—even something as simple as asking a trusted friend to check for typos—may trigger an honor code violation.

---

[8] Sharon D. Nelson, et al., *Using Generative AI in Your Practice? You Better Be Aware of Ethical Implications*, 48 Montana Lawyer 16 (April/ May 2023).
[9] Judge Mark W. Klingensmith, *Let's Talk ChatGPT: What Will the Judiciary's Future Look Like?* 97 Fla. Bar J. 26, 32 (May 2023).
[10] Sharon D. Nelson, et al., *Using Generative AI in Your Practice? You Better Be Aware of Ethical Implications*, 48 Montana Lawyer 16 (April/ May 2023).

> *Checklists seem to provide protection against such failures. They remind us of the minimum necessary steps and make them explicit. They not only offer the possibility of verification but also instill a kind of discipline for higher performance.*
>
> — Atul Gawande, *The Checklist Manifesto*

Once you have completed your strongest draft of your memo, the best way to guarantee that you approach the editing process thoughtfully and deliberately is through the use of a revision checklist. Developing a checklist that guides you through a detailed editing process will help you improve your writing. In *The Checklist Manifesto*, Atul Gawande describes the efficacy of checklists for improving baseline performance.[11] Everyone—from pilots to medical doctors—relies on checklists to ensure they have met minimum standards. The implementation of checklists, even among experienced professionals in routine activities, has made flying and hospitals safer. Imagine what a checklist can do for your writing!

If your instructor provides you with a checklist, great. If not, build your own. Start with the basics. Make sure that the checklist you develop reflects the requirements for the assignment. Effective revisions move from the large scale to the small scale to the downright picayune.

When building an editing checklist, incorporate any essentials that jump out of any rubrics you have been given. The most important step in using an editing checklist, though, is to personalize it based on your writing strengths and weaknesses. To get you started, a few sample checklists are listed below.

A Substantive Example

This checklist is a sample checklist for the argument section of your brief. This particular checklist forces you to engage actively in the editing process by underlining and circling important components. Some students also elect to use colored pencils or highlighters for emphasis.

ARGUMENT GUIDELINES

- ☑ Underline the introductory and transition words and the commas that follow them.
- ☑ Streamline your writing (e.g., replace phrases such as "due to the fact that" with "because").
- ☑ Underline conclusions at the beginning and end of each argument. Compare your first conclusion to your second conclusion. Are they identical? If so, make the needed corrections.

[11] Atul Gawande, The Checklist Manifesto: How to Get Things Right (2009).

- ☑ Underline any rules that appear in your argument. Are rules complete and stated in universal terms? Do they accurately synthesize the law? Are your rules persuasive?
- ☑ Include citations to any rules in the argument section.
- ☑ Underline any assertions in the rule explanation and application sections. Are they complete? Does your rule application assertion refer to the client's case? Does it incorporate a reference to the applicable legal rules?
- ☑ Draw an arrow from each subject raised in the application to the corresponding subject in the rule explanation section. Does the rule application track the order of the rule explanation?
- ☑ Bracket the analogies and distinctions. Are your analogies explicit?

A Style Example

This sample applies to any type of legal writing. It's a general checklist that's focused on style and easy-to-proof formatting requirements. It's sometimes helpful to tackle this less-demanding checklist when you have cognitive loads that may temporarily prevent you from unpacking more challenging tasks. The items on this list are important but are more easily evaluated. Tired of trying to develop a synthesized rules paragraph? Spend some time making sure your paper conforms to the general writing guidelines. The following checklist will get you started.

WRITING GUIDELINES

- ☑ Do your sentences flow smoothly?
- ☑ Are you using "plain English"?
- ☑ Is your writing grammatically correct?
- ☑ Is your writing free of bias?
- ☑ Did you update your research?
- ☑ Do you cite to relevant case law (binding, where available?)
- ☑ Do you use signals and parentheticals properly and where needed?
- ☑ Does each cite conform to *Bluebook* style?
- ☑ Is your paper within the page limit requirements?
- ☑ Are you following all format requirements (e.g., font, margins, spacing)?
- ☑ Is the document visually appealing?
- ☑ Did you proofread?
- ☑ Did you proofread again?
- ☑ Are you submitting your best work?

A Personalized Example

The best checklists are personally tailored to your individual writing strengths and weaknesses. You can use the form checklists or instructor-issued checklists to start the editing process, but do not rely only on such one-size-fits-all revision checklists.

A personalized checklist not only helps you with your editing, but helps you better identify your writing competency. And this process transforms you into a self-regulated learner, one who can objectively assess what she needs to address.

Your checklist can be as informal or formal as you like. (This is, after all, *personalized.*) You might want to make a checklist by hand on a sticky note, type it out and add bullets, create one on your laptop, or use a white board. As far as the content, the best way to develop your personalized checklist is to review your own submitted and edited work. Pay attention to the feedback that your professor has given you on prior assignments. Also consider writing challenges you have struggled with throughout your undergraduate education and career. Here is one example of what a personalized checklist might look like.

- ☑ Check spelling!!
- ☑ Improve parentheticals.
- ☑ Use active voice.
- ☑ Watch for pronoun agreement.
- ☑ Follow Bluebook for string cites.
- ☑ Double-check comma use.

SPECIAL POINTERS TO BOOST THE POWER OF PERSUASION

Editing and revision are an absolute must in any written product. Structural defects, typographical errors, and grammatical mistakes are always confusing. In the world of persuasive writing, however, they crush credibility. The goal of the brief is to persuade the judge.

A brief rooted in legal storytelling is even more sensitive to the need for strong writing and editing. The advocate must capture the judge's attention and trust. In addition to everything else you know about strong editing, review the following tips that are specifically aimed at boosting the power of persuasion.

Reduce Nominalizations

When verbs turn into nouns, bad things can happen. **Nominalization** is the process of converting a verb into a noun. Nominalizations can also spring from adjectives and, sometimes, other nouns. They are commonly signaled through a suffix (segment added to the end of a word) and a stilted sentence construction. Minimize the use of nominalizations because they make your writing wordy and less dynamic. Writer and teacher Helen Sword calls nominalizations "zombie nouns" because they "cannibalize active verbs" and "suck the lifeblood from adjectives."[12]

[12] Helen Sword, *Zombie Nouns*, N.Y. Times: Opinionator (July 23, 2012, 9:15 PM), http://opinionator.blogs.nytimes.com/2012/07/23/zombie-nouns/?_r=0.

TIP: LOOK FOR WORDS THAT END WITH:

"-tion"
"-ability"
"-ment"

For example, nominalizations include nouns such as "education," "formation," "dissection," and "enjoyment." These words are converted from their stronger verb forms: "educate," "form," "dissect," and "enjoy." Reality check: Even the word "nominalization" is a nominalization. Not all of these words must be eliminated, but you should examine them carefully to make sure they should not be restored as verbs. Can you find the nominalization in the following sentence?

The reporter conducted an investigation of the man's claim.

Here is one example of how the sentence might be rewritten to reduce the nominalization:

The reporter investigated the man's claim.

When you are revising to reduce these words, it isn't as simple as replacing a word with a stronger word. Usually, the remedy calls for sentence reconstruction. But this process is good because it makes your writing clear, concise, and persuasive.

Don't Be So Intense!

Ever tried to argue with a child who doesn't have a load of facts or strong reasoning to make a case? Chances are that at some point in the conversation you heard these words: "Well, obviously, that is my point." The use of intensifiers—here, the word "obviously"—is a common but ineffective way of trying to make a persuasive argument.

One simple way to boost your writing is to rigorously eliminate intensifiers. While a few well-placed intensifiers may strengthen your argument, too many undercut your credibility. They essentially invite the judge to look for the support needed to back a claim. They are also deployed when the writer has not taken the time to develop cogent, sound arguments. Further, one modest study showed a statistical relationship between the use of intensifiers and negative outcomes[13]—exactly the opposite of what you want to achieve.

Common intensifiers include the following:

- very
- certainly
- patently
- absolutely
- simply
- clearly

Still not convinced? Compare the following sentences:

Clearly, the use of intensifiers is simply not effective in persuasive writing.

Intensifiers are not effective in persuasive writing.

Not only do the intensifiers dilute your credibility, but they also take up more space. Removing the intensifiers in the example—"clearly" and "simply"—gives the sentence more impact. This issue takes us to the next specific suggestion for editing persuasive writing.

Cut, Cut, and Cut Again

Novice writers are notoriously wordy. And this is especially true for novice legal writers. One of the most common complaints first-year law students make is about the length of the assignments; most students say they need more space to make their point. But concision is key. This is a critical skill that must be developed for legal writing in practice.

First, local formatting rules may impose page length requirements on documents. Also, the attention span of the busy judge will be tested by lengthy briefs. Furthermore, in persuasive storytelling, readers will not be able to track the storytelling elements if they have to wade through superfluous, redundant material.

It takes work, effort, and time to make your writing concise. Revising with a checklist is one way to stay focused on the essential material. Eliminating dangling words at the bottom of the page will also open up more space. However, the most

[13] Lance N. Long & William F. Christensen, *Clearly, Using Intensifiers Is Very Bad–Or Is It?*, 45 Idaho L. Rev. 171, 184-185 (2008). "The results can be interpreted several ways. It may be that, in connection with appellate briefs, the traditional overuse of intensifiers actually renders them suspect and subject to increased skepticism by appellate court judges. It may also be that intensifiers function as powerless language in appellate briefs, resulting in a greater likelihood of a negative outcome."

important step toward streamlining your writing is the ability to be rigorous and ruthless in the editing.

Don't fall in love with anything you've written. There is always more than one way to say something effectively. When you must part with a favorite word or phrase, remember that its sacrifice will make the entire brief better. Editing adds another layer of complexity, but it is the only way to write a persuasive brief.

COGNITIVE CORNER

Editing

Consider the following questions about the editing process:

1. Would your work make sense to someone without the benefit of a "live narration"?
2. Have you been a ruthless reviewer of your own work?
3. Were you mindful of your narrative as you made edits and additions to the brief?
4. Did you tailor editing to your personal strengths and weaknesses?

Chapter 11

Organizing, Practicing, and Delivering an Effective Oral Argument to Sell Your Story

"The best way to sound like you know what you're talking about is to know what you're talking about." —Author unknown

Even the most seasoned attorneys experience some anxiety about public speaking. Studies consistently point to public speaking as one of the most anxiety-ridden activities human beings encounter. In one study, public speaking even outranked death as the number one fear for respondents.[1] Psychologists point out that public speaking, for many, invites an intense fear of public scrutiny and possible rejection. For lawyers, public speaking on behalf of a client's best interest also invites the possibility of rejection of the client's case. And no amount of flash, style, or natural speaking ability can overcome lack of preparation.

This chapter helps you prepare for oral arguments by taking you through the basics of what to expect in a motion hearing on your trial brief. Essentially, it helps you tell your story at oral argument through mastery of both style and substance. As the author of the quote above states, there is no substitute for preparation. This chapter

[1] Joe Queenan, *Joe Queenan's Guide to Public Speaking: How to Avoid Utterly Humiliating Yourself in Front of a Bored and Yawning Crowd*, WALL ST. J. (June 13, 2014), http://www.wsj.com/articles/joe-queenans-guide-to-public-speaking-1402683882; *see also* Preston Ni, *5 Tips for Reducing Public Speaking Nervousness*, PSYCHOL. TODAY: COMM. SUCCESS (May 14, 2013), https://www.psychologytoday.com/blog/communication-success/201305/5-tips-reducing-public-speaking-nervousness.

gives you a common structure to help you organize your oral argument, building on the structure you used in your motion brief. It then shares the best suggestions available for practicing your oral argument, with an emphasis on how technological advances can widen the scope and effectiveness of your practices. The chapter helps you understand how to respond on your feet as you deliver an oral argument. It concludes by identifying the most common mistakes new attorneys make in oral arguments, with tips on how to correct these mistakes. With the right preparation, oral arguments can be exciting and successful.

While some students prepare for an appellate oral argument, this chapter focuses on how to prepare an oral argument for a motion hearing. The fact is that most attorneys never handle appellate oral arguments, while more litigators prepare motions for summary judgment, the most common type of motion brief. Therefore, this chapter reflects the trends in practice today. However, most of the instruction easily translates from motion hearing to appellate argument. Further, global advice about effective communication will translate to any type of law practice. Indeed, lawyers must learn how to communicate effectively with the bench, the jury, opposing counsel, clients, business leaders, public officials, and the public. Refining communication skills will help any aspiring lawyer – regardless of the practice area.

> *It doesn't make any difference whether you want to go into transactional work, you want to be a litigator, or you want to be in business, your job is to communicate ideas effectively. At the end of the day, lawyers try to convince people that they are right, no matter the task.*
>
> —Judge Dorian K. Damoorgian, Florida's Fourth District Court of Appeal

ORAL ARGUMENTS AT A GLANCE

The Basics

A legal story—whether delivered on paper or from a podium—depends on a strong theory and theme.

Effective oral advocacy should build on a motion brief and allow the judge to rule in your favor. A clear theory and theme are essential components of a legal story. A good oral argument:

- ☑ Explains why your client should prevail
- ☑ Is easily understood and credible
- ☑ Is consistent with the core values reflected in the rule structure
- ☑ Emphasizes favorable facts and explains unfavorable ones
- ☑ Targets the weakest aspects of your opponent's case
- ☑ Applies the best forensic practices to deliver a polished, professional argument to the bench

Does this list look familiar? These are many of the same principles you were encouraged to consider as you worked through theory and theme in Chapter 4. As you move from the desk to the podium, do not forget what you know about building a strong narrative in your argument. Oral arguments that are *all style and no substance* are ineffective. It is important to incorporate the theory and theme of the case both explicitly and implicitly throughout the oral argument.

Style and substance are inextricably linked, but mastering the substance will give you the confidence to perfect your style. Before you start practicing in the mirror, recording yourself with your cellphone, or asking others to practice with you, you must sit down and write out a plan for your argument.

Once you have a general template as a work basis, you can further tease out minor points. Even after you start practicing the delivery, always remain flexible about how you want to best present the argument on your feet.

Oral arguments are an important opportunity for you to advocate on behalf of your client and answer the Court's questions. While they are meant to help you advance your client's story, they can also create new obstacles for you if you are not thoroughly prepared. The old adage holds: "You never win at oral argument, but you certainly can lose."[2] This chapter provides some concrete steps to help you feel prepared to confidently approach your oral agument.

What to Expect

As a first-year law student, you are likely doing your oral argument as part of your legal research and writing course or as part of a competition to earn an invitation to your law school's Moot Court Society. Either way, the oral argument is an excellent way for you to prepare for either trial court or appellate court arguments in practice. Though not the same—for instance, appellate court arguments are generally more formal—there are enough similarities between the two that are transferable. The goal of this chapter is to prepare you for the law school oral argument experience. As you map out your argument and complete this task, remember that this is still a pedagogical experience primarily aimed at getting you to refine your analytical skills. The same legal research, synthesis, policy arguments, and narrative techniques that shaped your memorandum of law or brief should inform your oral argument for class. The additional stress of public speaking should encourage you to make every effort to plan.

The oral argument experience for first-year law students typically involves students who are each assigned between 10 and 30 minutes to present an "argument" before a bench. The bench could be comprised of a single judge or a panel of several judges. Each student speaks, takes questions from the bench, and often receives a critique. Most of the time, the bench is also prepared with a bench memo that summarizes the applicable law, highlights strengths and weaknesses in each side, and provides some questions. You should be prepared, however, for judges who come

[2] Kyle R. Kroll, *Short, Sweet and Specific*, 78 Bench & Bar Minn.12 (Nov. 2021).

in with a full understanding of the material and those who are not familiar with the record or governing law. Being flexible will allow you to feel successful with either type of judge.

ORGANIZING YOUR ARGUMENT

A good starting place for your oral argument is a common template that allows you to introduce yourself and your client, relay your prayer for relief (this is what you want from the court), announce your theme, and provide a roadmap to help the court arrive at the result you seek. Imagine the key points looking something like this:

Introduction and Prayer for Relief:

May it please the Court. My name is _______, and I represent _______, the movant in this case. _______ respectfully requests that this Court [prayer for relief].

Theme:

[Insert a **BRIEF** description of your theme of the case here.]

Roadmap:

This Court should [prayer for relief] for three reasons:

First: [**Briefly** identify first point.]

Second: [**Briefly** identify second point.]

Third: [**Briefly** identify third point.]

Facts:

[**Briefly** state key, legally operative facts if required to do so.]

Argument: [Return to the large points identified in your roadmap and address each in turn.]

Closing:

[Incorporate theme, mention major points if time allows, and close with prayer for relief.]

The basic format will vary based on the complexity of the case and any local rules that govern your argument. Just as in practice, always check the local rules. For instance, some schools permit rebuttal in first-year oral arguments. If you are expected or allowed to do one, you should adjust the suggested format to add a section under the introduction to request time for rebuttal. You should also be able to adjust based on the needs of the bench.

Some judges will ask for a brief recitation of the facts. You should also speak with your instructor about specific rules governing the oral argument practice at your school. Just as local rules control in court, the "local rules" of your school or professor's oral argument will trump any general guidelines offered in this chapter. Part of your research preparation, then, is to get a clear understanding about what is expected of you.

Integration of Theme

The podium is no place to abandon the careful development of your client's story. Rather than move away from support of your theory and theme, you should announce the theme of the case and marshal the law, facts, and policy in support of your narrative. Former Chief Justice William Rehnquist once said that the successful oral advocate is willing to listen to questions and "has a theme and a plan for her argument."[3]

In Chapter 4, you learned about the importance of theory and theme development in your brief. Recall that an effective theme engages and resonates with the judge through its simple, accessible message. During oral argument, it is just as important to advance the theme of your client's story through both explicit and implicit methods. The goal is to appeal to the listener's sense of fairness and to reinforce your narrative. Rather than hide the theme or bury it at the end of the argument, reflect on how your use of facts, case law, and public policy arguments advance your theme. Also, write your own theme in one simple sentence on your roadmap. If you can't condense your theme and reduce it to a digestible chunk, it is likely too convoluted to be effective. Finally, evaluate your roadmap in light of the theme you have adopted. If the two are not a good "fit," you may need to do more research or make better selections. And don't just rely on a catchy phrase in place of a well-reasoned, accessible theme that supports your theory and case.

For instance, in a case about the application of U.S. antitrust law in foreign nations, one student reduced his argument to a much more palatable theme: "This is a case about the dangers of overreaching." For the other side, the theme was drilled down to reflect a justification for extraterritorial application of U.S. antitrust regulations: "This is a case about fairness." After the themes were announced, the judges were given the more specific, technical aspects of the law and policy implications. But even a judge unfamiliar with foreign application of U.S. trade law was poised to interpret an analysis of overextension or inequitable business practices.

[3] William Rehnquist, The Supreme Court: How It Was, How It Is (Morrow 1987).

Because you should have structured a memorandum or brief based on a well-developed theory and theme, you should be able to import the theme into your oral argument. But this is an oral argument, not a written document. Therefore, focus on making the theme concise and immediately understandable. If you have to explain to the judge what you mean by your theme, you have gone in the wrong direction. If your judge must be an expert in the field, you are also being too technical. Keep the theme as simple as possible. And write it at the top of your roadmap as you craft the outline. It is a good way to stay focused on the message you are relaying.

Notebooks and Folders

Experts split on whether advocates should bring notes or folders to the podium during oral argument. Some experts propose that the best attorneys walk to the podium with nothing. No notes. No paper. No folder. No binder. They suggest that delivering an argument with no notes demonstrates mastery of the material, exudes confidence, and relieves you from the temptation of reading anything, which is always a big mistake in moot court.

Others, however, including the authors of this text, propose that the advocate is better served by taking up a single triptych folder with the essentials for the argument neatly stacked inside. A well-organized folder gives you access to important information and reflects what real attorneys usually do in practice. The triptych can be purchased or inexpensively made in a few simple steps.

1. Get two standard manila folders. Use the standard color; the colored folders are too bright and distracting.
2. Cut off the index tab from one of the folders.
3. Place one side from the folder with the removed index tab inside the other. You should now have a tri-panel spread.
4. Staple the folders to each other at the top and bottom of the center panel. You should now have a triptych that closes right side, then left side down.
5. Staple only three pages to the folder, preferably in the following order:

   Center page: Introduction, theme, roadmap/bullet outline (refer to the box above), argument, closing

   Left page: Specific statutory provisions (with proper cites) and key facts. Best to write these facts in bullet form to avoid reading.

   Right page: A case matrix (only the key cases and holdings, plus a quick note about how to distinguish or discredit negative authority)

Suggested Triptych Folder Organization

Statute	Introduction	Case Matrix
Citation	Theme	(Make sure it is easy to read.)
	Roadmap	
Legally operative facts	Argument	
Needed cites to record	Closing	

Sample Case Matrix for Triptych

Case Name	Citation	Quick Facts Snapshot	Holding
Case Name	Citation	Quick Facts Snapshot	Holding
Case Name	Citation	Quick Facts Snapshot	Holding
Case Name	Citation	Quick Facts Snapshot	Holding

Don't forget to highlight, in two different colors, cases that help and cases that challenge your theme and theory so you can pull them easily when you are arguing. Also, list the cases on your matrix in alphabetical order so you can refer to them quickly when you are speaking. A table might be most helpful in helping you manage the cases quickly; just be sure to list only key words to help you with recall. You must do everything you can to resist the urge to write too much and potentially read from the podium.

PRACTICING YOUR ARGUMENT

You will never have "free time" to practice your oral argument. You are a law student, with briefs to do, cases to read, memos to write, study groups to attend, and family and friends to enjoy. You have so many demands on your time as a law student that you simply must be deliberate and intentional about blocking out time to practice your oral argument. (Chapter 12 discusses time management in more detail.) You must have a game plan. And you are lucky enough now to have access to technology that can help you with practices.

First, you should be active about locating and viewing YouTube videos of oral arguments. There are many, many student and professional oral arguments posted on the Internet for public consumption. Some are clearly better than others. But even the weak examples of oral argument are highly instructive. What is the advocate doing right? What is annoying? What is distracting? What is most effective? Also consider viewing videos with friends and classmates (if permitted by your instructor) to highlight the good, bad, and strange approaches to oral arguments.

> *I once had a team member who cocked his head whenever he was asked a question. Telling him about this for several weeks did no good. The first time he saw himself on camera, however, he immediately recognized the problem and was able to correct it quickly thereafter.*
>
> —Ronald J. Rychlak, Distinguished Professor of Law, University of Mississippi School of Law

Next, you should take advantage of technology to record and review your own practices. Luckily, most of us have smartphones, laptops, or tablets that will allow us to easily record ourselves. It is incredibly instructive to practice in front of a camera. You can easily record yourself with one of your own devices. Then you can play the self-recordings back for critique. Keep notes on your performance so you can improve with each subsequent practice. As you watch the recordings or review your live practices, however, use an evaluation tool to make sure you assess all of the different aspects of your presentation. One evaluation rubric is included in this chapter.

You should also spend as many practice rounds as you can in front of real people. Of course, confirm with your instructor that this is permitted under your school or classroom rules. If the rules allow you to do so, don't be shy about asking friends and family beyond the law school community to moot you. Even experienced advocates say they learn a great deal from practicing oral arguments in front of non-lawyers. Attorney Bruce Rogow, an expert in Constitutional Law who has argued 11 cases at the Supreme Court of the United States, says he regularly does some practices in front of lay people when he is preparing for his oral arguments. The extra practice and novel questions are helpful even to someone with vast experience and expertise.

> *Do dry run preparation before anyone who will listen. And let them ask questions. Often a lay person will hear something that is discordant and that can be helpful in preparation. The more often you get to be on your feet and hear yourself the more confident you will be when you get up for real.*
>
> —Bruce Rogow, Attorney and frequent advocate before the Supreme Court

You should also be mindful of time. Some students spend 30 minutes on every practice, even though they are given only 15 minutes for their arguments in class. This only increases the likelihood that they will not be able to effectively manage their time during the actual presentation. Limit the length of practice rounds to the amount of time allocated for the real round. And stay in "character" as you work through your arguments during the practices.

Below are some concrete guidelines to use in evaluating your own performance. You may also want to share with classmates and friends who volunteer to bench you.

PRACTICE CRITIQUE GUIDELINES FOR ORAL ARGUMENTS

Effectiveness

- ☑ Familiar with the record
- ☑ Understands legal issues
- ☑ Makes clear, concise points
- ☑ Builds effective analogies and distinctions with case law
- ☑ Cites to specific authority

Questions from the Bench

- ☑ Listens and responds to questions

Organization

- ☑ Has a prayer for relief
- ☑ Announces a clear theme of the case
- ☑ Articulates roadmap in distinct points

Forensics

- ☑ Speaks clearly and at a reasonable volume
- ☑ Uses eye contact, posture, and body language appropriately
- ☑ Acts professionally and doesn't talk over judge
- ☑ Listens attentively and politely when opponent speaks

DELIVERING YOUR ARGUMENT

Even though the bulk of your oral argument preparation occurs before your first "dress rehearsal," you must set aside some time to practice the delivery. A recent study by a communication analytics firm found that a speaker's "tone, appearance, and demeanor" were more salient than the actual content presented.[4]

[4] Anett Grant, *How to Command a Room Like Stephen Colbert,* Fast Company: Hit The Ground Running (Aug. 11, 2014), http://www.fastcompany.com/3034166/how-to-be-a-success-at-everything/how-to-command-a-room-like-steven-colbert.

Forensics

The term "forensics" refers to the art of argumentative presentations. Because you are not merely having a casual conversation with a friend, you should employ more formal rhetoric to make your argument more persuasive. While there may be particular stylistic preferences for your oral argument, always remember that this is not truly a "performance." That is, you are not acting. You are to stay in the "character" of an oral advocate both during all practices and on the big day. But you are not memorizing a speech. Such efforts will most likely fail under the pressure of the big day and frustrate your authenticity.

More important, the discussion points on style here are not meant to overshadow the importance of substance. Though this chapter and your instructor will address style format for the argument, you should expect to spend a lot of time preparing to tackle the substance. Preparation is still more important than natural speaking flair.

That said, one of the lawyering skills you are developing is the art of public speaking. Even if you plan to work as a transactional lawyer or in a JD-preferred field, you must learn how to present concise and cogent arguments orally. It is equally important to learn how to effectively field questions from judges, clients, or partners.

The same things that make you an effective communicator in interpersonal exchanges—good eye contact, excellent listening skills, appropriate tone, and responsiveness to questions—make you a successful oral advocate.

The Eyes Have It

The number one way that people understand that you are paying attention to them is through eye contact. However, several nervous students will avoid eye contact when they are faced with a panel of judges. Further, overreliance on notes will sometimes tempt students to read their outline and never look up to the bench. Some students actually roll their eyes or look up in frustration when they are faced with a challenging question. Use eye contact to convey confidence and interest with the bench. People assume that other people with shifty eyes or those who avert their gaze have something to hide. Don't hurt your credibility with the judges by refusing to look them in the eyes.

Also, when you are answering questions, remember that you are always speaking to a whole panel. Even if the judge sitting on the right side of the bench asks the questions, make sure that you make eye contact with all of the judges (even the one on the far left side) as you respond. If you are truly stumped and don't know how to answer a question, pause to think. But when you do so, do not look up to the heavens for divine intervention. That single move relays frustration and confusion. And it happens quite often in oral argument practice! Instead of looking bewildered, look at the podium for a second or two as you collect your thoughts. If it will not make you more nervous, you can also look at the panel as you sort through your response.

Listen Up

Just as eye contact demonstrates engagement and interest, so does attentive listening. It relays to others that what they say matters to you. Most class evaluation sheets, in fact, rank whether student advocates listen to questions posed during oral arguments. Of course, listening carefully to what the judges ask is impossible if you are so determined to plow through your roadmap and arguments that you talk over them. Always stop talking when a judge starts to speak. Always stop talking if a judge looks like he is going to speak. If, for some reason, you hear yourself talking when a judge is talking (perhaps he interrupted you), stop speaking even in midsentence.

If a judge asks a long, rambling question, do not interrupt him to try to clarify. Also listen for multi-part questions that require several answers. If in the course of fielding questions from the bench you forget one part or question, don't be afraid to ask for clarification. Asking for clarification shows that you actually care about the question and that you want to respond properly.

Voice Control

Use your own voice as a tool in oral argument. This means that in addition to the words that are coming out of your mouth, be aware of the way in which your responses are relayed. Do not sound adversarial. Do not sound defensive. Do not try to challenge the judge. Do not sound defeated. Be very careful not to answer in a sing-songy tone. Though you may think this is cute or deferential, it merely shows a lack of confidence. Uptalk—adding a rising intonation at the end of a declarative sentence so that it sounds like a question—is particularly harmful to your credibility. Use your voice to control the room. But don't go overboard and silence the bench, forgetting that this is a dialogue.

The best oral advocates sound like they are having a healthy conversation with the bench. Think about your professors who are effective when leading a class discussion, prompting good questions and answering them effectively. These professors not only know their substance, but they relay expertise by having a strong and confident voice pitch.

Questions, Anyone?

The distinguishing feature of oral arguments are the questions that come from the bench. Some students hope that the bench is "cold"—meaning no one asks any questions and the student is able to deliver a speech, sit down, and be done. That is possible, but rare. And it is actually more challenging than you might anticipate. The oral argument is designed to give the judges a chance to clarify or address issues that emerged from the briefs. It is another opportunity for you to persuade. A cold bench strips you of the ability to respond to any questions that judges have. It also robs you of the chance to showcase your ability to respond extemporaneously to questions. Finally, a cold bench can make even 15 minutes seem like forever. If you have a bench that asks nothing of you, be even more mindful of their facial expressions to see how you are doing. Also, slow down and walk through your roadmap step by step. Don't forget to CREAC on your feet to help the quiet judges see analogies and make distinctions.

Now for the hot bench. This is where the fun begins. Let's say you get through your introduction, but now the judges begin to chime in with questions. Remember, listen carefully to the questions and respond. Easiest point: Answer a yes-or-no question with a "yes" or "no." Then follow up with reasoning, facts, or case law.

Also, do not avoid a difficult answer to a difficult question. Judges can spot a staller and are likely to go in deeper on you for trying to be evasive. If the question is challenging, try to use facts or public policy to help your client.

Furthermore, remember that not all questions are alike. Some judges will hit you hard and fast with rapid questions. Sometimes the questions are direct and relatively simple to manage. Other questions are incredibly complex and multilayered. There are also "softball" questions that are meant to help you.[5] Judges want you to answer their questions. One former federal law clerk said: "The best oral arguments I saw were ones in which the attorneys effectively answered all of the judge's questions; they were not the ones in which the attorneys gave the best speeches."[6]

THE MOST COMMON MISTAKES

Rookie mistakes are expected from novices who may never have delivered a public speech, much less an oral argument rooted in exchange about complex legal issues. Although your advance preparation should allay some of your fears, do not take lightly the challenge of succeeding at oral argument. You should also be careful to avoid the most common mistakes that new law students make when they move from the desk to the podium. Review the common mistakes that follow and develop and commit to a plan now to avoid these traps.

"I can wing it!"

Short answer: No way. It does not matter if you won your high school's Lincoln-Douglas debates or placed every year at your undergraduate mock trial team. Oral arguments

[5] J. Stephen J. Dwyer, Leonard J. Feldman & Robert G. Nylander, *Effective Oral Arguments: Six Pitches, Five Do's, and Five Dont's from One Judge and Two Lawyers*, 33 Seattle U. L. Rev. 347, 349 (2010).

[6] Rachel Clark Hughey, *Effective Appellate Advocacy Before the Final Circuit: A Former Law Clerk's Perspective*, 11 J. App. Prac. & Process 401, 434 (2010).

belong to a very specialized system that rewards those who are prepared for the special rules and customs that govern it. Even though you have competing demands on your time, do not attempt to "wing" an oral argument.

It isn't reflective of the work you have devoted to a strong legal memo or brief. It is not good practice as you near graduation and representation of real clients. Finally, your reputation is too valuable and the law school community too small for you to turn in a substandard presentation. Take pride in the work that you are doing and commit to working on a thorough, impressive oral argument.

"I wrote a good brief, so I will just take it up and read that!"

One advocate notes, "If you come to court with a prepared script, you will quickly learn what it is like to be dropped from a plane without a parachute."[7] This analogy perfectly captures the irony of trying to read a script during oral argument. Even with a "cold" or nonresponsive bench, you cannot expect to follow a script once you face the bench. So the very step you took to be uber-prepared will backfire when the judges begin to throw questions, comments, and more questions at you. Do yourself a favor and don't even plan on reading a memo or brief. Instead, prepare an outline with easy-to-read bullet points that you can quickly scan for a prompt.

"I am going to win by showing everyone I'm smarter than the judge!"

The term "oral argument" is a bit of a misnomer. There is no place in the oral argument to argue with, bicker with, or challenge the judge.

The judge has the ability to interrupt you, pose hypotheticals, and take you away from your carefully crafted roadmap. It is your job, then, to reestablish control of the room through a professional, authoritative, well-reasoned argument. You can do so by being deferential but assertive. You will not win any points by challenging the judge. You will also lose credibility by personally attacking opposing counsel. Though you may know more about your specific case than anyone in the room, oral arguments are not won by advocates who can't control their egos.

[7] David M. Gersten, *Effective Brief Writing and Oral Argument: Gaining the Inside Track*, 81 Fla. B.J. 26, 28 (2007).

FINAL TIPS

The big day is here, and you finally get the chance to do your thing. Make it count. Oral arguments are usually the capstone of many first-year legal research and writing programs. Below are a few parting tips to make sure your oral argument is a success.

Look the Part

People will show up dressed professionally and excited to step into the role of "lawyer" for an hour or so. Because you want the focus to be on what you are saying rather than what you are wearing, dress appropriately and avoid anything flashy or novel. You are in graduate school and you understand what professional dress means. You also know that the latest trends on music videos and fashion pages are not the best attire for a mock courtroom experience. Leave the funky T-shirts under velour blazers at home. Save the leopard-print halter top for the club. Wear shoes that are comfortable but polished. Your dress is a means to help bolster your credibility.

> *There are two types of speakers, those who get nervous and those who are liars.*
>
> —Mark Twain

Relax

One of the biggest challenges for law students approaching their first oral argument is the overwhelming fear many have about public speaking. The fear of facing a panel of judges and the possibility of not knowing how to answer a question can be debilitating. Even new lawyers and seasoned advocates can be overwhelmed by anxiety associated with public speaking. And many people let their nerves get the best of them – therefore compromising the effectiveness of solid substantive arguments. If preparing for your first oral argument makes you feel like you have "butterflies in your stomach," you are not alone.

Release the pressure of perfection and commit yourself to doing your personal best. Further, recognize that it is okay to be nervous. Your charge, of course, is learning which steps are most effective to help you manage your anxiety and perform at your best level. In addition to the substantive practice on content and forensics, spend some time figuring out how to calm your nerves when you get anxious. There are several short breathing and meditation exercises online you can try to help you manage your anxiety about oral arguments. Ideally, you will learn how to channel your nervousness into excitement about the task at hand.

By the time you are ready to walk to the podium and present your oral argument, you will have no doubt devoted great time and energy to the preparation. But what if you still feel "butterflies" despite all of your preparation and enthusiasm?. Even if your hands shake and your voice quivers, those things will last only a moment. Take a breath and remember that you are there to demonstrate your mastery of the material. Remember that you are prepared. (Score!) And remember that this is not a real client. Consider this a very sophisticated game that everyone in the room—all advocates and judges—are eager to play.

Be You

Have your own style. Study the samples, but don't try to reinvent yourself. Polish your own style and make improvements. Even if you are incredibly impressed with the student advocate on YouTube who won the national competition, you cannot necessarily transform yourself into him. We each bring our own strengths, weaknesses, and personalities into the room with us. Striving to make self-improvements—even those rooted in the presentation of another person—is vastly different from striving to be someone else. The judges want to see you. Be your best self. But still be yourself.

Have Fun

Despite all of the anxiety that may be created by public speaking, competing for good grades, or making it on to moot court, try to enjoy the experience. Let's face it, only a handful of students are thrilled by the prospect of digging through the Bluebook for citation rules, but more than a few actually enjoy the oral argument exercises. This may be the capstone of your first-year law school experience. Have fun with it and give yourself credit for getting up there.

Even if you dread the thought of speaking in public, you may be surprised at how much fun you have once you get up to the podium and start speaking. You will certainly feel relief once the argument is over and you've done a good job. Your classmates are also anxious and excited. Ditto for your professor. Even the judges in the room—who may be upper-class students or local attorneys and judges—are volunteering their time to come bench you because they are invested in your success.

The one thing you can control now is to spend time preparing for success. To make sure this is an enjoyable experience for you, lay a proper foundation, build a strong roadmap, do not skimp on research, and budget time to prepare. Because you will be as prepared as possible, you might actually have fun. It's okay to enjoy yourself. And don't forget to smile!

COGNITIVE CORNER

Oral Argument

Consider the following questions about oral arguments:

1. Why is it important to develop a clear roadmap for your oral argument?
2. Why should you incorporate a theme into your oral argument?
3. What steps can you take to help you manage any anxiety you may feel about oral arguments?
4. Even if you don't plan to be a litigator, why is it important to develop oral advocacy skills?

Chapter 12

Managing the Story: Developing Effective Time Management Skills

"A goal without a plan is just a wish." —Antoine de Saint-Exupery, author

What good is a story that's never told? Sometimes compelling legal stories aren't presented to the judge because the advocate had poor time management skills. The following scenario illustrates the importance of developing effective time management skills while in law school.

You're a newly minted lawyer, all fresh and shiny from passing the bar. The boss, a short-tempered curmudgeon, gives you two weeks to write an appellate brief. In your legal writing class, you had an entire semester to complete this very same task. The idea that you might not be able to write a supreme court–worthy brief in two weeks sends you into a tailspin. How many days should you spend researching, outlining, writing, and revising? What if you fail? Will you be fired? Reprimanded?

This chapter helps quash these nagging voices and equips you with strategies for effectively managing any legal writing project.[1]

[1] Many of the recommendations contained in this chapter are adapted from Camille Lamar Campbell, *Timing Is Everything: Teaching Essential Time Management Skills for "Real-World" Legal Writing*, 22 PERSPECTIVES: TEACHING LEGAL RES. & WRITING 125 (2014).

THE IMPORTANCE OF TIME MANAGEMENT

Time is an advocate's most valuable commodity. As the introductory scenario suggests, in the world of law practice attorneys are frequently required to draft briefs under intense time constraints. Although you typically won't be asked to write a brief in two weeks as a law student, law school is the time to begin cultivating effective time management skills.

For law students, time management is more nuanced than a to-do list or simply vowing not to wait until the last minute to begin a writing assignment. Instead, begin thinking about time management as involving two discrete components: (1) project management and (2) stress management.

Project management requires a realistic assessment of the time you have to complete a project and a strategy for maximizing that time. Stress management acknowledges the psychological obstacles that can impede effective time management. Often, these psychological barriers are premised on an unrealistic view of the writing process. Writing is difficult. It's difficult for law students; it's difficult for advocates; it's even difficult for legal writing professors. Instead of embracing a writing assignment as an opportunity for improvement, some students erect psychological barriers that prevent them from becoming their best "writing selves." Students with poor stress management skills might tell themselves some version of the following.[2]

"I don't know what I want to say, so I can't start writing."

"I have to read more before I can start writing."

"I'm sad/lonely/upset/tired/bored/busy/confused, so I can't work."

"I don't have the right skills or resources to do this perfectly, so I won't do it at all."

These kinds of counterproductive statements almost always lead to procrastination. Procrastination is the nemesis of effective time management and "occurs when there's a significant time period between when people intend to do a job and when they actually do it."[3] Some forms of procrastination are obvious while others are more subtle. Take a look at the following examples from the procrastination hall of fame.[4]

- Opting to complete low-priority tasks first, ones that aren't immediately pressing. The sudden urge to complete low-priority tasks begins any time you think about the assignment.
- Consistently saying "yes" to unimportant tasks that others ask you to do and filling your time with these tasks instead of beginning the assignment.

---

[2] Sheila M. Reindl, *A Procrastinator's Guide to Writing: Reconsidering Beliefs that Keep Us from Engaging with Our Work* (Bureau of Study Counsel, Harvard Univ., 2015), http://bsc.harvard.edu/files/procrastinators_guide_to_writing_ revised_august_2012.pdf; *see also Overcoming Procrastination*, MINDTOOLS: TIME MANAGEMENT BLOG, http://www.mindtools.com/pages/article/newHTE_96.htm (last visited Nov. 9, 2016) (internal quotations omitted).

[3] *Id.*

[4] *Id.*

- Convincing yourself that you can catch up on a neglected task by spending an unrealistic amount of time on the same task in the future.
- Failing to acknowledge the immediacy of a deadline or having only a vague awareness of it.

If you recognize yourself in some of these scenarios, don't be discouraged. The key to managing stress is acknowledging its existence and taking concrete steps to move past the psychological barriers described in this section. Implementing the strategies described next will give you the confidence to begin improving your time management skills.

EFFECTIVE TIME MANAGEMENT STRATEGIES

The three strategies described in this section are illustrative, not exhaustive and will give you a manageable approach for tackling any writing project.

Strategy #1: Make a Written Plan

At first blush, this first strategy may seem obvious. However, your plan should be written for three reasons. First, a written plan is a tangible sign of your commitment. Second, a written plan is a visual reminder, especially when prominently displayed, of your progress and a powerful motivator should you encounter obstacles or be tempted to procrastinate. Third, a written plan puts the assignment squarely in the center of your consciousness, forcing you to begin thinking about and planning for its completion.

To write an effective time management plan, you'll need to do the following: (1) determine the net completion time, (2) break the assignment into intermediate tasks, and (3) devise a strategy for completing intermediate tasks.

Determine the Net Completion Time

How much actual time you have to complete the assignment is called the net completion time. Calculate the net completion time by selecting a date to start the assignment and then recording that date on a print or electronic calendar or organizer. Next record the due date and any intermediate deadlines assigned by your professor (e.g., the due date of a research log, annotated outline, first draft). Now count the number of days between the start date and the date of any final and intermediate deadlines. This calculation is your gross completion time.

To calculate the net completion time, subtract the number of days that you won't be able to work on the assignment—because of known or unknown contingencies—from the gross completion time. Known contingencies are events such as other classes, family and other social obligations, leisure activities, and hobbies. Acknowledging and honoring these kinds of obligations will prevent burnout. You're a person, not a robot, and your time management plan should reflect this reality. You'll also need to plan for unforeseen contingencies such as illness, computer malfunctions, or other unanticipated emergencies. What follows is one student's calculation of the net completion time for a particular assignment.

Brief Writing Assignment

Assigned:	February 29
Assignment Due:	April 4
Start Date:	March 2
Gross Completion Time:	Approximately 4½ weeks/34 days
Net Completion Time:	**3½ weeks/25 days** [St. Patrick's Day; torts midterm; sister's engagement party; possible illness (flu affecting the entire section)]

Notice two things. First, the student has adjusted the gross completion time by nine days because of a holiday, an important deadline in another class, an important family obligation, and what appears to be a high likelihood of contracting a contagious illness. Second, the student has conceived of the time in days instead of weeks. Conceptualizing time in days instead of weeks makes breaking the assignment into smaller, more easily scheduled pieces much easier. Furthermore, thinking of the net completion time in days minimizes the risk of procrastination by reinforcing the assignment's limited time frame.

Break the Assignment into Intermediate Tasks

Armed with the net completion time, you're now ready to execute the next step: breaking the assignment into intermediate tasks. Noted writing expert Anne Lamont describes this crucial time management step as tackling a writing assignment "bird by bird."

To begin tackling an assignment "bird by bird," ask yourself what discrete intermediate tasks are necessary to complete the project. Of course, how you answer this question depends on many factors. For example, some students might be guided by their past writing experiences.

Let's assume that those prior experiences suggest the need to research, read, and synthesize research results; complete some rudimentary form of an outline; complete at least one draft; and assemble citations. Another student might identify intermediate tasks in relation to preliminary assignments identified in the syllabus. For example, if the professor requires students to submit rough drafts, case charts, or outlines, then that student might elect to use those deadlines to brainstorm intermediate tasks. If you're unsure about how to identify intermediate tasks or if you simply want feedback, ask your professor for guidance.

No matter which identification technique you use, be specific. The more detailed your description of the intermediate task, the more likely you'll be to appreciate how long it will take you to perform the particular task. For example, indicating that you will "outline the arguments" won't help you appreciate subtasks such as categorizing cases based on issues, determining which cases to use for each issue, and creating an annotated outline.

Lastly, don't forget to identify intermediate tasks such as proofreading, revising, and cite checking. Making sure to account for these ancillary tasks ensures a polished final product. Most attorneys will tell you that they *never* have enough time to write a brief and that they *always* feel that the perfect sentence, paragraph, or insightful observation about a particular case would magically appear if only they had a bit more time. However, these very same attorneys know the importance of creating an illusion for the reader that the particular writing assignment was completed weeks before the actual deadline. Savvy writers create this illusion by avoiding obvious proofreading and citation errors. In short, even if the assignment isn't perfect or even if you didn't fully adhere to your time management plan, *always* incorporate time for proofreading and cite checking. Even if you think the brief is crap, make it pretty crap. Consider the following evolving time management plan.

Brief Writing Assignment

Assigned:	**February 29**
Assignment Due:	**April 4**
Start Date:	**March 2**
Gross Completion Time:	**Approximately 4½ weeks/34 days**
Net Completion Time:	**3½ weeks/25 days** [St. Patrick's Day; torts midterm; sister's engagement party; possible illness (flu affecting the entire section)]

Intermediate Tasks

- **Research Tasks**
  - Eleventh Circuit case law
  - Factually similar Fifth Circuit case law
- **Synthesize Case Law**
  - Chart & synthesize relevant cases
  - Outline rule structure

- **Determine Issues**
  - Scrutinize facts
  - Identify number of issues
  - Brainstorm arguments
  - Brainstorm theory/theme
- **Outlining**
  - Sort cases based on issues
  - Determine which cases to use for each issue
  - Create annotated outline
- **Writing Tasks/ Small Scale**
  - Draft point headings
  - Draft argument for issue 1
  - Draft argument for issue 2
- **Writing Tasks/Large Scale**
  - Draft statement of facts
  - Draft introduction & conclusion
- **Revising/Editing**
  - Create citation matrix
  - Proofread argument for issue 1
  - Proofread argument for issue 2
  - Eliminate excess words

Note how many intermediate steps are required to write one brief. Also note how each intermediate task can be further subdivided into additional intermediate tasks. Just imagine if this student had lumped all of these discrete tasks under the general term "complete brief" or "research law"? If the student hadn't specifically described these intermediate tasks, then he or she wouldn't have any idea about the real number of intermediate tasks required to complete the project.

Devise a Strategy for Completing Intermediate Tasks

Strategizing the completion of intermediate tasks can be particularly challenging because each student's writing process is unique. Unlike the process of baking a cake where each intermediate step has a definite sequential order, the writing process typically reflects individual preferences. For example, some students approach the writing process in a linear way; they *always* attempt some sort of outline before writing. But other students *never* start with an outline and use a "brain dump" or free-writing method where they jot down random thoughts and impressions.

Other students are a bit more systematic, beginning the writing process where they feel most comfortable, where they feel the least comfortable, or with the task that they think will take the most or least amount of time. In short, avoid a one-size-fits-all approach, and opt for one that's tailored to your individual preferences.

Time is the next consideration. And your strategy should also include a realistic time estimate for each intermediate task. Formulating a realistic assessment is strikingly similar to the process of computing the net completion time for the project. For example, your strategy should account for known and unknown contingencies and be specifically described. Furthermore, estimating a completion time in terms of hours or minutes will exponentially increase the likelihood of fitting intermediate tasks into a hectic schedule. Consider the following plan.

Brief Writing Assignment

Assigned:	**February 29**
Assignment Due:	**April 4**
Start Date:	**March 2**
Gross Completion Time:	**Approximately 4½ weeks/34 days**
Net Completion Time:	**3½ weeks/25 days** [St. Patrick's Day; torts midterm; sister's engagement party; possible illness (flu affecting the entire section)]

Intermediate Tasks

- **Research Tasks**
  - Eleventh Circuit case law
  - Factually similar Fifth Circuit case law
- **Synthesize Case Law**
  - Chart & synthesize relevant cases
  - Outline rule structure
- **Determine Issues**
  - Scrutinize facts
  - Identify number of issues
  - Brainstorm arguments
  - Brainstorm theory/theme
- **Outlining**
  - Sort cases based on issues
  - Determine which cases to use for each issue
  - Create annotated outline
- **Writing Tasks/Small Scale**
  - Draft point headings
  - Draft argument for issue 1
  - Draft argument for issue 2
- **Writing Tasks/Large Scale**
  - Draft statement of facts
  - Draft introduction & conclusion

- **Revising/Editing**
  - Create citation matrix
  - Proofread argument for issue 1
  - Proofread argument for issue 2
  - Eliminate excess words

<u>**Completion Strategy**</u>

Week One

Monday

- Research Eleventh Circuit case law on first issue **(1-2 hours)**
- Read cases for Torts
- Work out
- Skim Eleventh Circuit cases for relevancy **(30 min–1 hour)**

Tuesday

- Meeting with professor re: research questions
- Read and chart ½ relevant Eleventh Circuit cases re: first issue **(2-3 hours)**

Wednesday

- Read and chart other ½ Eleventh Circuit cases re: first issue **(2-3 hours)**
- Review case file **(30 min–1 hour)**

Thursday

- Review case file **(30 min–1 hour)**
- Meet with Con Law study group
- Research factually similar Fifth Circuit case law on first issue **(1 hour)**

Friday

- Read and chart Eleventh Circuit cases re: second issue **(2-3 hours)**
- Happy Hour

Saturday

- Sister's engagement party (all-day)

Sunday

- Synthesize case law re: first issue **(2-3 hours)**

This student's strategy is to complete various intermediate tasks in two- to three-hour blocks. Also notice that the student has not indicated *when* she will complete a particular intermediate task, only that a particular task will be completed on a particular day. Another student might be even more specific, opting to research relevant Eleventh Circuit law from 8:00 am to 11:00 am on Monday. Yet another student might prefer to work only in one-hour increments or in four- to six-hour increments.

Don't be afraid to experiment with different completion strategies. The more you experiment, the more adept you'll become at creating a plan that meets your individualized needs and that won't languish in an unopened computer file.

Strategy #2: Develop an Accountability System

Much of what you have just read about time management sounds good in the abstract, doesn't it? However, people who struggle with time management often have trouble implementing their time management plans. Often students will make written time management plans only to leave them in unopened files on their computers or on the most obscure part of their desks, where the plans never again see the light of day. Failure to adhere to the plan often leads to a cycle of shame, detachment, and anxiety that ultimately culminates in more procrastination and avoidance behaviors. To break this cycle and remain committed to your plan, you must hold yourself accountable. What follows are some suggestions for developing an accountability system.

Trick yourself into compliance. For example, you might create a system of healthy rewards such as a movie, dinner at a favorite restaurant, or similar treat each time you complete an intermediate deadline.

Find a time management partner. Select someone whose personality strikes the appropriate balance between kindness and firmness. Kindness is important because you don't want someone who will make you feel like a loser if you fall short of your time management goals. Firmness is important because you don't need a partner who won't hold you to any kind of standard, blithely accepting any reason for noncompliance.

Find a time management mentor. In addition to providing a basic system for accountability, a time management mentor is a person proficient in time management who can offer concrete time management strategies. Mentors can come from a variety of sources and can run the gamut from second- or third-year students recommended by your professors to attorneys actively engaged in law practice who you encounter in your work or extracurricular experiences.

Use technology. Time management apps such as Things, AwesomeNote, and Alarmed are widely available on the Internet. Other free resources such as the Pomodoro Technique (www.pomodorotechnique.com) and Mytomatoes (www.mytomatoes.com) allow users to break intermediate tasks into timed segments.

Strategy #3: Visualize the Finish Line

Visualization harnesses the power of the subconscious by focusing your attention on the benefits or rewards of a particular action instead of on likely obstacles. For example, you might think of how good you'll feel when your classmates are pulling all-nighters and gnashing their teeth the day before the brief is due, while you're at

home watching television, anxiety-free. Admittedly, this imagery may be a bit obnoxious, but the point is this: Select an image of success that motivates you to work through inevitable obstacles. The following image is a personal favorite.

It captures the sense of accomplishment after successfully implementing a time management plan. Pick an image that motivates you and then harness the power of the subconscious to obliterate any obstacles. Now, go forth, and exercise those time management muscles.

Chapter 13

Modifying the Story for the Workplace: Guidelines for Strong Letters and Professional E-mails

"I have received no more than one or two letters in my life that were worth the postage."—Henry David Thoreau

Letter writing is not a lost art. But it is certainly reimagined. In the age of e-mails, text messages, group chats, social media, the art of written communication has changed—and not always for the better. People have become less practiced in communicating their wants and needs through written communication. Hashtags, GIFs, and emojis have muddied the water. But as the quote from Thoreau indicates, the "good old days" of letter writing weren't as good as they seemed. Even with old-fashioned pen and paper, people sometimes wasted the space provided to them in a traditional letter.

In the past, a primary challenge of drafting an effective letter was overcoming the tendency to obfuscate our meaning with formalities. Today, we must be careful not to become too informal in our written communication with clients and partners. We must also work hard to make our correspondence effective and individualized. Form letters are a fact of life, but as professional writers and storytellers, lawyers must be mindful of the time and money spent drafting communication.

Effective advocates should actively incorporate effective storytelling techniques into their shorter written products. In the workplace, storytelling techniques can be modified and implemented to help you achieve your desired goal. This chapter addresses the most common letter-writing vehicles attorneys use to communicate. It focuses on the demand letter; it also offers advice about how to draft professional e-mails. In addition to covering the mechanics of drafting professional correspondence, it examines these items through the lens of storytelling.

A change in form doesn't mean that you should abandon your efforts to develop a consistent message as a legal writer. Chapter 4 described a theory as a unifier that brings your legal argument together. And just as your trial brief benefits from a central theory and theme that appeal to both reason and emotion, your workplace correspondence is more effective with a central theory. Like judges who may need motivation to rule in your favor, workplace readers (whether attorneys, clients, or prospective employers) also need motivation to agree with you.

theory

For the purposes of this chapter, we will focus on implicitly incorporating a theory into your correspondence. The "theme" here will be supplied by the details and supporting facts in your correspondence. The correspondence is typically less formal and does not require an explicit announcement of a theme. But the central legal storytelling components that inform effective advocacy—logos, pathos, and ethos—are critical in even the shortest correspondence. Readers want it all: They want you to create a logical argument rooted in a rule of law. They want subtle emotional appeals. And they want you to be credible. A tall order for a single letter.

By deliberately incorporating a theory in your correspondence, you can build effective workplace communication. Writing persuasively and integrating storytelling principles will help you secure the opposition's agreement, the client's consent, or a job offer.

WHAT'S YOUR MOTIVATION?

Remember the elevator speech? That term was used in Chapter 2 to describe the theory of the case. It is the unifier that you can relay in under a minute to explain why your client should prevail. The theory also connects your client's mission to societal values, which are often reflected in the prevailing rule. When you are drafting correspondence, the theory connects the purpose of the correspondence to broader values. In each of the sections that follow, we connect the dots for you in an example to show how an effective legal letter writer is motivated by a clear understanding of a theory that is being relayed to the reader.

THE DEMAND LETTER

The demand letter is a staple of the correspondence that often occurs between opposing parties. Depending on the complexity of the legal dispute at issue, the demand letter can be as simple as a call for the return of an apartment rental deposit or as involved as the termination of an advertising campaign.

No matter how simple or complex the actual demand, however, the key component is to relay *clearly* and *convincingly* the steps you need taken. The theory for compliance is reinforced by everything from your basis for demand (such as contractual or statutory) and your word choice. Sometimes, the "demand" is that another party take steps (repair the tenant's washing machine as specified in the contract). Other times, the "demand" is that another party cease certain behavior (do not park in an assigned parking space as specified in the homeowner's regulations).

The demand letter is adversarial in nature. It is needed when there is an unresolved conflict between the parties that has not yet required intervention through litigation. A persuasive, effective demand letter can eliminate the need for subsequent litigation—which is always expensive, time-consuming, and stressful. The organization for the demand letter follows a four-part format that succinctly captures the objective.

1. An introductory paragraph that states the purpose of the letter
2. Presentation of persuasive facts that support your purpose
3. Presentation of persuasive law that supports your position with an application of the law to the facts
4. Concluding statement that clearly states demands and consequences for noncompliance

The demand letter should clearly relay the theory that animates the demand. If the issue is equity, it should emerge from a simple reading of the letter. If the demand is a legal mandate, this should be clear from a simple reading of the letter. Because the letter should convey a message to readers without more explanation, it must be organized. Before you start drafting, be sure that you understand your client's goals.

There are a few other important factors to consider:

Write a Strong Opening. Remember that you are not writing a murder mystery. Get to the point quickly in the opening paragraph by identifying yourself and the exact issue in dispute. Relay the demand and summarize the basis for the demand.

Choose Your Facts Wisely. You need to keep the reader engaged by presenting the most compelling facts for your client. Follow the basic principles of storytelling and relay facts in a narrative order. But you must also cut and choose the facts that are persuasive and supportive of your position.

Apply the Law to the Facts. Once you have identified and relayed all of the legally operative facts that carry an emotional appeal consistent with your theme, explain the controlling law. Make sure you state the law accurately and persuasively; make it easy for the reader by applying the law to the facts.

Advocate. Have you made a convincing case rooted in facts and law that would compel your opponent to meet your demands? Would a neutral reader think that your demands are fair and appropriate? Have you attempted to be a zealous advocate on behalf of your client to achieve a positive resolution?

Consider Your Audience. Who is the recipient of your letter? Although you are writing with a unifying theme and a clear purpose, consider your audience. Are you addressing another attorney? An experienced business executive? A college student? The audience will dictate the sophistication and complexity that characterize your letter. It will also govern how much more additional explanatory material is needed to make the letter easy to understand.

> *In legal writing, as in any form of communication, tone is crucial. What you say is no more important than how you say it.*
> —Savannah Blackwell, *Bar Association of San Francisco Bulletin* contributor

Remember Your Tone. The tone should be firm, not unsure or uneasy. It should still be professional. Even the most serious demands are only weakened by shallow threats or unprofessional writing. Name-calling is strictly off limits. Threats are also banned.

Clarity. You cannot be too explicit in relaying your demands. You don't want the reader to read the demand letter and ask: *What am I supposed to do now?*

Format. Don't neglect the basic mechanics of letter-writing. Is the demand letter printed on firm letterhead? Is the letter properly dated? Is there a subject line? Is it signed? Does it indicate that you have sent a copy of the letter to the client?

Compliance. Also, make sure the essentials are covered. If you need money, make it easy for the reader to comply by telling them when, where, and how to convey the money.

Good: *Please return the rental deposit immediately.*
Better: *Deliver $500 in the form of a cashier's check by certified mail to 1234 Ivory Street by 5 p.m. EST April 15, 2024.*
Ridiculous: *Return the money or else!!!*
Do you see the difference?

Don't Make Baseless Threats. Although it is not improper to raise the possibility of civil litigation if the demands are not met, demand letters do implicate ethical rules that could expose lawyers to sanctions. For instance, a lawyer cannot threaten criminal charges to obtain an advantage in a civil dispute.

E-MAILS IN THE WORKPLACE

Leave the emojis on your cellphone. That's the short and sweet lesson you must learn about drafting shorter communication—such as letters or e-mails—in the legal workplace. Based on the speed and ease of transmitting letters online, the reality is most attorneys will spend a great deal of time communicating through e-mails. The frequency with which attorneys write e-mails, however, does not impact the standards that should be used in drafting professional communication—no matter the medium.

There is absolutely no room for informal, cutesy, or inappropriate e-mails within the law office culture. Your client doesn't want to see them. Your partner doesn't want to see them. And opposing counsel doesn't want to see them.

To help you appreciate the differences between a typical e-mail and a workplace e-mail for the legal office, compare the following two examples.

Personal E-mail

From: Marta Gomez

Sent: May 30, 2024

To: Kayleigh Champion

Subject: ← No subject here

Hey there! I know that you said you wanted to check out the "Greatest Hits" album from Prince. Actually bought a copy and it is everything!!!! ☺☺☺

Exclamation marks relay excitement on a personal level, but they can appear unprofessional. The emojis create visual interest. But happy faces aren't appropriate in workplace e-mails.

That's one bad boy.
XXOO

Colloquialisms are okay among friends, but not among coworkers. Ditto for "hugs and kisses."

Professional E-mail

From: Marta Gomez

Sent: June 1, 2024

To: Glenn Jameson

Subject: Research re: Noncompete Agreements ←

> Subject field helps keep sender and receiver organized.
>
> Note that relevant attachments are also included and clearly labeled.

Attachment: Patel v. Juste.doc ←

Dear Glenn,

You asked me to research the law on noncompete agreements under Georgia law.

I found that the noncompete provisions in employment contracts have to be reasonable in terms of time, territory, and scope. More important, Georgia recently adopted a "blue pencil" rule that allows courts to correct certain provisions that may otherwise be unreasonable. ←

> This e-mail begins by identifying the legal issue the writer was asked to review and a brief answer.

A copy of the Georgia Supreme Court case summarizing the change is attached. Please let me know if you have any questions or additional issues you would like to be addressed.

Thank you, ←

> Professional tone is maintained throughout. Even in closing. (Not Love, Yours Truly, or XXOO.)

Marta

This message contains information that may be confidential and privileged. If you are not the intended recipient, you may not copy, use, or forward the information contained in this message. If you have received this message in error, please delete. ←

> Use the automated signature block to attach a confidentiality warning to your e-mail. Your firm will likely have standard language you can use.

Though not always persuasive, the e-mail is an extremely common tool for attorneys to communicate with each other in today's culture. In one recent survey, 92 percent of graduates said that they use substantive e-mails (as opposed to briefs and letters) to communicate with their clients.[1] When drafting e-mails for the workplace—whether to opposing counsel, your supervisor, or a client—remember that e-mail messages are easily shared.

That means taking extra steps to be professional. Do not import the e-mail practices you use in your personal communication. Non-negotiable rules: Avoid WRITING IN ALL CAPS (comparable to yelling) and using emojis (comparable to texting your bestie). Another good rule of thumb with e-mails: Keep your messages short. If an e-mail is too long, people may not read it. Your message will never be relayed if it is not received.

COVER LETTERS

Cover letters are another example of persuasive writing. Though you may not need to draft a cover letter in class, you will likely be asked to produce a cover letter for your summer internship or job placement. A compelling cover letter should persuade the reader to hire you—or at the very least to give you an interview.

Cover letters should not merely repeat the information in your resume; after all, most cover letters will be accompanied by your resume. Cover letters should also move beyond merely restating the job description. The best cover letters employ the techniques described in this chapter that encourage you to develop a unifying theory in your document. After reading the job description and reviewing your resume, what is the narrative pull that should compel someone to hire you?

Do all of your work experiences, school interests, and personal commitments point to someone who is a proven leader? Are you committed to social justice? Do you have a passion for work with abused animals? Whatever the unifying theory is about your energy and expertise, relay that through the cover letter.

You may need to brainstorm with a trusted mentor to help you identify a unifying theory. It may take some time. For instance, if you have experience working with soldiers struggling with PTSD, foster children, members of the LGBT community, and hurricane survivors, it may be difficult to develop a unifying theory for your work history. But consider what these various groups have in common. One possible unifier may be that each group represents a vulnerable community. The theory of showing a

[1] Kristen Konrad Robbins-Tiscione, *From Snail Mail to Email: The Traditional Legal Memorandum in the Twenty-First Century*, 58 J. Legal Educ. 32, 32 (2008).

work history focused on vulnerable populations is one possible *common ground* you can thread in your cover letter to bring together diverse experiences.

Your professor or staff in the Career and Professional Development Office will probably have a standard cover letter format to address the technical aspects and organization, but it is up to you to make the cover letter personal and persuasive. A simple web search will also yield hundreds of format examples you can follow. Do not merely cut and paste the forms and substitute your own name. That is likely copying a movie review and blindly substituting one movie name for another. There is a big difference between the review for *Everything Everywhere All At Once* and the review for a *Mission Impossible* movie, right? There is also a big difference between any form letter you get from the web or career services and one personalized to reflect you.

Take the time to study your resume, reflect on your experience—whether it is for pay, volunteer hours, or social interests—and develop a unifying theory that will amplify your cover letter. This extra step can make your letter stand out from all of the others—a critical step in this very competitive market.

A COUPLE OF CAVEATS

Take Time to Edit with Human Eyes

Even though we have shared this advice in multiple places within this text, it bears repeating: Do not rely on the computer to do your editing for you. Take the time—even in a brief letter or e-mail—to edit the material with human eyes. Spell check can only do so much. Grammar checkers on laptops are also limited. Furthermore, there is no suitable technological substitute for the tone relayed through sentence structure, word choice, and decisions about what to place in your copy. Finally, in shorter copy, a careless typo will likely be even more apparent. The reader will doubt your credibility, and your bargaining position will be weakened. This will hurt you if you are seeking a demand for a client or a job interview for yourself.

Forever Is a Long, Long Time

In his book *So You've Been Publicly Shamed*, Jon Ronson makes a critical point about the ways in which the Internet era has transformed human frailty.[2] Thanks to e-mail, blogs, and social media, a simple mistake between two parties can go "viral" and end up in front of millions of people. Instead of being limited to one's immediate community, mistakes that end up on the computer (such as unprofessional e-mail rants) can

[2] *See* Jon Ronson, So You've Been Publicly Shamed (2015).

reach a very wide and often permanent audience. Ronson describes today's climate as a "great renaissance of public shaming" fueled by social media mobs and e-mail chains. Before hitting Send, remember that e-mails are easily shared and hard to erase. (Even after the pesky Delete key is activated.) But public shaming isn't the only negative consequence lawyers face for unprofessional communication. There are also sanctions.

Some lawyers have been hit with bar violations for drafting unprofessional e-mails. For instance, the Florida Supreme Court suspended a lawyer for rude conduct based on e-mails he sent to opposing counsel. The e-mails included personal attacks, called the opposing counsel disingenuous, and said his motions were "laughable and scurrilous."[3] Another attorney from New Mexico was sanctioned for unprofessional behavior stemming from an e-mail claiming a judge and opposing counsel were "bosom buddies."[4] Such conduct clearly crosses the line and moves into unprofessional conduct. Because these attorneys hit Send on insulting, unprofessional e-mails, they jeopardized their practice and were seriously disciplined.

You Are Still a Professional

Writing a brief to the court necessarily invokes a level of formality and professionalism. The structure of the brief, the court rules, and the very fact that you are writing to a judge will put you on notice that a high level of professionalism is required. With less formal documents, however, the risk is that you will write in a less professional tone.

Make a deliberate effort to be polite and professional in your letters and e-mails. One common caveat is to imagine anything you've written being splashed across the front page of the *New York Times*. In today's culture, you might imagine it popping up on a first hit on Google. Although the format may be less formal, your professional and ethical duties as an attorney have not disappeared. Letter writing is not a lost art, but it has changed. A commitment to professionalism and the incorporation of narrative techniques can make those changes for the better.

---

[3] Debra Cassens Weiss, *Lawyer Who "Incessantly" Disparaged Opposing Counsel Gets Two-Year Suspension*, A.B.A. J. (Nov. 25, 2013), http://www.abajournal.com/news/article/lawyer_who_incessantly_disparaged_opposing_counsel_gets_two-year_suspension/.

[4] Emil J. Kiehne, *Calling Judge a "Drunken Idiot on the Bench," Among Other Things, Earns Attorney Sanction from NM Supreme Court*, N.M. App. L. Blog (June 24, 2013), http://nmappellatelaw.com/calling-judge-a-drunken-idiot-on-the-bench-among-other-things-earns-attorney-sanction-from-the-new-mexico-supreme-court/.

COGNITIVE CORNER

Letters and E-mails

Consider the following questions about drafting professional letters and e-mails:

1. Did you consider a unifying theory when drafting your demand letter?
2. Would your letter appear persuasive and fair to a neutral party?
3. Why is it so important to be professional in e-mails?
4. How can you take steps to ensure that your shorter correspondence is professional and persuasive?

Part IV

Sample Briefs

IN THE DISTRICT COURT OF DENVER COUNTY
2ND JUDICIAL CIRCUIT
CIVIL DIVISION

HAILEY GIDEON, Plaintiff, vs. FIRST UNION ANGLICAN CHURCH OF COLORADO, Defendant.	No. 16-CV-1534-HLA

DEFENDANT'S BRIEF IN SUPPORT OF SUMMARY JUDGMENT

The advocate uses Baskerfield Old Face, a traditional serif font, to subtly communicate the client's theory and theme.

Thomas J. Clark
Attorney for Defendant
3200 Divine Way
Boulder, Colorado 55523
(303) 315-4916

TABLE OF CONTENTS

> The Table of Contents gives the judge a comprehensive snapshot of the advocate's story.

> Plot headings (1) outline the plot of the emerging legal story, (2) subdivide the SOF into easy-to-read digestible chunks and (3) subtly introduce the judge to the advocate's theory and theme.

> Notice the difference between the defendant's argument section and the plaintiff's argument section. Unlike the plaintiff's brief, which has three arguments, the defendant makes a strategic choice to present only its strongest argument. This approach simplifies the argument in the ways discussed in Chapter 3.

INTRODUCTION

The introduction is analogous to an opening statement at a trial and to the summary of argument in an appellate brief. Its goal is to grab the court's attention by succinctly presenting the client's theory and theme.

The First Union Anglican Church of Colorado is one of state's largest providers of social services to homeless children. Consistently ranked as one of the "Top Ten Best Places to Work in Colorado," the Church is proud of its youth ministers who are role models to the homeless children they serve. Colorado's employment at-will doctrine permits the Church to end its relationship with employees like the plaintiff whose sexual practices not only violate its religious teachings but jeopardize its mission of community service.

The writer uses context to personalize an institutional client.

The advocate avoids using the plaintiff's name to dehumanize her. Dehumanizing the opposing party is a soft-sell persuasive technique.

The Church demonstrated its intent to maintain Colorado's long-standing presumption of at-will employment by including a prominently placed at-will employment disclaimer in its employment handbook. That at-will employment disclaimer conspicuously conditioned the availability of a pretermination hearing to employees embroiled in genuine workplace disputes.

Notice the second function of the introduction, which is to summarize the advocate's arguments and to highlight its theme: Protection, not Perfection.

A reasonable juror evaluating the facts of this case could reach only one conclusion: The handbook does not create an unconditional right. Instead, pretermination hearings are reserved for employees involved in genuine workplace disputes, not for those who would use them as a forum to criticize the Church's religious teachings.

Given Colorado court's long-standing adherence to the employment at-will doctrine, a reasonable juror could conclude only that plaintiff was an at-will employee whom the Church had the legal authority to release from her employment.

STATEMENT OF FACTS

As a space-saving measure, this SOF does not include any citations. However, your professor or managing partner will typically require their inclusion.

Following the widely publicized scandals of the late 1990s involving inappropriate sexual conduct between clergy members and the children whom they were entrusted to protect, the Church amended its employee handbook. The handbook advises employees that they cannot separate their personal personas from their workplace personas, cautioning that "[w]hat happens at a secretary's desk, in an administrator's office, or around the table in the cafeteria can affect the Church's ability to discharge its mission of public service." The morals clause echoes this language, warning employees that "behavior . . . in violation of Church teachings . . . is particularly offensive to the Church and will not be tolerated."

The level of detail about this section of the handbook emphasizes the writer's theme of the case: a religious employer's right to make personnel decisions based on its religious teachings.

Hired as a Role Model for Homeless Children

Plaintiff received a copy of the amended handbook on her first day of work. She also signed a form acknowledging that she had read, understood, and would comply with the Church's employment policies and religious teachings. During his deposition, the plaintiff's immediate supervisor described the relationship between the Church's fundamental mission of service and its morals clause:

Q. Does the morals clause require perfect employees?

A. Absolutely not. It only requires that counselors deserve a child's respect.

Q. What happens when a counselor loses a child's respect?

A. You lose them to the streets.

Notice the effective use of detail, a soft-sell persuasive technique discussed in Chapter 7, to justify the client's need to strictly enforce its policies.

An Admitted Violation of the Morals Clause

Plaintiff admits that she was aware of the morals clause and that she violated the Church's religious teachings. No discharged employee has ever received a pretermination hearing for violating the morals clause. The progressive discipline policy, including the provision mentioning pretermination hearings, provides that it is designed to "foster a fair and equitable resolution of workplace disputes." Plaintiff concedes that the crux of her dispute with the Church is based on what she describes as "its prehistoric teachings on premarital sex"

The advocate uses the soft-sell persuasive technique of juxtaposition to subtly diffuse the opponent's argument about how the provision should be interpreted.

An At-Will Employment Disclaimer Below the Plaintiff's Signature

The acknowledgment page is the only section of the handbook requiring employees to affirmatively acknowledge compliance with their signatures. Plaintiff signed the handbook on her first day of employment.

A half inch below the plaintiff's signature is the following phrase: "I ACKNOWLEDGE THAT THIS EMPLOYMENT HANDBOOK IS NOT A CONTRACT OF EMPLOYMENT AND THAT MY EMPLOYMENT IS AT-WILL." This phrase is the only portion of the disclaimer written in all capital letters. By signing, plaintiff acknowledged that: "AT-WILL EMPLOYMENT MEANS THAT A CHURCH EMPLOYEE DOES NOT HAVE AN UNLIMITED CONTRACTUAL RIGHT TO PROGRESSIVE DISCIPLINE PRIOR TO TERMINATION." Plaintiff admits that (1) she selectively read only certain portions of the handbook and (2) did not read the handbook in its entirety until after she was released from employment.

The plaintiff subsequently filed suit claiming that the Church's employment handbook created an unlimited contractual right to a pretermination hearing. After several unsuccessful negotiation attempts, the Church filed this summary judgment motion.

ARGUMENT

The Church Is Entitled to Summary Judgment Because Clear, Conspicuous At-Will Employment Disclaimers in Its Employee Handbook Preclude Any Implied Contractual Right to a Pretermination Hearing.

Summary judgment is appropriate. No reasonable juror could conclude that the language of the Church's handbook requires that it provide a pretermination hearing to a disgruntled employee like the plaintiff who (1) concedes that she violated the Church's religious teachings on premarital sex and (2) would only use that hearing as a forum to voice her displeasure with the Church's prohibition on premarital sex. Summary judgment is properly granted in wrongful discharge cases, despite its being a drastic remedy, when there is no genuine issue as to material fact and the moving party is entitled to judgment as a matter of law. Abrahamsen v. Mountain States Tel. & Tel. Co., 494 P.2d 1287, 1288 (Colo. 2006); Morlan v. Durlan Trust Co., 252 P.2d 98, 102 (Colo. 1952).

The advocate obscures unfavorable information about the procedural rule by placing it in the middle of the sentence.

The U.S. Supreme Court has recognized in other contexts that religious employers have a right "to decide for themselves free from interference, matters of church government as well as those of faith and doctrine." Kedroff v. St. Nicholas Cathedral of Russian Orthodox Church, 344 U.S. 94, 116 (1952); see also EEOC v. Catholic Univ. of Am., 907 U.S. 455, 457 (1996).

This traditional deference to decisions of religious employers reflected in U.S. Supreme Court jurisprudence is also reflected in Colorado's employment at-will doctrine. In Colorado, an employer's decision to release an employee cannot subject it to civil liability for wrongful discharge when an employee handbook clearly and unambiguously proclaims the employer's intent to bypass the judicially created exceptions to the doctrine. Churchey v. Adolph Coors Co., 759 P.2d 1336, 1348, 1349-51 (Colo. 1988); Evenson v. Colo. Farm Bureau Mut. Ins., 879 P.2d 402, 405 (Colo. App. 1993). Consequently, a conspicuous contract disclaimer in an employee handbook insulates an employer from a wrongful discharge claim based on an implied contract theory of liability. Churchey, 759 P.2d at 1349-51; Evenson, 879 P.2d at 405.

The writer uses context from a Supreme Court decision in a similar kind of case as a foundation for a persuasive articulation of the governing substantive rule.

Broad rather than detailed references to the exceptions obfuscate unfavorable information.

Colorado appellate courts typically grant employers' motions for summary judgment when a disclaimer — conspicuously placed in an employee handbook — is easily recognizable and would attract the attention of a reasonable employee. See Fejes v. Gilpin Ventures, 960 F. Supp. 1487, 1495 (D. Colo. 1997); George v. Ute Water Conservancy Dist., 950 P.2d 1195, 1198 (Colo. App. 1999); Dell v. Montgomery Ward & Co., 811 P.2d 974, 976 (Colo. App. 1998).

Note the strategic use of punctuation to attract the court's attention.

In Colorado, disclaimers are more likely to attract the attention of a reasonable employee when they contain distinct formatting features. See George, 950 P.2d at 1198 (holding that boldfaced capital letters in the disclaimer demonstrated that the employer intended for the handbook not to constitute a binding offer); Schur v. Storage Tech. Corp., 878 P.2d 51, 52 (Colo. App. 1994) (determining that a disclaimer using italicized letters was sufficiently conspicuous); Evenson, 879 P.2d at 409 (determining that, because employer did not emphasize the disclaimer with distinct formatting features, the disclaimer did not attract the attention of a reasonable employee). No Colorado court has ever held that a handbook with internally inconsistent font size is inconspicuous as a matter of law.

First R/E assertion. Note that it has a point of view and is written in way that advances the client's argument.

The writer uses explanatory parentheticals instead of case illustrations to explain this fairly simple rule.

Three At-Will Disclaimers Designed to Attract Attention

Because the advocate has only one argument, impact headings reenforce the point heading and provide the judge with visual relief in a sea of text.

The Church is entitled to summary judgment because the disclaimers used various formatting tools to attract the attention of a reasonable employee. The Church's at-will disclaimer reads as follows:

First R/A assertion. Here, the writer alters the CREAC formula. Instead of explaining and then applying all the rules, he explains one part of the argument and then applies that part to the facts of the case. In short, the structure is R/E>>> R/A for each assertion.

> I have entered into my employment relationship with the Church voluntarily and for no specified length of employment. I ACKNOWLEDGE THAT THIS EMPLOYMENT HANDBOOK IS NOT A CONTRACT OF EMPLOYMENT AND THAT MY EMPLOYMENT IS AT-WILL. AT-WILL EMPLOYMENT MEANS THAT A CHURCH EMPLOYEE

DOES NOT HAVE AN UNLIMITED CONTRACTUAL RIGHT TO PROGRESSIVE DISCIPLINE PRIOR TO TERMINATION.

The entire handbook is formatted in 12-point font while the disclaimer is in 11-point font. However, this disclaimer contains almost an entire paragraph in all capital letters. Consequently, a reasonable juror evaluating this case is likely to conclude that this distinctive formatting style would attract a reasonable employee's attention.

Furthermore, a reasonable employee would have seen the two other at-will employment disclaimers contained in the employee handbook. The plaintiff had **three** opportunities to recognize the status of her at-will employment. Two of these expressions were located under boldface type headers that specifically said things such as "Prohibited conduct" or "Work Rules." A reasonable employee would take a moment to look at what immediately proceeds these headers — the conditions of at-will employment. Although plaintiff claims that she did not see the disclaimer, the relevant inquiry focuses on the actions of a reasonable employee. A reasonable juror would most likely find that a seven-page handbook asserting in three separate locations the employer's right to maintain the presumption at-will employment would attract the attention of a reasonable employee.

Placing the disclaimer in a prominent position, such as an acknowledgment page, is a design choice that suggests that the disclaimer would attract a reasonable employee's attention. In Silchia v. MCI Telecommunications, the federal district court — applying Colorado law — granted the employer's motion for summary judgment on the plaintiff's implied contract claim. 942 F. Supp. 1369, 1375 (D. Colo. 1996). The handbook contained a disclaimer on the last page, directly above the plaintiff's signature. Id. Although the disclaimer was not highlighted by capital letters or bold print, the court nevertheless held that the signature block — immediately above the disclaimer — served to place a reasonable employee on notice that the handbook was not an employment contract. Id.; see also Ferrera v. Nielsen, 799 P.2d 458,461 (Colo. App. 1990) (holding that the disclaimer

Second R/E assertion. Note that it is not objectively written but has a point of view and is written in way that advances the client's argument.

was conspicuous as a matter of law when placed on the acknowledgment page immediately below the plaintiff's signature). But see Durtsche v. Am. Colloid Co., 958 F.2d 1007, 1010 (10th Cir. 1992) (holding that disclaimer was inconspicuous because it was buried in an appendix to the employment handbook).

A reasonable juror could conclude that the Church's at-will disclaimer would attract the attention of a reasonable employee because it was prominently placed on the acknowledgment page of the employee handbook. The facts in this case are remarkably similar to the facts in the Silchia. Just like the plaintiff in Silchia, the plaintiff in this case signed and dated documents with disclaimers located directly above her signature, a prominent location that a reasonable employee would have noticed and read immediately. Also like the disclaimer in the Silchia case, the Church's disclaimer is located on the last page, entitled acknowledgment page, immediately below the plaintiff's signature. Based on these similarities, a reasonable juror could conclude that the at-will employment disclaimer insulates the Church for any liability on the plaintiff's implied contract claim.

Second R/A assertion. The writer sticks with the R/E>>R/A format.

Employment Practices Consistent with a Mission of Community Service

Another impact heading reenforces a different aspect of the advocate's point heading.

To circumvent the Church's reliance on its conspicuous at-will employment disclaimer, the plaintiff relies on language from the Colorado Appeals Court in Evenson. The rule announced in Evenson is a limited exception that permits an employee to potentially invalidate a conspicuous handbook disclaimer only if the employee has specific, concrete evidence that an employer had a custom of using progressive disciplinary procedures prior to every instance of termination despite the language of the at-will employment disclaimer. Evenson, 879 P.2d at 402. In Evenson, the employee argued that the conspicuous handbook disclaimer did not prevent the

Transition from primary argument to a counterargument. The writer primarily uses analogical reasoning to support this counterargument.

formation of an implied contract entitling her to progressive discipline. Id. Plaintiff's contention relied on deposition testimony from several high-ranking corporate officers, including the Chief Personnel Officer, who testified about their belief that the pretermination hearing was an absolute precondition to an employee's termination. Id. The court denied the motion for summary judgment because the deposition testimony of high-ranking managerial employees established a factual dispute about the availability of a pretermination hearing despite the existence of an at-will employment disclaimer. Id.

This case is easily distinguishable from Evenson. Unlike the Evenson plaintiff who presented evidence from several managers, including the Chief Personnel Officer, that established that they regarded the availability of a pretermination hearing as an absolute condition limiting the employer's right to discharge an employee, the plaintiff in this case has no evidence from any supervisory employee that the Church has ever provided progressive discipline to any employee who violated the morals clause. The plaintiff's inability to produce evidence of employment practices at odds with its employment practices invalidates her reliance on Evenson and reinforces the underlying rationale of the Church's morals clause: to protect the homeless children that it serves.

In further support of her argument, plaintiff contends that the Church reprimanded two of its supervisory employees for terminating employees without a pretermination hearing. However, those employees were embroiled in legitimate workplace disputes with their supervisors. For example, one employee was engaged in a dispute about the applicability of various safety regulations, and the other employee was accused of sexually harassing another coworker. Upon the occurrence of a genuine workplace dispute requiring additional fact-finding measures, the Church applied the progressive discipline policy according to its custom, which is evidenced by its immediate reprimand of these two supervisory employees. Unlike the employees identified as comparators, the plaintiff admits that she engaged in premarital sex despite her knowledge that this conduct was in direct violation of the Church's teachings. Consequently, her conduct falls squarely within the morals clause, and she was not entitled to a pretermination hearing.

CONCLUSION

The brief conclusion provides one last opportunity to present the client's theory and theme.

The Church demonstrated its intent to maintain Colorado's long-standing presumption of at-will employment by incorporating a prominently placed at-will employment disclaimer into its employment handbook. That at-will employment disclaimer clearly and conspicuously conditioned the availability of a pretermination hearing to employees embroiled in genuine workplace disputes. Given these facts, a reasonable juror could conclude only that plaintiff was an at-will employee who the Church had the legal authority to release from her employment.

Respectfully Submitted,

Thomas J. Clark
Thomas J. Clark
Attorney for Defendant
3200 Divine Way
Boulder, Colorado 55523
(303) 315-4916

CERTIFICATE OF SERVICE

I hereby certify that a copy of this Motion Brief in Support of the Defendant's Motion for Summary Judgment was sent by regular U.S. Mail, postage prepaid, to Ms. Raffaela Wilson, 100 East Eighth Street, Suite 1000, Fort Lauderdale, Florida 33321.

Thomas J. Clark

IN THE DISTRICT COURT OF DENVER COUNTY
2ND JUDICIAL CIRCUIT
CIVIL DIVISION

HAILEY GIDEON, Plaintiff, vs. FIRST UNION ANGLICAN CHURCH OF COLORADO, Defendant.	No. 16-CV-1534-HLA

PLAINTIFF'S BRIEF IN OPPOSITION TO SUMMARY JUDGMENT

The advocate uses a modern sans-serif font to subtly communicate her theory and theme.

Raffaela Wilson (WIL200)
Attorney for Plaintiff
100 East Eighth Street
Suite 1000
Fort Lauderdale, Florida 33321
(954) 421-3133

TABLE OF CONTENTS

The Table of Contents gives the judge a comprehensive snapshot of the advocate's story.

Plot headings (1) outline the plot of the emerging story, (2) subdivide the SOF into easy-to-read digestible chunks and (3) subtly introduce the court to the advocate's theory and theme.

The writer begins and ends with the strongest arguments and buries the weaker argument in the middle (the "sandwiching principle").

INTRODUCTION

The introduction is analogous to an opening statement at a trial and to the summary of argument in an appellate brief. Its goal is to grab the judge's attention by succinctly presenting the theory and theme.

Plaintiff Hailey Gideon is a 35-year-old woman who was fired from her job as a youth minister without the benefit of a pretermination hearing because she opted to raise her unborn child as a single mother. In this case, a reasonable juror could conclude that the defendant strategically used promissory language in its handbook to lure talented job applicants with unconditional promises of a pretermination hearing.

The advocate uses context to create a favorable image to personalize the client and highlight the "bait and switch" theory and theme.

Summary judgment is a drastic remedy that is warranted only when the defendant carries its two-part burden of demonstrating (1) the absence of a material factual dispute and (2) that clearly established Colorado law entitles it to judgment as a matter of law. When viewed in the light most favorable to Ms. Gideon, a reasonable juror could conclude that the defendant's employee handbook created an implied contractual promise to a pretermination hearing. Furthermore, a juror could reasonably conclude that the at-will employment disclaimer is contradicted by the defendant's documented employment practices. The potential for disagreement about whether the progressive discipline policy created an unlimited contractual right to a pretermination hearing and about its effect on the validity of the at-will employment disclaimer renders summary judgment inappropriate.

The advocate uses persuasive techniques to explain the procedural governing rule. For example, language such as "drastic remedy," "warranted only," "two-part burden" and numbering subtly emphasize the stringency of the MSJ standard.

Notice the second function of the introduction, which is to summarize the advocate's arguments. Compare this introduction with the defendant's introduction. Notice how each introduction develops a theory and theme that is consistent with the party's arguments

STATEMENT OF FACTS

As a space-saving measure, this SOF does not include any citations. However, your professor or managing partner will typically require their inclusion.

In the minutes following her arrival to work on February 14, 2016, Plaintiff Hailey Gideon was summoned to her immediate supervisor's office, interrogated about rumors that she was pregnant, and then terminated. Ms. Gideon's supervisor did not (1) provide written notice of the reasons for termination, (2) mention the defendant's progressive

Compare the use of language in this brief with that in the plaintiff's brief. Here the advocate uses "terminated" while the defendant's advocate uses "released from employment." Strategic word choice is a powerful soft-sell persuasive technique.

discipline policy, or (3) reference the pretermination hearing procedures outlined in that policy. All of these procedures are outlined the employee handbook.

This paragraph is an executive summary. Executive summaries are powerful soft-sell persuasive techniques that quickly grab the judge's attention with the most salient and relevant facts.

An Award-Winning Youth Counselor

Ms. Gideon worked as a youth counselor at the defendant's Colorado Springs shelter for homeless teenagers. During her decade-long employment, Ms. Gideon was either nominated for or won "Counselor of the Year" for nine of those ten years. She has never been reprimanded, and none of the homeless teenagers whom she served complained about her work performance. Two months before she was terminated, the defendant awarded Ms. Gideon its Award of Excellence for service to the homeless community.

The advocate effectively uses word choice by describing this group as "homeless teenagers." The defendant's brief uses "homeless children."

A Multisection Progressive Discipline Policy

The defendant is one of only five employers in the state with a progressive discipline policy. Each section of the progressive discipline policy has a heading written in boldface type. On her first day of work, Ms. Gideon read each heading. The progressive discipline policy mandates that the defendant "shall discharge its fact-finding mission at a pretermination administrative hearing where the employee . . . shall have an opportunity to present evidence." The policy has no exceptions.

The advocate emphasizes the absence of a fact, a particularly effective soft-sell persuasive technique.

The policy has three subsections and spans five handbook pages. None of the subsections cross-reference the conduct clause. The conduct clause, prohibiting non-work-related activities that violate the defendant's religious teachings, is a four-line paragraph buried within a subsection relating to work rules. The progressive discipline policy has its own heading and spans two handbook pages.

The small-scale persuasive technique of juxtaposition subtly diffuses one of the defendant's potential arguments.

A Disclaimer at Odds with Employment Practices

The at-will employment disclaimer has no heading identifying it as a disclaimer, is not written in boldface type, and is located on the last page of the handbook. No one discussed any of the handbook provisions with Ms. Gideon. No one directed her attention to the disclaimer. No one even mentioned a disclaimer until Ms. Gideon filed this lawsuit.

> The soft-sell persuasive technique of repetition highlights favorable facts.

The defendant has reprimanded supervisors for terminating employees without a pretermination hearing despite language in the disclaimer noting that "an employee does not have an unlimited right to pretermination hearing." After receiving the pretermination hearing referenced in the progressive discipline policy, several terminated employees were reinstated. After months of requesting a pretermination hearing, Ms. Gideon sought relief from this Court, filing suit against First Union Anglican Church of Colorado and several codefendants:

Reverend Aaron Lewis	Chief Executive Officer
Reverend Jonathan Ozeki	Council of Bishops President
Reverend Dominick Vanderbilt	Plaintiff's Immediate Supervisor

> A simple two-column chart streamlines the delivery of key background facts.

Seven days after Ms. Gideon filed suit, the defendant filed this summary judgment motion.

ARGUMENT

> The roadmap unifies the advocate's multipart argument and has a distinct point of view. The advocate creates a favorable context for the governing rule by presenting a "story" where she characterizes the at-will employment doctrine as antiquated.

A Reasonable Juror Could Conclude that the Plaintiff Had an Unconditional Implied Contractual Right to a Pretermination Hearing.

This Court should deny the defendant's motion for summary judgment. Under Colorado law, the issue of whether an employer voluntarily modified the presumption of at-will employment is typically a question for the jury. See, e.g., Cronk v. Intermountain Rural Elec. Ass'n, 765 P.2d 619, 630 (Colo. App. 1988); Salimi v. Farmers Ins. Grp., 684 P.2d 264, 265 (Colo. App. 1984). More than two decades ago in Continental Air Lines v. Keenan, the Colorado Supreme Court rejected a rigid interpretation of the employment relationship that would preclude employers like the defendant from voluntarily altering the presumption of at-will employment. 731 P.2d 708 (Colo. 1987). The underlying rationale of the implied contract theory is that the law should respect an employer's decision to create a more equitable employment relationship, one that is more reflective of modern employment relationships than the restrictive at-will employment doctrine. See Silchia v. MCI Telecommc's Corp., 942 F. Supp. 1369, 1372 (D. Colo. 1996); Jaynes v. Centura Health Corp., 148 P.3d 241, 250 (Colo. App. 2006).

Notice the strategic use of language. Subtle persuasion dictates that the writer use the phrase "implied contract theory" instead of implied contract exception. Why? Because the writer doesn't want to emphasize that the theory is the exception instead of the rule.

Progressive discipline policies are one judicially recognized way that employers alter the harsh consequences of the at-will employment doctrine. See McGuire v. Sampson, 210 F.3d 1141, 1145 (10th Cir. 2000); Churchey v. Adolph Coors Co., 759 P.2d 1336, 1347 (Colo. 1988). Colorado courts consistently hold employers contractually liable for promises contained in employment handbooks when (1) those provisions could reasonably be construed as an offer to limit the employer's ability to immediately terminate an employee and (2) the employee's initial or continued employment constituted acceptance and consideration for the handbook provisions. See Churchey, 759 P.2d at 1348.

Creating a favorable context is another soft-sell persuasive technique that is particularly persuasive in roadmaps.

In the first two sections of this brief, Ms. Gideon argues that, given the defendant's linguistic and formatting choices, a reasonable juror could interpret the defendant's progressive discipline policy as an offer to modify the presumption of at-will employment that Ms. Gideon accepted with ten years of dedicated service as a youth counselor. The last section of the brief makes an alternate argument: A juror could reasonably conclude that the disclaimer was contradicted by other handbook provisions promising equitable employment practices and by the defendant's documented employment practices. The potential for disagreement about the policy's interpretation renders summary judgment inappropriate.

This is an effective example of mapping arguments. Mapping techniques are particularly helpful in roadmaps.

A. The Mandatory Language of the Progressive Discipline Policy and Its Comprehensive, Detailed Enforcement Scheme Was an Offer to Provide All Employees with a Pretermination Hearing.

The promissory language in the preamble to the progressive discipline policy and its detailed, comprehensive enforcement scheme created an unconditional implied contractual obligation to a pretermination hearing. To determine whether the handbook created an offer of progressive discipline, the relevant inquiry is not whether the employer subjectively intended to create an implied contractual obligation. Churchey, 759 P.2d at 1348-49 (citing Toussaint v. Blue Cross & Shield, 292 N.W.2d 880, 892 (Mich. 1980)). Instead, the relevant inquiry is whether the handbook objectively created an atmosphere "instinct with an obligation" where the plaintiff reasonably anticipated some limitation on the employer's common law right to unilaterally terminate employees. Id. Employers create an atmosphere instinct with an obligation by making strategic choices when designing their employment handbooks. See, e.g., Churchey, 759 P.2d at 1349; Tuttle v. ANR Freight Sys., 797 P.2d 825, 827 (Colo. App. 1990).

The employer's decision to create a detailed progressive discipline policy is a strategic design choice that creates an atmosphere instinct with an obligation. In Churchey, the employer enacted a progressive discipline procedure with a detailed two-step appeals process entitling the employee to an administrative hearing. 759 P.2d at 1349. The Colorado Supreme Court denied the motion for summary judgment, reasoning that the employer's deliberate choice to include such a detailed progressive discipline policy could convince a reasonable juror that it objectively created an atmosphere

First R/E assertion. Note that it has a distinct a point of view that emphasizes the client's arguments.

where an employee could reasonably believe that he or she was entitled to an administrative hearing. Id.

The writer uses a case illustration here instead of explanatory parentheticals because this case is a favorable "Ferrari" case.

Similarly, the inclusion of promissory handbook language is another strategic design choice that creates an atmosphere instinct with an obligation. Compare Tuttle, 797 P.2d at 827 (reasoning that the use of words like "pledge" and "commit" and other promissory handbook language created a genuine issue of material fact about the creation of an implied contract), with Mariani v. Rocky Mountain Hosp. & Med. Serv., 902 P.2d 429, 435 (Colo. App. 1995) (reasoning that the frequent use of discretionary language such as "may" or "can" was evidence of the employer's intent to maintain the presumption of at-will employment).

Second R/E assertion. The advocate follows the traditional CREAC structure of explaining the R/E assertions in their entirety before applying them to the facts of the case. This traditional organization is most helpful when rule explanations are relatively short and easy to understand.

Ms. Gideon is entitled to present her implied contract claim to a jury because the detailed progressive discipline policy created an atmosphere of instinct with an obligation. The progressive discipline policy has three distinct subsections that provide a wide range of progressive discipline, including a three-step notification process commanding supervisors to (1) provide written notification of the termination recommendation to the employee, (2) send a copy of the written notification to the Council, and (3) inform the employee of the right to request a pretermination hearing with the Council of Bishops. Given this level of detail, Ms. Gideon was understandably shocked by her supervisor's refusal to grant her request for a pretermination hearing or to provide her with written notice outlining the reason for her termination.

This sentence is the R/A assertion. Notice how the R/A assertion references the case's procedural posture and asks the court take a specific type of action.

The proactive measures taken by the Church to design a detailed progressive discipline policy strongly mirror those measures taken by the employer in Churchey. Like the employer in Churchey who created a progressive discipline procedure to be administered by an appeal board, the defendant authored an employee handbook containing progressive discipline procedures and created the Council of Bishops to enforce the policy. Just as the court in Churchey held that summary judgment was inappropriate based on the dispute over the formation of an implied employment contract, this Court should deny summary judgment based on a similar factual dispute.

A reasonable juror could also conclude that the handbook's mandatory and promissory language created an atmosphere instinct with an obligation. The first page welcomes new employees with the following promise: "This employment handbook is the *definitive source of [your] rights and responsibilities* as a Church employee and applies to all supervisory and non-supervisory employees." (emphasis added). The welcome page contains no exceptions to this mandatory language.

The preamble to progressive discipline policy contains even more promises. The policy's fundamental purpose is to ensure "*fundamental fairness* consistent with the Employer's policy of treating all employees with dignity and worth" and is designed to "foster a *fair and equitable resolution* of workplace disputes." (emphasis added). These references to fairness and equity are reinforced by a provision mandating that "the supervisor *shall* seek guidance from the Council of Bishops . . . before terminating employment under this progressive discipline policy." (emphasis added). The requirement that immediate supervisors consult the Council before terminating an employee has no exceptions. Furthermore, the policy gives the Council "ultimate authority to determine if the facts of a particular workplace dispute warrant termination or a lesser form of discipline," and requires that the Council "shall discharge its fact-finding mission at an administrative hearing." These provisions contain no exceptions to this promissory and mandatory language.

Because a reasonable juror could conclude that the combination of mandatory and promissory language creates an atmosphere instinct with an obligation, summary judgment is inappropriate.

B. The Inconspicuous At-Will Employment Disclaimer Buried at the Bottom of the Handbook's Last Page Did Not Prevent the Formation of an Offer.

The defendant's disclaimer would not attract the attention of a reasonable employee and thus did not negate the defendant's unconditional obligation to provide progressive discipline. Under Colorado law, an at-will employment disclaimer must conspicuously negate an implied contract. Cronk, 765 P.2d at 623 (reversing the trial court's grant of summary judgment for the defendant notwithstanding the written disclaimer contained in the policy manual). Colorado courts have refused to classify a disclaimer as conspicuous as a matter of law when it (1) contains no editorial enhancements and (2) is not located in a position of prominence. See, e.g., Jaynes, 148 P.3d at 247; Evenson v. Colo. Farm Bureau Mut. Ins., 879 P.2d 402, 409 (Colo. App. 1994); Ferrera v. A.C. Nielsen, 799 P.2d 458, 459 (Colo. App. 1990).

Boldface or italicized type written in a large, distinctive font is an editorial enhancement that makes a disclaimer conspicuous. Compare Jaynes, 148 P.3d at 247 (reasoning that disclaimer was sufficiently conspicuous where it was on the second page of the handbook, under a boldface heading labeled "**Employment at Will**"), and Ferrera, 799 P.2d at 459 (reasoning that disclaimer sufficiently conspicuous where it appeared on the first page of the handbook under a distinct capitalized heading labeled "IMPORTANT"), with Evenson, 879 P.2d at 409 (reasoning that the disclaimer was inconspicuous because it contained nothing designed to emphasize it).

First R/E assertion.

Notice the writer's strategic choice to support the assertion with explanatory parentheticals instead of case illustrations. These explanatory parentheticals streamline the delivery of important information.

In Colorado, disclaimers are prominently positioned when they appear in the first few pages of the handbook and when they are emphasized with a distinctive heading. Colorado courts do not evaluate the number of disclaimers but whether they are designed to attract the attention of a reasonable employee. For example, in Fejes v. Gilpin Ventures, the federal district court applied Colorado law to invalidate an at-will employment disclaimer. 960 F. Supp. 1487, 1495 (D. Colo. 1997). In that case, the defendant's employee handbook had three disclaimers. Id. The second disclaimer was buried in a paragraph titled "AUTHORIZATION." Id. Despite this capitalized heading and the presence of three at-will employment disclaimers, the court held that the entire handbook could not prevent the formation of a contractual obligation because the second disclaimer was buried in a section of the handbook under a heading that would not attract the attention of a reasonable employee because it bore no logical relationship to the at-will employment doctrine. Id.

Second R/E assertion.

This case illustration has a distinct point of view. The advocate gives more "airtime" to facts she wants to emphasize and downplays facts she wants to deemphasize.

Although the disclaimer in this case is clear, a juror could reasonably determine that it is inconspicuous because it contains no editorial enhancements and because it is obscured by an uninformative heading that bore no logical relationship to the at-will employment doctrine. First, the disclaimer contains no editorial enhancements to attract the attention of a

First R/A assertion.

reasonable employee. Although some of the disclaimer language is written in all capital letters, it contains no boldface or italicized typeface and is written in typeface that is a whole font size smaller than the text contained on the rest of the page.

Second, the defendant's disclaimer is obscured by an uninformative heading. This case and the Fejes case both feature obscured and uninformative headings. Like the disclaimer in Fejes that was buried under a heading titled "AUTHORIZATION" that bore no logical relationship to the presumption of at-will employment mentioned in the disclaimer, the disclaimer in this case is buried on the last page of the handbook under an uninformative heading titled "Employee Acknowledgment Form" that bears no relationship to the at-will employment doctrine. The uninformative heading located six paragraphs above the disclaimer makes it inconspicuous. For example, a juror evaluating the relative positioning of the heading and the disclaimer would not expect anything in that subsection to restrict the unconditional right to progressive discipline referenced numerous times in the handbook.

Third, the disclaimer does not contain the distinctive bolded and underlined heading that so prominently announces other sections of the handbook such as the "**Conduct and Work Rules**" section and the "**Progressive Discipline Policy**." As the author of the handbook, the defendant had the opportunity to emphasize its disclaimer by using the same distinctive heading featured so prominently in other portions of the handbook. Furthermore, had the defendant employed the same labeling techniques as it did for the other major sections of the handbook, then Ms. Gideon might have seen the disclaimer on her first day of work when she read all of the handbook's major headings.

At best, the issue of the conspicuousness of the disclaimer is subject to multiple interpretations, making summary judgment inappropriate.

C. A Reasonable Juror Could Conclude, Even If the Disclaimer Was Conspicuous, That Its Mandatory Language and the Employer's Custom of Providing Employees with Pretermination Hearings Invalidated the Disclaimer.

A reasonable juror could surmise that the disclaimer's absolute language is contradicted by the mandatory, promissory language riddled throughout the handbook and by the defendant's actual employment practices. In Colorado, even a conspicuous disclaimer does not insulate an employer from contractual liability when legally sufficient evidence creates a jury question about whether it modified the presumption of at-will employment articulated in the disclaimer. See, e.g., Jaynes, 148 P.3d at 247; Evenson, 879 P.2d at 409 (reasoning that "[e]ven if there is a disclaimer in the manual, an employer may nevertheless be found to have manifested an intent to be bound by its terms").

An employee can invalidate a disclaimer when it conflicts with relevant handbook provisions. In Allabashi v. Lincoln National Sales Corp. of Colorado-Wyoming, a handbook's "just cause" provision limited the employer's unilateral right to immediately terminate an employee via the at-will employment doctrine. 824 P.2d 1, 3 (Colo. App. 1991). However, the handbook also contained a disclaimer affirming the employer's intent to maintain the presumption of at-will employment. Id. The employer filed a motion for summary judgment, arguing that the disclaimer prevented the creation of an implied contract. Id. In denying the motion for summary judgment, the court reasoned that the conflict between the disclaimer and the handbook's "just cause" provision negated the disclaimer. Id.

An employee can also invalidate a disclaimer when it conflicts with the employer's personnel practices. The leading case on this issue is Evenson. In that case, the Colorado Court of Appeals determined that the employee's at-will status was a question of fact precluding summary judgment despite the existence of several conspicuous disclaimers, including one near the employee's signature. Evenson, 879 P.2d at 409. Although the disclaimer indicated that the language in the handbook "was not intended to alter the traditional rule of at-will employment and thus, is not a binding contract," the appellate court nevertheless held that the employer was obligated to provide the employeer with a pretermination hearing. Id. The court's reasoning was based on the testimony of several employees who testified about their belief that the pretermination hearing was an absolute precondition to an employee's termination. Id. The court denied the employer's motion for summary judgment because the disclaimer was at odds with the employer's actual employment practices. Id.

Notice how the writer's description of this case differs from the defendant's description of the same case.

Handbook Language at Odds with Employer Custom

Despite the relatively compact nature of this argument, the advocate uses impact headings to reenforce the point heading and to visually remind the judge of the client's theory and theme.

Interpretative conflicts between the promissory language in other sections of the handbook, the progressive discipline policy, and the disclaimer negate any preclusive effect the disclaimer might otherwise have had and preclude summary judgment. This case is strikingly similar to the contradictory handbook language in Allabashi. Like the just cause provision in Allibashi conflicted with the plain language of the disclaimer upholding the presumption of at-will employment, the mandatory language of the progressive discipline policy requiring that supervisors "shall seek guidance from the Council of Bishops" and establishing that the Council of Bishops "shall have the ultimate authority" conflicts with the disclaimer's pronouncement that employees do not have a "contractual right to progressive discipline."

Furthermore, a juror could reasonably conclude that the defendant's at-will employment disclaimer was contradicted by the behavior of its employers. Like the plaintiff in Evenson, who produced deposition testimony establishing that high-ranking supervisory employees regarded the pretermination hearing as an absolute right unconditionally available to all employees, Ms. Gideon has evidence that the defendant disciplined two supervisory employees for firing employees without first providing them with the pretermination hearing promised in the progressive discipline policy. These factual similarities are important because Evenson's holding that the plaintiff was entitled to a jury trial on her implied contract claim was based on tangible evidence of a contradiction between the disclaimer and the defendant's conduct. Consequently, a jury in Gideon's case would likely find that there is conflicting evidence about whether the handbook created an implied contractual obligation to a pretermination hearing.

Nothing in the handbook logically conditions the right to a pretermination hearing on an employee's personal sexual practices. The immorality clause in the defendant's employment handbook is a four-line paragraph in a subsection

Here, the advocate transitions to a counterargument.

relating to work rules while the progressive discipline policy contains its own heading and spans two handbook pages. Furthermore, nothing connects the immorality clause to the promissory and mandatory language contained in the progressive discipline policy. For example, although indicating that immoral conduct is "particularly offensive to the Church and will not be tolerated," this language is not cross-referenced or even repeated in the progressive discipline policy. Instead, the language of the progressive discipline policy is absolute and provides that it is "designed to ensure fundamental fairness" and "foster a fair and equitable resolution of workplace disputes." The policy contains no exceptions to this guarantee of fairness and equity.

At best, a reasonable juror could conclude only that the relationship between the immorality clause and the promise of a pretermination hearing contained in the progressive discipline clause is ambiguous. Under general contract principles, ambiguous contract language must be construed against the drafter. See, e.g., Kuta v. Delta, Gunnison, & Montrose Joint Dist. 50(J), 799 P.2d 379, 390 (Colo. 1990). As the handbook's drafter, the defendant had the flexibility to design its handbook to unambiguously convey its intent to condition the availability of progressive discipline on an employee's personal sexual practices. In short, the very existence of an interpretive ambiguity makes the resolution of this case on summary judgment inappropriate.

CONCLUSION

Hailey Gideon is an example of the kind of qualified employee whom the defendant attempted to lure with its promises of progressive discipline. A reasonable juror reading the promissory handbook language in the context of the detailed, comprehensive progressive discipline policy could easily construe the policy as an unconditional offer of progressive discipline. To prevent the fundamental unfairness that would result from the defendant's unilateral decision to deny Gideon the procedural safeguards guaranteed by the policy, this Court should deny the motion for summary judgment.

Respectfully Submitted,

Raffaela Wilson

Attorney for Plaintiff
100 East Eighth Street
Suite 1000
Fort Lauderdale, Florida 33321
(954) 421-3133

CERTIFICATE OF SERVICE

I hereby certify that a copy of this Motion Brief in Opposition to the Defendant's Motion for Summary Judgment was sent by regular U.S. Mail, postage prepaid, to Mr. Thomas J. Clark, 3200 Divine Way, Boulder, Colorado 55523.

Raffaela Wilson

Glossary

Analogical Reasoning: A hard-sell persuasive technique that substantiates a desired conflict resolution assertion by comparing legally relevant facts from the client's case to legally relevant facts from a prior case (i.e., one that has previously been identified and discussed in the status quo section of the argument).

Antagonist: A secondary character in the statement of facts whose actions threaten to undermine the client's desired conflict resolution.

Appellate Brief: A document presented to a group of judges containing arguments about the validity of a lower court's ruling on an issue related to procedure, substance, or a combination of both.

Argument: A group of ideas arranged logically to convince a reader or listener to do a particular thing or to adopt a particular belief.

Case Illustration: Supports a status quo assertion by clarifying the meaning of ambiguous rules in a logos argument or core societal values in an ethos or pathos policy argument with an in-depth discussion of legally relevant facts, holdings, and rationales from a case.

Core Societal Values: Things, ideas, or concepts embedded in legal rules, statutes, regulations, local ordinances, and public policy that a society believes to be so important that they justify legal protection.

Counterargument: A hard-sell persuasive technique in the desired conflict resolution section of the argument that explicitly identifies adverse facts and explains why they won't undermine the client's requested relief.

Desired Conflict Resolution: The section of the argument where the advocate substantiates the client's desired relief using hard-sell persuasive techniques such as rule-based, analogical, and policy-based reasoning.

Desired Conflict Resolution Assertion: Begins the desired conflict resolution section of the argument and succinctly articulates why the client is entitled to relief.

Economic Policy Argument: Arguments about core societal values that place economics at the center of judicial decision-making.

Ethos: A rhetorical device that appeals to an audience's respect for authority, character, credibility, or to its preference for organization and reader-friendly formatting features.

Ethos Policy Argument: A type of policy argument premised on core societal values related to tradition, custom, or precedent.

Executive Summary: A short paragraph at the beginning of the statement of facts that succinctly captures the most compelling legally and emotionally relevant facts of the client's case.

Explanatory Parenthetical: Supports a status quo assertion by clarifying ambiguous rules in a logos argument or core societal values in an ethos or pathos policy argument with a succinct (typically no more than 35 words) description of a case.

Fact Application Logos Argument: An argument about how the facts of the client's case should apply to the clearly established law.

Hard-Sell Persuasive Techniques: Ones that overtly tell the judge why the client is entitled to relief.

Impact Heading: A reader-friendly formatting feature in the desired conflict resolution section of the argument that visually reinforces core components of a point heading while providing visual relief from dense paragraphs of text.

Institutional Competence Policy Argument: Arguments about core societal values that focus on which branch of government should address a particular issue.

Inverse Policy Argument: A type of policy argument memorializing a core societal value by advocating for a new rule or significantly expanding or limiting an existing rule.

Judicial Administration Policy Argument: Arguments about core societal values that focus on the role of courts or on the difficulty of judicial enforcement.

Juxtaposition: A soft-sell persuasive technique that arranges two or more ideas to suggest comparison, contrast, rhetorical effect, suspense, or character development.

Legal Interpretation Logos Argument: An argument about what the law should be or how judges should resolve issues of first impression or splits among the appellate courts.

Logos: A rhetorical device that appeals to an audience's respect for logic and reason.

Logos Argument: An argument about law such as how the legally relevant facts of the client's case should apply to the clearly established law, what the law should be, or how the law should be interpreted.

Memo: A interoffice document, also known as a memorandum, memorializing the counselor's objective predictive analysis.

Motion: A request filed in a trial or appellate court for a procedural or substantive ruling.

Motion Brief: Also known as a trial memorandum or trial brief, is a document that contains arguments about why the client is entitled to relief on pre-trial or post-trial motions.

Narrative Hook: A sentence at the beginning of an introduction that captures the audience's attention.

Nonprimary Secondary Character: A character in the statement of facts whose presence helps fully develop the client's story.

Normative Policy Argument: An argument about core societal values that focuses on broad concepts such as morality, social utility, and corrective justice.

Packaging: The second phase of the legal storytelling process where the writer infuses the brief with ethos-generating navigational tools and utilizes an eclectic mix of soft- and hard-sell persuasive techniques to showcase the client's theory, theme, and arguments.

Pathos: A rhetorical device that appeals to an audience's emotions.

Pathos Policy Argument: An argument premised on core societal values related to real-world concerns such as how the resolution of the client's case might impact the court system, society, or future litigants.

Persuasive CREAC: A mnemonic device for substantiating a logos argument in a motion or appellate brief.

Plot Headings: A reader-friendly formatting feature consisting of short, nonargumentative phrases that outlines the plot of the client's story, captures the judge's attention, and subtly foreshadows the client's arguments.

Point Heading: A reader-friendly formatting feature in the table of contents and the desired conflict resolution section that announces the advocate's best arguments about why the client is entitled to relief.

Policy-Based Reasoning: A hard-sell persuasive technique that substantiates a desired conflict resolution assertion by referencing core societal values at the root of legal rules instead of the rules themselves.

Preemption: A hard-sell persuasive technique used in the desired conflict resolution section that subtly refutes adverse facts in the advocate's primary argument instead of refuting them in a counterargument.

Preemptive Case Selection Strategy: A soft-sell persuasive technique that discusses favorable cases or non-legal information at the beginning and end of sentences and paragraphs and buries unfavorable cases and non-legal information in the middle of sentences and paragraphs.

Primacy and Recency: The theory that people best remember information that's presented first and last.

Procedural Posture: The case's stage in the legal process.

Processing: The first phase of the legal storytelling process where the advocate creates the client's story by extracting core societal values from legal and non-legal sources, scrutinizing the facts of the client's case, and using those facts to brainstorm arguments and to craft a unifying theory and theme.

Protagonist: The main character (typically the client) featured in the statement of facts.

Roadmap: An ethos-generating navigational tool for streamlining complex, multi-part arguments.

Rule-Based Reasoning: A hard-sell persuasive technique that substantiates a desired conflict resolution by applying a rule to legally relevant facts from the client's case that aren't analogous to a prior case (i.e., one that has previously been identified and discussed in the status quo section of the argument).

Soft-Sell Persuasive Techniques: Ones that prime a judge for a favorable response to the client's story by subtly referencing the client's theory, theme, and arguments.

Standard of Review: Dictates the level of deference that an appellate court must give to a lower court's decision.

Status Quo: The section of the argument that persuasively identifies and discusses information that's integral to the advocate's argument using a combination of soft-sell persuasive techniques.

Status Quo Assertion: Begins the discussion of the status quo section of the argument and succinctly and persuasively clarifies the meaning of ambiguous rules or core societal values.

Stock Characters: A universally recognized character type that advocates use as a template for subtly conveying the client's theory and theme in the statement of facts.

Stock Stories: A universally recognized story type that advocates use as a template for subtly conveying the client's theory and theme in the statement of facts.

Summary of the Argument: The component of an appellate brief that succinctly summarizes the advocate's best arguments.

Theme: A short, memorable phrase that summarizes the theory and functions as the pathos or emotional component of the client's story.

Theory: The central idea or thesis that unifies the advocate's arguments.

Visual Rhetoric: The symbiotic relationship between persuasion and document design, encompassing everything from the sequence of the components in a brief; font selection; and the effective use of white space and reader-friendly formatting features such as headings, bullet points, charts, and graphs.

Index

Index